IONESCO and GENET

IONESCO and GENET

Playwrights of Silence

by JOSEPHINE JACOBSEN
and WILLIAM R. MUELLER

A DRAMABOOK

HILL AND WANG · NEW YORK

STANDARD BOOK NUMBER (CLOTHBOUND EDITION): 8090-5885-5
STANDARD BOOK NUMBER (PAPERBACK EDITION): 8090-0544-1
Library of Congress catalog card number: 68-14782

FIRST EDITION APRIL 1968

Manufactured in the United States of America
34567890

For
Richard H. Hart
and
Nathan A. Scott, Jr.

Contents

This study of Eugène Ionesco and Jean Genet is a sequel to the authors' *The Testament of Samuel Beckett,* published by Hill and Wang in 1964 and by Faber and Faber Limited in 1966. This book, like the last, is written for the intelligent lay reader. It is not, of course, conceived as a replacement for the plays about which it speaks, but, hopefully, as a study which will help its readers in their understanding and enjoyment of those plays.

We wish to acknowledge gratefully that the first chapter of this book appeared in the March 1967 issue of *The Kenyon Review*. For our many quotations from Ionesco and Genet we are indebted to the following publishers: Bantam Books, Grove Press, John Calder.

J.J.
W.R.M.

Abbreviations

In references to Ionesco's works,* the following abbreviations will be used:

A	*Amédée, or How to Get Rid of It* (*Three Plays,* tr. Donald Watson. New York: Grove Press, 1958.)
BS	*The Bald Soprano* (*Four Plays,* tr. Donald M. Allen. New York: Grove Press, 1958.)
C	*The Chairs* (*Four Plays.*)
EK	*Exit the King* (*Plays,* Volume V, tr. Donald Watson. London: John Calder, 1963.)
FE	*The Future Is in Eggs, or It Takes All Sorts to Make a World* (*Rhinoceros and Other Plays,* tr. Derek Prouse. New York: Grove Press, 1960.)
I	*Improvisation, or The Shepherd's Chameleon* (*The Killer and Other Plays,* tr. Donald Watson. New York: Grove Press, 1960.)
J	*Jack, or The Submission* (*Four Plays.*)
K	*The Killer* (*The Killer and Other Plays.*)
L	*The Lesson* (*Four Plays.*)
MM	*Maid to Marry* (*The Killer and Other Plays.*)
NCN	*Notes and Counter Notes,* tr. Donald Watson. New York: Grove Press, 1964.
NT	*The New Tenant* (*Three Plays.*)
R	*Rhinoceros* (*Rhinoceros and Other Plays.*)
SA	*A Stroll in the Air* (*Plays,* Volume VI, tr. Donald Watson. London: John Calder, 1965.)
VD	*Victims of Duty* (*Three Plays.*)

In references to Genet's works,* the following abbreviations will be used:

Bal	*The Balcony,* tr. Bernard Frechtman. New York: Grove Press, 1960.

* For a chronological list of Ionesco's and Genet's works, see pages 236–237.

Bl   *The Blacks: A Clown Show,* tr. Bernard Frechtman.
        New York: Grove Press, 1960.

D   *Deathwatch* (*The Maids and Deathwatch,* tr. Ber-
        nard Frechtman. New York: Grove Press, 1954.)

M   *The Maids* (*The Maids and Deathwatch.*)

OLF   *Our Lady of the Flowers,* tr. Bernard Frechtman.
        New York: Bantam Books, 1964.

S   *The Screens,* tr. Bernard Frechtman. New York:
        Grove Press, 1962.

TJ   *The Thief's Journal,* tr. Bernard Frechtman. New
        York: Grove Press, 1964.

IONESCO and GENET

The absurd is born of that confrontation
between the human need and the unreasonable
silence of the world.

Camus' *The Myth of Sisyphus*

NAGG. Our Father which art——
HAMM. Silence! In silence!
Beckett's *Endgame*

ROBERTA II. All we need to designate things
is one word: cat.
Ionesco's *Jack, or The Submission*

ARCHIBALD. . . . we shall even have the decency . . .
to make communication impossible.
Genet's *The Blacks*

The Absurd Quest

THE MOST EXCITING theatre of our mid-century is that of the absurdists, particularly Samuel Beckett, Eugène Ionesco, and Jean Genet. They dazzle us, first, with a fine control of craft, with the precisely appropriate setting, stage dynamics, and language. Beckett's near-empty landscapes, his reduction of physical movement to a minimum, his sparse, austere, and wonderful poetry; Ionesco's multifarious and imaginative settings, his wild proliferation of persons and things in their snowballing confusion of ceaseless movement back and forth, up and down, around and around, his profusion of words regressing from nonsense to the no-words of syllables and letters; Genet's elaborate and eye-arresting sets, reaching four distinct levels in one of the scenes of *The Screens,* his shuttling between appearance and reality as props come and go, as characters shift roles, as play gives way to play-within-play, which in turn reverts to play, his poetry which sparkles on occasion with a sensuous, concrete richness—all these qualities make for the finest theatre of our day.

But Beckett, Ionesco, and Genet are more than masters of a craft: their artistry is equaled by their vision. From their plays we gain a perceptive composite portrait of the contemporary man for whom God is either dead or dying, of the man who sees himself in that strange twilight land between life and death. Beckett's *Waiting for Godot,* Ionesco's *The Killer,* and Genet's *The Balcony* form, in this respect, the perfect trilogy. Beckett's protagonists wait with the flicker of hope that approaches despair. Ionesco's Bérenger, first spun to ecstasy by his surface view of the Radiant City, then learns its utter, death-spawning rottenness, and finally can only surrender to the Killer with the "What can we do . . . What can we do" (*K*, 109) which paces the falling curtain. And Genet's players give Bérenger their heartening and victorious answer. The would-be Bishop speaks for many of them when, at the beginning of *The Balcony*, he describes his path as "a skilful, vigorous heading towards Absence. Towards Death" (*Bal*, 1). We *cannot*, as Bérenger learned, battle Death on equal terms, but we *can*, Genet affirms, beat Death at his own game, by seeking him out and gaining control over him through our very surrender to him. It is no rarity, in the history of political warfare, for conquered peoples to absorb and gain ascendancy over forces that in a frontal attack they never could have overcome. The three plays do give us a familiar portrait of the contemporary man who, first reduced to the faintest of hopes, asks the question of what he can do, and then resigns himself to the seeming inevitability of cosmic nothingness. Such is not the whole story, and not all men have laid down their arms before the forces, conscious or unconscious, which oppress them. But only the blind can deny that, in the thoughts of many men, it is the prevailing story. And though there are indeed those among us who are convinced that one's waiting for Godot will be crowned with success—through supernatural or human intervention, through a divine breakthrough or a reassertion of nobility, courage, and wisdom in man—the predominant disposition of our time is toward holocaust. It is this temperament which the theatre of the absurd has engraved with precision tooling.

Great prophets of doom have always served to shake their hearers into an awareness of the times. The greatest —at least the most inspiriting—of them have issued tentative, conditional proclamations: "Our people are, in evil and ignorance, moving disastrously toward destruction; they will be destroyed *unless* . . ." So, for example, spoke those earliest Hebrew prophets, Amos and Hosea. It is sometimes difficult to discern the dividing line between the prophets of conditional disaster and those who proclaim, with finality: "Our people are moving toward destruction and will be destroyed." Was George Orwell saying that 1984 will inevitably come? Or that 1984 will come unless, awaking to the sweeping encroachment of totalitarianism, we recognize the enemy and fight it? The same question may also be asked of Ionesco and Genet, the principal subjects of this study. And we will conclude that Ionesco, amid and despite a welter of contradiction, sees his calling in part as that of summoning mankind back to its humanity, back to an emotional responsiveness in which man may once again come to know man through the kind of communication that inevitably springs from love and compassion. With Genet, the answer is different. With a "Come, sweet death," he celebrates man's ultimate goal as the triumphant arrival into the silence and darkness of nothingness.

Initial productions of Beckett, Ionesco, and Genet came within six years of one another: Genet's *The Maids* in 1947, Ionesco's *The Bald Soprano* in 1950, Beckett's *Waiting for Godot* in 1953. The large majority of their plays were written during the 1950's. Their productivity has decreased during the 1960's and may be approaching its end. Perhaps Beckett has no more to say after *Happy Days* and *Play,* or Ionesco after the Bérenger plays, or Genet after *The Screens.* Even if this is true, their achievement of a decade and a half has been immense. No other twentieth-century "school" of playwrights has been more theatrically and philosophically effective; none has more vividly and deeply represented its age—an age conscious, perhaps above all else, of life's absurdity.

Albert Camus' *The Myth of Sisyphus* offers the most extended and precise definition of the word *absurd,* certainly as it applies to those dramatists so brilliantly analyzed in Martin Esslin's *The Theatre of the Absurd.* The sense of absurdity is born in a man, Camus affirms, when he no longer takes his habitual, mechanical, routine life (or death-in-life) for granted, when he begins to ask "why." Such thoughtfulness, introspection, and questioning give rise to a series of disquieting epiphanies. This startling awakening, which passes many men by, comes to the more sensitive, the *Myth* tells us, at the age of thirty—and so it does, in literature at least: Camus' "stranger," Meursault, is thirty at the time of his self-revealing trial; and Kafka's Joseph K. awakes to his trial on the morning of his thirtieth birthday. Man awakes, Camus tells us, to three potentially shattering discoveries.

First, a man comes to realize at thirty that *he* is going to die. He has long known that death *is,* that *one* dies, but he now recognizes that even he will be death's victim, that time, the *sine qua non* of mortality, is his fatal enemy. One of the most impressive literary expressions of this discovery is Tolstoy's "The Death of Ivan Ilyich," though Ivan is over thirty when he comes to his knowledge. And in Shakespeare's *Richard III* Ionesco finds that most profound truth before which all men must bow, a truth which "is simple and absolutely commonplace: I die, he dies, you die" (*NCN,* 31). Man's first step into consciousness of the absurd is the realization that he, who has taken life for granted and enjoyed some of its pleasures, will die.

If the sensitive man's first discovery is his true relationship to time, his second is his relationship to nature. The young are often Wordsworthians or Thoreauvians or Emersonians, feeling at home in the cosmic order, seeing in the natural world of earth and sea and sky, of grass and trees and flowers, of birds of the air and beasts of the field a personal kinship and compatibility. But they come to realize either, with Tennyson, that nature is "red in tooth and claw" (or, with Camus, plague-ridden), or that nature is indifferent, with neither care for nor consciousness of the descendants of Adam. The natural world comes to be viewed no longer as a home, but as a chilling, unfeeling complex oblivious to its human and transient dwellers.

Become aware of time's destructiveness and nature's indifference, man may turn with some hope to himself, only to find no solace there either. Formerly confident of his humanity, of his freedom to choose his way and guide gracefully his movements in a constant flux of activity, of his capacity to exercise that *élan vital* so dear to Henri Bergson, he now sees himself as a machine, bound to repetitive and fatuous gestures that deny his human beingness. Observe the unheard man in the telephone booth, turn off the sound but not the picture of the television, and, behold, the machine is at work. Etched in today's memory is the Charlie Chaplin of *Modern Times,* who, having spent his day tightening bolts on an assembly line, then walks home with his right arm still repeating the rigid movement of the day's unvarying labor.

To come to believe that time is his destroyer, that the natural world observes him not, and that he is brother to the machine—such is the way by which man arrives at a knowledge of the absurdity of this world, an absurdity born of the juxtaposition of all that he would wish life to be, with the way that life actually seems to be. Man yearns to defy time, to feel at home in the world, to rest confident of his humanity, but he comes to know his mortality, his loneliness, his machinelike rigidity. The absurd is, Camus writes, "that divorce between the mind that desires and the world that disappoints."

Camus presents an expository definition of absurdity. The playwrights of the absurd, as they speak to us across the footlights, transport us into the fabric of absurdity itself. They do not, as Mr. Esslin has remarked, tell us what the condition is—they enable us to experience it. And in most cases the experience into which we are drawn is that of the disparity between the life man hopes for and the life he endures. This observation, to be sure, is not so fully applicable to Genet as it is to Beckett and Ionesco.

Waiting for Godot, of all plays, perhaps best exemplifies "that divorce between the mind that desires and the world that disappoints." From their bleak and joyless world Vladimir and Estragon seek relief. They recall that, according to one of the gospels, one of the two thieves who flanked Jesus on the cross was saved. In Godot's promised arrival they place their hope for salvation. The first intruder upon their solitary and anxious waiting is the monstrous Pozzo, whom they initially mistake for Godot, but who, with his grotesque servant Lucky, is the epitome of all that is most vicious and degrading. Throughout the play the near-desperate waiting continues, in spite of all the frustrations and disappointments which the world heaps upon the protagonists. Despite their mutual impatience and offensiveness, they remain together, finding solace in each other's companionship and conversation, sparse and nagging as the latter frequently is. They are the perfect prototypes of Beckett's world, together comprising the Everyman sunk in the misery of this universe and, though seemingly powerless in themselves to amend their condition, awaiting a miraculous intervention of a supernatural force. They weather two ghastly meetings with Pozzo and Lucky, and two messages (there have been others antecedent to the play's action) from Godot that he will not appear on that evening, but certainly on the next. The last words of each of the two acts, first spoken by Vladimir and next by Estragon, are "Yes, let's go," but the final stage direction of each act is *They do not move*." The protagonists are remarkable for their tenacious clinging to a slim skein of hope, the threads of which seem difficult to weave in this world.

Other Beckett dramatic protagonists are less markedly waiting, but the juxtaposition of hope and disappointment, and, sometimes, of past joys and present miseries, is persistent. In *Endgame* the weary Hamm, miserably confined to his armchair, pathetically voices his hopes: "If I could sleep I might make love. I'd go into the woods. My eyes would see . . . the sky, the earth. I'd run, run, they wouldn't catch me." But he is sleepless, loveless, sightless to nature, and motionless. His servant Clov also has his vain dreams: "I love order. It's my dream. A world where all would be silent and still and each thing in its last place, under the last dust." Despite the seeming failure of all hopes, however, they share with Vladimir and Estragon a bold persistence to continue. Both Hamm and Clov, three-quarters of the way through the play, speak the same sentiment: "Keep going, can't you, keep going!" And certainly Winnie of *Happy Days,* finally buried up to her neck in the dirt, displays the most persevering quality of endurance, happy that her near-moribund husband Willie can respond to her conversation by so much as a wiggling of his fingers.

Other Beckett characters, mired in their wretchedness, can look back to better times when hopes were realized. Hamm's parents, Nagg and Nell, though trapped in their ash bins, remember happier days when, betrothed, they went rowing on Lake Como and capsized through their ecstatic motions. Krapp, who at seventy plays and replays those tapes which chronicle his earlier life, listens with particular fondness to the account of his one relationship approaching love, enjoyed three decades earlier and still his most precious memory: "I lay down across her with my face in her breasts and my hand on her. We lay there without moving. But under us all moved, and moved us, gently, up and down, and from side to side."

Ionesco, no less than Beckett, evokes from us that feeling of the wide gap between our hopes and our disappointments. *The Bald Soprano,* a "tragedy of language" (*NCN,* 175) as Ionesco calls it, strikes immediately a most unnerving truth for humanity, the truth that communication through language and feelings, the most basic necessity for human joy, simply does not exist—that persons impart nothing to each other because they no longer have anything to impart. And perhaps the most hilariously funny dialogue in the whole theatre of the absurd—the one spoken by Mr. and Mrs. Martin as they sit across from each other at the Smiths' and have the strange feeling they have met before—is also one of the most tragic. They recall in rigorous detail every material facet of their recent lives, every detail of their trip from Manchester to London, and every furnishing of their flat, but of each other neither spouse remembers anything. In what one would hope to be the most intimate of human relationships is found only the most profound ignorance and indifference.

Of all Ionesco's plays, perhaps *The Chairs* portrays most vividly the wide margin between human aspirations and the bitter truth of the way things are. The Old Man, in the leisurely seclusion of his lighthouse, has devoted most of his adult life to formulating and phrasing the message which will save the world. He would serve as the Godot for those millions who, he is convinced, would be lost without him: "I have a message, that's God's truth, I struggle, a mission, I have something to say, a message to communicate to humanity, to mankind" (*C*, 119). The message ready, he and his wife invite the citizens of the world to visit them and hear the saving words. No talented speaker, he has, as a last precaution to insure the success of his message, summoned the Orator to deliver the proclamation to the assembled guests. But when the curtain falls, we have beheld an orator who is mute and capable only of writing nonsense words and letters on the blackboard at his side. Nor can the Old Man try again. For made confident by the arrival of the Orator in whom he had such trust, he has happily leaped through the window to his death in the awaiting sea, mistakenly assured that the world would now be saved.

The Bérenger of *The Killer* is still another example of one whose highest hopes are completely negated. With wondrous memories of the joys of his youth, as well as more recent experiences of the bleakest and most depressing of worlds, he first sees in the Radiant City the epitome of all that life should be. But once he pierces the spurious decor of the city, penetrating deeper and deeper into its cancerous reality, he learns that death, not life, is dominant. Of the innumerable arguments he musters in trying to dissuade the Killer from his murderous ways, not one is sufficient either to convert the hideous adversary or to maintain his own faith in his ability to withstand the Killer's voiceless power. At the play's end, the helpless Bérenger can only stammer: "Oh God! There's nothing we can do. What can we do . . . What can we do" (*K,* 109). The final action shows the chuckling Killer moving toward his latest victim— most discouragingly, a victim whose resistance has been greater than that of many men.

The plays of Beckett and Ionesco present vividly the disparity between the characters' yearnings and their accomplishments, yet with an important difference. The viewer or reader of a Beckett play feels little distance between himself and the protagonist. Vladimir and Estragon, Hamm and Clov, Krapp, Winnie—all of them may at first be viewed with some distaste or condescension, but not for long. For anyone who is moved to return to Beckett (and not everyone is) comes to suffer the most intensive empathy with his characters. Their longings, as well as their bitter disappointments, mirror our own hopes and responses to the daily round of life. More than this, the Beckett character is conscious of his predicament, much as we like to believe we are conscious of our own. There are, of course, various kinds of irony in Beckett's plays, but there is seldom the irony conveyed by the author's looking over the shoulder of his character, catching the eye of the reader, and entering into a tacit complicity, an unspoken "you and I, dear reader, are sufficiently intelligent, sophisticated, and sensitive to see what a fool I have created." Ring Lardner's "Haircut" is a fine example of this kind of irony; Gulliver's voyage to Brobdingnag, though more subtly and compassionately presented than "Haircut," has something of the same tone. The portraits of Lardner's monologist barber and Swift's Gulliver are ironic because the characters are ignorant, in different degree, of themselves. But Vladimir and Estragon and other Beckett protagonists know themselves as well as we know ourselves, which is not to say that they have all the answers to the ultimate problems of life but that they are aware of the highly problematic and mysterious condition of their lives.

Ionesco and his audience, however, usually stand above the characters, viewing them sometimes with Olympian detachment, frequently with condescension. The irony is greater, the sympathy less, than in Beckett. Bérenger comes closest to being the exception to the general rule, a fact which helps account for the power of *Rhinoceros* and the even greater power of *The Killer*. But the distance between the playgoer and, say, the Martins and the Smiths is immense. We hardly feel in empathy with the characters of *The Bald Soprano*. We find them funny and pathetic by turn (or simultaneously); we find some of our traits mirrored in them. But we view them more as caricatures than as human beings with whom we sense close kinship. We feel quite superior to them and, with Ionesco, look down upon them as we would upon dancing, erratic marionettes. But if we do not identify with Ionesco's characters, we do at least see them as he would have us see them. They succeed well in conveying to us his vision of the world, a vision set early in life, as Ionesco makes clear in recounting a memory of childhood:

. . . when I was a child, I can still remember how my mother could not drag me away from the Punch and Judy show in the Luxembourg Gardens. I would go there day after day and could stay there, spellbound, all day long. But I did not laugh. That Punch and Judy show kept me there open-mouthed, watching those puppets talking, moving and cudgeling each other. It was the very image of the world that appeared to me, strange and improbable but truer than true, in the profoundly simplified form of caricature, as though to stress the grotesque and brutal nature of the truth. (*NCN*, 20)

Although Beckett and Ionesco do not stand in the same relationship to their respective characters, they share a wide area of agreement about the ways of the world and man's hopes and disappointments. They lament together the difficulties of human communication and the consequent terrible estrangement which separates man from his fellows and results in loneliness. They see man as a victim of circumstances, of the persistent assault of malign forces that seem beyond his control. And their areas of agreement are shared by many men who, with Beckett's characters in particular and certainly with the Bérenger of *Rhinoceros,* would resist the hovering presence of despair and continue to fight against the dark pressures which threaten every hope. Whatever the differences between Beckett's and Ionesco's interpretation of and response to life, they share far more in common than either has in common with Genet. Whereas they would, each in his own way, resist the demonic forces that plague humanity, Genet would join hands with the powers of darkness and set up his altar to them.

Genet's response to life's absurdity exhibits a most fascinating twist. He would stay "that divorce between the mind that desires and the world that disappoints" by changing man's desires. If communication is difficult, he would pride himself on the joy of noncommunication. If the mind finds its desire for honesty, fidelity, and heterosexual love difficult of attainment, he would direct the mind's desire toward the glories of theft, betrayal, and homosexuality. If Godot seems reticent, unseeing, and unhearing, Genet would remind us that Satan stands ready to receive the frustrated men-in-waiting. The gears must simply be reversed—love must give way to hate, creation to destruction, persuasion to power, God to Satan. In sum, if the juggernaut which is the world will not yield to man, then let man surrender to the world and, in the very process, gain power over what hitherto had been overpowering. Genet is the great accommodator.

Accordingly, the absurdist dimension of most of Genet's drama lies in the disparity between what the character holds as his ideal and what most of the theatre-goers see as their own. In terms of Camus' definition of absurdity, what distinguishes the Genet character most radically from that of Beckett or Ionesco is the nature of his desire. He desires what would, to say the least, bitterly disappoint a Vladimir or a Bérenger. It is difficult, for example, to conceive of Genet's writing a play which does not celebrate at least one murder. And whereas the Killer is one of the great antagonists of Ionesco's work, Genet's murderers are habitually the protagonists. Genet's love of death, preferably violently accomplished, is profound and passionate. Moreover, it is significant that, of all the murders committed in his plays, only one—Lefranc's strangling of Maurice—fails to bring a rich satisfaction to its perpetrator.

Among Genet's many protagonists, Lefranc of *Deathwatch*, the first play composed though performed and published after *The Maids*, is the single unequivocal failure. His murder of Maurice is the only gratuitous one in Genet's dramatic corpus. He commits the deed in emulation of his idol Green Eyes, whose wanton and seemingly unprovoked strangling of a girl had won him the plaudits of his prison community. Lefranc's violent act, on the other hand, reduces him to a cipher—and all because it was committed for the wrong reason. He is condemned to personal defeat not because of committing the act of murder *per se* but because of doing so without the vocation to murder, thus countering his destiny rather than bowing to it. But over *The Maids* and the suicide-murder involving Claire, Solange, and Madame hangs the aura of success. The maids were called to the deed, and the absurdity lies not in the disappointment of their desires, not in their being unwilling pawns, but in the disparity between their goals and the at least conscious goals of their audience. And Genet's most fully realized character, Saïd of *The Screens*, makes of his poverty, his wife's ugliness, his mother's offensiveness, and his fellows' violence and rapacity the steppingstones to his own long-sought and perfectly accomplished annihilation—by way of five revolver shots. Genet and his players join forces with the world's malignity and, in most cases, win the salvation and peace which, Genet insists, come with annihilation. The Genet formula, then, is the opposite of that of Beckett and Ionesco.

Camus has written of the absurdity man perceives as he recognizes the fatal power of time, the indifference or hostility of the natural world, and the machinelike rigidity of the human being. Each recognition is the bridge from hope to disappointment, and each has influenced the theatre of the absurd in its preoccupations with death, with man's sense of homelessness, and with his tragicomic rigidity. Yet these preoccupations, in the minds of men and in their literature, have a many-centuried history. Of more recent date and also of considerable influence on the absurdists is another recognition, a complex one, having almost as many meanings as it has adherents and yet summed up in the simplest of statements: "God is dead." No sentence of the prolific Friedrich Nietzsche is more widely remembered, and perhaps no sentence ever written has had greater influence on our century.

The most common meaning of the phrase is that the biblical God is no longer a force in the lives of men. It does not assert that there never was a God and does not necessarily imply that there is not now a God. Most commonly, it means that even if God does exist "out there," he is not seen or heard or felt by mankind; that, so far as contemporary man is concerned, God might just as well not exist. In order to discover what difference this fact may make, it is necessary to ask who is or who was this God now dead to us. Of the many descriptions and identifications of the biblical God, two are of paramount importance to man. First, in both the Old Testament and the New, God is he who has created every man in his image and with a purpose, and has called each man to the fulfillment of his unique purpose. Second, in the New Testament, God is he who, through Christ, has promised an eternal life in his presence to those who faithfully fulfill their purposes by means of his grace.

To the Jew and Christian, past and present, the *living* God has the most profound influence on the life-in-this-world of every man. The believer rests confident, not because it is easy to discover and carry out God's will, but because there is such a thing as a vocation—a calling he must seek through prayer and meditation. Very solacing is a man's conviction that life has a meaning and he a purpose, that there is an omniscient, loving Creator and Sustainer of all things human and earthly. However fully such a believer may recognize the hostility of his fellows, the seeming indifference of the universe, and his own human deficiencies, he is constantly sustained by his belief in a merciful God who wills his good. And of equal importance is the conviction that, through the Old Testament prophets and through Christ and the apostles, God has made known the rules and spirit, in terms of law and love, whereby a man should live. However outrageous a man's fortune, he must not be distracted from righteous ways but must courageously endure through the knowledge that God too is in history.

The New Testament's promise that there is a life to come in which the faithful will forever enjoy God's presence has, of course, exerted an immense influence (a malign one in the judgment of both Camus and Jean-Paul Sartre) on the Christian's response to this earthly existence. God is believed to be not only in history, constantly by the side of the heavily yoked; he is also outside history, there to await his chosen ones in the fullness of his glory.

But the fact is, as Nietzsche's "God is dead" intimates, that many men do not live as if the biblical God is in and beyond history. By Nietzsche's time there were many voices crying, without belief, in the wilderness; many others professed faith but did not act upon it. And even Søren Kierkegaard, who predated Nietzsche by almost half a century, found few Christians in Christendom. For him the professing Christian was often like an unthinking machine, merely going through the empty, rigid motions of what he proclaimed as his faith. In our own time, of course, one of the most prominent schools of religious thought finds various theologians, ecclesiastics, and laymen bound together, in spite of much diversity among them, under the rubric of death-of-God theology.

The most terrifying absurdity of our century is expressed in the phrase "God is dead." To come to the belief, after many centuries in which the world's order, meaning, and purpose have been predicated on God's being, that God has absented himself is to feel a strange emptiness, homelessness, and disappearance of familiar guides and landmarks. The "mind's deepest desire," Camus asserts in *The Myth of Sisyphus,* "is an insistence upon familiarity, an appetite for clarity." A striking example of the quest for familiarity and clarity is Jacob's wrestling with the angel. Jacob, seeking the identity of his assailant, forced the angel to speak to him and thereby was brought, as he affirmed, to a direct vision of God's being. But the man for whom God is dead meets no angel and hears no angel's voice. *His* need is answered only by silence. Camus, again, puts it with exactness: "The absurd is born of that confrontation between the human need and the unreasonable silence of the world." If there is no desire deeper than man's insistence on familiarity and clarity, there is no disappointment greater than the silence which confronts our questions. The phrase "God is dead" expresses well that awful disparity between our most anxious hope and our most desperate disappointment. W. B. Yeats, in "The Second Coming," defines the structurelessness of a universe without God: "Things fall apart; the centre cannot hold; / Mere anarchy is loosed upon the world."

The theatre of the absurd bears witness not only to man's sense of mortality, alienation, and robotization but also to his sense of God's death. Much of contemporary literature is predicated on the assumption that God is dead, just as the literature of medieval and Renaissance times was written with the assumption that God was very much alive. Whether Godot will, in time, appear to Vladimir and Estragon is problematical; that he remains beyond eye and ear within the context of the play is clear. Clov's opening line in *Endgame* is certainly meant to recall the dying words of Christ recorded in the Fourth Gospel: "It is finished." Clov is simply not quite so certain: "Finished, it's finished, nearly finished, it must be nearly finished." And Nagg's attempt at prayer, "Our Father which art——," is quickly countered by Hamm's "Silence! In silence!"; this response is to be construed both as a silencing of Nagg and as a reminder that "Our Father" is "in silence." Beckett's twilight world is brooded over by God's absence and silence.

Ionesco has not among his characters any who even so much as wait for God. The one extended argument intimating the possibility of a living God forms a part of Bérenger's monologic attempt to halt the Killer. But even here, by means of stage directions calling for Bérenger to speak with a hollow, unconfident eloquence, Ionesco makes clear that references to the brotherhood of man, the vicarious sacrifice of Christ, and the intercession of the saints have no firm place in Bérenger's beliefs. And in a more recent Bérenger play, *Exit the King,* a highly allegorical drama written in 1962, the character Bérenger may, among other things, represent the dying God. Marie's twice-repeated "Oh God" (*EK,* 22, 26) could be merely an exclamatory remark but in its context it could also refer vocatively to Bérenger, the King who has lived seemingly forever and who fades into a mist at the curtain. The death of that religious impulse which formerly nourished Western civilization is felt not only in the plays of Ionesco. His most explicit statement, expressed with regret, is found in a brief essay on one of Kafka's short stories:

This theme of man astray in the labyrinth, without a guiding thread, is primordial, as we know, in Kafka's work: if man has no guiding thread, it is because he no longer really wanted one. Hence his feeling of guilt, his anguish, the absurdity of history. Anything without a goal is absurd: and this ultimate goal can only be found outside history, it ought to guide the history of mankind, in other words give it meaning. Whether we like it or not, this reveals the profoundly religious character of Kafka's work; when man is cut off from his religious or metaphysical roots, he is lost, all his struggles become senseless, futile and oppressive.

But why in Kafka does man suffer? Because in the last resort he exists for something other than material comfort or the ephemeral: his true vocation, from which he has turned aside, must lie in his quest for the imperishable. It is the world unsanctified that is denounced by Kafka; and this is exactly what is meant by a world without Goal; in the dark labyrinth of the world, man now reaches out only unconsciously and gropingly for a lost dimension that has completely vanished from sight. (*NCN,* 256–257)

Both Beckett and Ionesco convey nostalgia for a human community convinced of the presence of a meaning, purpose, and clarity—legacies of the biblical tradition. Both writers present the absurdity of a godless world. But whereas Ionesco's characters are generally oblivious to any sense of God, in Beckett's plays biblical and theological references are many, particularly in *Waiting for Godot, Endgame,* and *All That Fall.* In the last, the dramatic action is played off in ironic counterpoint against the Psalmist's verse which is the text of the play: "The Lord upholdeth all that fall, and raiseth up all those that be bowed down" (Psalm 145:14). If Beckett is very much concerned with the *question* of God's being, Genet is obsessed by the *fact* of God's being. Genet's plays—or certainly the philosophical and theological premises on which they rest—would collapse if God were in fact dead.

Genet sees the whole of life as a complex of polar opposites, with both units of each pair of opposites mutually and absolutely dependent on the other for its being. We have already suggested that, with Genet, love must give way to hate, creation to destruction, persuasion to power, God to Satan. But if any one of them were to give way completely, to be negated, the other would cease to exist. Destruction, for example, presupposes creation, and should creation come to a stop, the Genet protagonist would soon be deprived of the ecstasy of destruction. In *The Balcony,* the make-believe priest remarks to the make-believe penitent whom he has just shriven: ". . . our holiness lies only in our being able to forgive you your sins" (*Bal,* 4). And the man who plays judge tells the woman who plays thief: "You need only refuse . . . to be who you are . . . for me to cease to be . . . to vanish, evaporated" (*Bal,* 14). This concept of polar opposites, of what may be called the reverse mirror image, is central to Genet's thought.

Genet's initial aim is to exalt the reverse of the major values and principles of the biblical tradition. "Saintliness," he writes in *Thief's Journal,* "means turning pain to good account. It means forcing the devil to be God. It means obtaining the recognition of evil" (*TJ,* 205). Genet's system of values is easily understood: it is necessary only to transpose every biblical affirmation into its opposite. But if Genet would celebrate the perfect diabolism, he must, to continue to write, affirm the presence of God. If God, as well as the imperatives of law and love, ceases to exist, Genet and his whole prescription for action would vanish. His opposition is his nourishment, and his satanism would have neither meaning nor life if deprived of its reverse image. Although Genet's initial aim is to exalt the satanic, his ultimate goal is the annihilation of *everything.* Each successive play is a further step toward *The Screens,* in which the protagonist Saïd reaches the ultimate state of bliss—a complete void in which there is room for neither God nor Satan. *The Screens,* celebrating and attaining this supreme nothingness, is the only Genet play in which the implicit presence of God is, finally, not needed.

The theatre of the absurd is the product of many forces and influences. And certainly among the most significant of these is the disappointment of man's hopes, a condition most clearly described in *The Myth of Sisyphus,* and all that the proclamation of God's death implies—in particular, the loss of faith in traditional values. Beckett's protagonists lament the loss; Ionesco's either lament it or are oblivious to it; most of Genet's clasp the loss to them and, by making it their own, rise above it. The plays of all three writers are explorations, quests for a new way of life (or death) in a world which seems to hold little hope, light, or clarity.

Directly related to the disappearance of certain commonly accepted values is the breakdown of communication. Throughout the theatre of the absurd, Camus' "unreasonable silence" is loudly and passionately proclaimed. Communication depends upon certain norms, the kinds of basic, mutually held assumptions so generously bequeathed by the biblical tradition. The biblical ideals long served as canons, as measuring sticks according to which human dispositions and actions could be judged. But the dispossessed contemporary man can neither look back to such guidelines nor forward to the promise of new ones. The absurd man is an exile from all that was familiar and clear. Again, we can turn to Camus for a description of the dilemma: ". . . in a universe suddenly divested of illusions and lights, man feels an alien, a stranger. His exile is without memory since he is deprived of the memory of a lost home or the hope of a promised land." In such an exile, communication—the ability to be, and the feeling of being, in touch with another—is frighteningly difficult of attainment.

Beckett's characters are intensively aware of near incommunicability. And if their imperative is to wait, to continue, to keep going, it is also to keep talking. One almost always thinks of Beckett characters in indivisible pairs, with each person feeling a strong compulsion to speak and/or to be spoken to. Vladimir and Estragon, although they threaten on various occasions to leave each other, *cannot* do so. At one point in *Waiting for Godot,* after a long silence, Vladimir pleads, "Say something!" to which Estragon replies, "I'm trying." After another extended silence Vladimir begs, "*in anguish,*" "Say anything at all." Krapp, cut off completely from the company of another person, listens to the recorded voice of his earlier self. In *Happy Days* Winnie's greatest anxiety is that she will be deprived of her *hearer,* Willie, before she finds the peace of death. Her only joy is found in some flickering sign of her husband's responsiveness: "Raise a finger, dear, will you please, if you are not quite senseless. [*Pause.*] Do that for me, Willie please, just the little finger, if you are still conscious. [*Pause. Joyful.*]—Oh all five, you are a darling today, now I may continue with an easy mind."

Probably no writer in the history of literature has been more obsessed than Ionesco with the incommunicability which defines the distance between men. As was previously mentioned, he describes *The Bald Soprano* as "the tragedy of language." The Smiths and the Martins move from an initial exchange of banal sentences, to nonsense, to syllables, to letters. Their disease is clearly diagnosed by Ionesco:

The Smiths and the Martins no longer know how to talk because they no longer know how to think, they no longer know how to think because they are no longer capable of being moved, they have no passions, they no longer know how to be, they can become anyone or anything, for as they are no longer themselves, in an impersonal world, they can only be someone else, they are interchangeable: Martin can change places with Smith and vice versa, no one would notice the difference. (*NCN*, 180)

The Bald Soprano is not the only tragedy of language. In *The Lesson* the Maid vainly and prophetically warns the Professor: "Philology leads to calamity!" (*L*, 60) Roberta II of *Jack, or The Submission* can reduce all words to the sound *cat* without entailing any great loss in her communicability with Jack. The Orator of *The Chairs* is a mute. The Killer responds to Bérenger only with a chuckle and a shrug of the shoulders. And by the end of *Rhinoceros,* Bérenger alone has a voice— and no one to whom he can direct it.

With Genet, there is once again a difference. If he cherishes any kind of communication, it is that of invective. His characters desire to achieve a distance from others so that ultimately they can exalt the silence of the void. In *Deathwatch,* Lefranc seeks the utter isolation of Green Eyes and climaxes whatever communication he endured with Maurice by murdering him. The perfect relationship among the maids and their Madame is achieved when Madame departs and Claire is a victim both of her own suicide and of Solange's murderous intent. The make-believe Bishop, Judge, and General of *The Balcony* seek nothing more passionately than a severance from the whole round of life which is normally theirs. In *The Blacks* Archibald thoughtfully promises his white audience that they will in no way be disturbed or embarrassed by the insult of communication:

This evening we shall perform for you. But, in order that you may remain comfortably settled in your seats in the presence of the drama that is already unfolding here, in order that you be assured that there is no danger of such a drama's worming its way into your precious lives, we shall even have the decency—a decency learned from you —to make communication impossible. We shall increase the distance that separates us—a distance that is basic—by our pomp, our manners, our insolence—for we are also actors. (*Bl,* 12)

And it is, again, Saïd of *The Screens* who epitomizes the ultimate achievement for Genet, as this supreme unhero attains in the void a silence that is absolute.

Among the influences, then, on the drama of Beckett, Ionesco, and Genet are man's sense of his mortality, alienation, and inhumanity; the proclaimed death or silence of God; and the loss of communicability through words or feelings. By means of a surrealistic, nightmarish style and tone, their plays convey to us the very feeling of absurdity itself, an absurdity so congenial to mid-twentieth-century life. Certainly, the plays are in this way *de*scriptive of the life of our times. We might ask finally, in these opening statements, to what extent they are *pre*scriptive. Given the world as it is in the experience of these dramatists, do they go beyond its description and prescribe a response to it, some way of action or passion which may help man to live in or with it or to counter its problems? An attempt at an answer may be made, with the understanding that there is no tidy summary that will encompass all of the plays of any one of the dramatists.

Waiting for Godot, of all Beckett's dramatic works, expresses most clearly and explicitly the fundamental tension—to wait or not to wait—found to a lesser degree in his other writings. We have written elsewhere that the human predicament described in Beckett's first play is that of man living on the Saturday after the

Friday of the crucifixion and not really knowing if all hope is dead or if the next day will bring the new life that has been promised.[1] Vladimir and Estragon ponder the wisdom or vanity of waiting, twice tempted to the suicide that haunts despair and tempted also to leave the scene; yet they decide to wait and see what the morrow brings. Thus they vacillate between despair and hope, settling finally for what might be described as a desperate hope. In the plays that follow, the ratio of despair to hope seems to increase, if such is possible without expunging hope altogether. Yet the Beckett characters do keep going, do show compassion for their fellows, and do continue to talk. Winnie keeps her revolver—as well as her toothbrush, umbrella, and mirror—by her side, but she does not use it and declares the day a happy one when she can elicit even a minimum response from Willie.

The most common denominator shared by most of Ionesco's characters is that of being a victim of duty. The "duty" is invariably that of conforming to whatever the prevailing winds may decree. His characters differ from one another both in the extent of their consciousness of being victims and in the extent of their resistance to victimization. The Smiths and Martins, for example, are so far gone that they have no introspective knowledge and consequently are able to offer no resistance to the banal quality of life engulfing them. The Pupil of *The Lesson* and Jack, in the Jack plays, at least put up strong resistance, the Pupil to the point where she must be murdered in order to be subdued. Amédée of *Amédée, or How to Get Rid of It* and Choubert of *Victims of Duty* share memories of a time when life was more generous, but their nostalgia is not sufficient to bring those days back. By the ends of their respective plays, Amédée's problem is "solved" as he is wafted into space by a ballooning corpse, and Choubert is reduced to an automaton who can only chew the bread which is being

[1] Josephine Jacobsen and William R. Mueller, *The Testament of Samuel Beckett* (London: Faber & Faber, 1966), pp. 177–192.

nauseatingly stuffed into his mouth. Ionesco's most substantial and impressive protagonists are the Bérengers of *The Killer* and *Rhinoceros*. Bérenger is the most conscious and introspective of Ionesco's characters, and he offers in his roles differing responses to the fact of absurdity. He falls to the wordless blandishments of the Killer but holds out against the many vocal and urgent invitations to rhinoceritis. Thus some of Ionesco's characters are more helpless, unaware, and indifferent than the more consistently drawn Beckett protagonist, while others are less so. On the whole Ionesco would seem to offer less hope than Beckett and to find less reason to wait. Yet he would hardly have undertaken the role of playwright if he had seen no salutary purpose in presenting to us his sense of man's nature, perhaps as a shocking revelation, a call to self-awareness, a first step toward a possible amendment of condition.

Genet is by far the most prophetic of the three. He writes with a confidence which reaches arrogance. He possesses at once no hope and every hope: no hope—indeed, no desire—that man can or should approach the condition whose absence grieves both Beckett and Ionesco, and every hope that man may capitalize on what would at first seem his most tormenting defeat. He would conquer not by opposition but by joining his adversaries and seducing them to work in his behalf. Of Snowball, mighty king of the prison in *Deathwatch*, Lefranc asserts, "His chains carry him" (*D*, 107); in other words, the astute man is he who transforms what would normally be considered his oppressor into his slave. Part of the underlying philosophic position of *Deathwatch* Genet soon discards, but certainly *The Maids, The Balcony, The Blacks,* and *The Screens* form a systematic, step-by-step guide to success. Genet's formula is based first on the doctrine of polar opposites, the concept of the reverse mirror image. "*Her* joy feeds on *our* shame" (*M*, 81), Solange says of Madame; to remove one is to remove the other. And when the "white" Queen of *The Blacks* threatens death to the Negroes, the black Felicity shrewdly remarks: "You fool, just imagine how flat you'd be without that shade to set you off in high relief" (*Bl*, 104). Genet, working toward hate and destruction, polar opposites of love and creation, comes to realize that the process, carried to its logical conclusion and seemingly complete victory, would be ultimately self-defeating. Without the reverse images of love and creation to feed upon, parasitic hate and destruction must come to annihilation. But this realization, far from deterring him, gives him a new impetus. Finally, all of Genet's power is directed toward the goal of annihilation. This quest takes on its first embryonic form in the last speech of *The Maids*, as Solange boasts that she and Claire have been resurrected into "the delicate perfume of the holy maidens which they were in secret" (*M*, 100). The Bishop of *The Balcony*, as we have noted, sees his goal as Absence. And *The Screens* presents in Saïd that character who in fact achieves not the beatific but the demonic vision. When stripped of all accidental, contingent characteristics, he is the embodiment of sordidness; and the next logical step is indicated as one of the characters says to him: "We're embalming your sordidness" (*S*, 192). Saïd has moved from a living to a dead and embalmed sordidness on his way to the nirvana of nothingness. It is toward this ideal nothingness that Genet has carried us step by step; it is the ultimate nay-saying, the ultimate defiance of the world. And from here, it would seem, there is no place to go. It is difficult to see how Genet could write another play.

What, then, is prescribed? Beckett would have us await, for a while longer at least, some superhuman intervention; Ionesco would have us continue to seek a way out of our labyrinth; Genet would pipe us to the void.

Eugène Ionesco and the
Loss of Paradise

EUGÈNE IONESCO is the most nostalgic of the absurdist playwrights. Genet's world is predominantly present and future—the present despised and the future, vaporized into nothingness, yearned for. Beckett's characters occasionally look back: Nagg and Nell to their blissful afternoon on Lake Como, Krapp to that day three decades earlier when he came closest to the experience of love. Pozzo too recalls more felicitous times, and at one point Vladimir pleads in his behalf: "Let him alone. Can't you see he's thinking of the days when he was happy." Yet such reminiscences in Beckett do not constitute a major theme.

In Ionesco's works, recollections of a Golden Age, a prelapsarian Eden, are many. His world is a fallen one, in a way that Genet's most certainly is not and that Beckett's is in only a limited degree. Things were not always, Ionesco's characters suggest on many occasions, as they are now. If we live at present in a bleak and barren world—a world which, to quote Matthew Arnold, "Hath really neither joy, nor love, nor light, / Nor certitude, nor peace, nor help for pain"—humanity has not always suffered such darkness. And if the persons inhabiting Ionesco's world have lost the motions of the heart and mind which are the bases of human communication, mankind has not always been so sterile. It is the memory of this past radiance, this paradisiacal state pervaded by light and warmth and love, which gives to this

present of darkness, cold, and alienation so chilling a
horror and sadness.

With Ionesco, then, the beginning of things is defined
in this nostalgic memory of a paradise, long lost but
hardly forgotten. And it is this paradise which provides
the great foil and contrast to the present fallen world.
There is no better point of departure toward an understanding of Ionesco than to begin with this realm of
memory. It is the first of the four stages of his panoramic view of man's history, which may be divided
into the happy memory, the fall, the present, the future.
There are four major thematic questions: (1) What
was the nature of the original paradise? (2) How was
that paradise lost? (3) What is the nature of the present
fallen world? (4) What is the way, if any, of regaining
paradise?

Ionesco has, in the course of his plays, created his
own comprehensive myth, having recourse not to literal
history but to psychic exploration, which would attempt
to account for man's present death-in-life. But to trace
the myth, to work from past to present and then project
to future, is not to follow the plays chronologically.
Genet's great myth does unfold chronologically, as he
presents his themes embryonically in *Deathwatch* and
The Maids and then develops them systematically until
they reach their climax in *The Screens*. Such is not true
of Ionesco, whose first play, *The Bald Soprano,* is not
a memory play. It is in *Victims of Duty,* whose produc-
ion (1953) followed that of the first play by three years,
that we initially encounter the theme of a lost paradise.
The myth of the paradisiacal state is also presented in
the almost contemporaneous *Amédée, or How to Get
Rid of It,* and in *The Killer,* first produced in 1959.
What was the nature of that paradise?

It is significant that *Victims of Duty* and *Amédée*
are not only about the memory of paradise but also
about marriage, with the intimation that the failure of
what should be the most intimate and loving of human
relationships is the first cause of the loss of paradise.

The unattractive, complaining, domineering wives in both plays are named Madeleine; their husbands, Choubert and Amédée, are among those Ionesco characters who form the link between present and past, as each, in his present misery, nostalgically recalls a time of keen joy. At the very beginning of *Victims of Duty* Choubert speaks a line which characterizes well the dominant malaise of the world of the play: "Nowadays men have lost the peace of mind they had in the past" (*VD,* 117–118). At a later point in the action, an old and debilitated Choubert, surveying the ruins of his once lovely wife and lamenting their shared wretchedness, reflects upon a time markedly different from the present. His urgent words to Madeleine, his expressed hopes for a turning back of the clock, comprise Ionesco's first extended playing upon the theme of a lost paradise, of that age of joy before men had lost their peace of mind:

Is that you, Madeleine? Is it really you, Madeleine? What a terrible misfortune! How did it happen? How could it happen? We never noticed . . . Poor old lady, poor little faded doll, it's you just the same, but how different you look! When did it happen? Why didn't we stop it? This morning our path was strewn with flowers. The sky was drenched in sunshine. Your laughter rang clear. Our clothes were brand new, and we were surrounded by friends. Nobody had died and you'd never shed a tear. Suddenly it was winter and now ours is an empty road. Where are all the others? In their graves, by the roadside. I want our happiness back again, we've been robbed and despoiled. Oh, when will the light be blue again? Madeleine, you must believe me, I swear it wasn't I who made you old! No . . . I won't have it, I don't believe it, love is always young, love never dies. *I* haven't changed. Neither have you, you're pretending. Oh, but no! I can't deceive myself, you *are* old, so terribly old! Who made you old like that? Old, old, old, old, little old woman, old little doll. Our youth, on the road. Madeleine, little girl, I'll buy you a new dress, primroses, jewels. Your skin will find its bloom again. I want, I love you, I want, oh, please! We don't grow old when we're in love. I love you, grow young again, throw away that mask and look into my eyes. You must laugh, laugh, little girl! To smooth away the wrinkles. Oh, if only we could go singing and skipping and jumping again! I am young. We are young. (*VD,* 130)

Thus Choubert moves from his confrontation with the terrible present to thoughts of the early joyful life he shared with Madeleine, to the desperate hope for the past's revivification. And the reason for the fall from the presence of morning and sunshine and laughter into the now joyless darkness of old age is explicitly stated: "We don't grow old when we're in love." The death of love was the fall from paradise. Precisely what occasioned the deterioration *Victims of Duty* does not detail, but it is clear that Madeleine, who can hardly even recall love's presence, is primarily responsible for its absence.

A large number of Ionesco's plays present variations on the theme of marital dissonance, and the wives he portrays are an impressively grim gallery of shrews. The Madeleine of *Amédée* is not significantly different from her namesake in *Victims of Duty*. And in at least one very important respect Amédée is like Choubert, for Amédée too recalls a past which had seemed to promise a joyous paradise. Significantly too, his marriage to Madeleine, the very basis of his high hopes, had spelled the death of every expectation. The growing corpse, which has during the years spread through their entire apartment and has by its presence both cut them off from the outside world and smothered any possibility of love between them, appeared at the very beginning of their marriage. "We put him in the best room, *our* bedroom when we were first married" (*A,* 21), Amédée reminds his wife. Marriage, in short, was the entrance to death.

The action of the play takes place fifteen years after the marriage. In a surrealistic dream sequence and by means of a flashback, two characters, designated as Amédée II and Madeleine II, appear, representing the present spouses as they were on the day of their wedding. Even then Madeleine clearly repulsed every hope of love embraced by her husband:

AMÉDÉE II.   Madeleine, Madeleine!
MADELEINE II.   Don't come near me. Don't touch me.

THE LOSS OF PARADISE

You sting, sting, sting. You hu-urt me! What do you wa-ant! Where are you going, going, going?

AMÉDÉE II. Madeleine . . .

MADELEINE II [half wailing, half shouting]. Aaaah! Aaah! Aaah!

AMÉDÉE II. Madeleine, wake up, let's pull the curtains, the spring is dawning . . . Wake up . . . the room is flooded with sunshine . . . a glorious light . . . a gentle warmth! . . .

MADELEINE II. . . . night and rain and mud! . . . oh, the cold! . . . I'm shivering . . . dark . . . dark . . . dark! . . . you're blind, you're gilding reality! Don't you see that you're *making* it beautiful?

AMÉDÉE II. It's reality that makes us beautiful.

MADELEINE II. Good God, he's mad! he's mad! My husband's mad!!

AMÉDÉE II. Look . . . look . . . gaze into your memories, into the present and the future . . . look around you!

MADELEINE II. I can see nothing . . . It's dark . . . there's nothing . . . I can see nothing! . . . You're blind! (*A,* 47–48)

The dialogue continues, structured on the juxtaposition of contrasting images. To Amédée II the world is a "green valley" where there is "dancing in a ring, hand in hand"; to Madeleine II it is a "damp dark valley, a marsh that sucks you down until you drown." And when the bridegroom speaks of love gone mad and of the blaze of joy, the bride's response makes clear her erotic fears: "Don't shoot! . . . Bayonets and machine-guns . . . Don't shoot, I'm afraid!" The counterpointing imagery is resumed—from "a bed of flowers" to "desert sand"; from churches, bells, and the voices of children, and from fountains and spring to "oaths and toads"; from the "morning [that] never grows old" to "Heavy shades of night." Even Amédée II's anguished cry, "You've lost your memory, find it again, find your memory," fails to stir his bride to reminiscences of happier days and thus efface her present horror. And in a climactic and most ingenious exchange, one in which Amédée II sees life in terms of glass and light whereas Madeleine II sees it in terms of brass and night, Ionesco indicates the victory of the dark world:

AMÉDÉE II.   We love each other. We are happy. In a
  house of glass, a house of light . . .
MADELEINE II.   He means a house of brass, brass . . .
AMÉDÉE II.   House of glass, of light . . .
MADELEINE II.   House of brass, house of night!
AMÉDÉE II.   Of glass, of light, of glass, of light . . .
MADELEINE II.   Of brass, of brass, of night, of brass, of
  night . . .
AMÉDÉE II.   Of glass, glass, glass . . .
MADELEINE II.   Brass, night, brass, night, brass, night . . .
  brass, brass, brass, brass, brass . . .
AMÉDÉE II [*as though beaten*].   Glass, light, glass, light
  . . . brass, light, brass, night, night, brass . . .
TOGETHER.   Brass, night, brass, night, brass, night, brass,
  night . . .
AMÉDÉE II.   The brass and the night, alas . . . (*A*, 47–52)

As the dream fades away and the present action is
resumed, Amédée affectionately addresses his wife in
much the same tone and sentiment as Choubert had
spoken to his Madeleine:

Poor Madeleine! What a terrible time you've had. [*Looking as though he wishes to approach her.*] Do you know,
Madeleine, if we loved each other, if we really loved each
other, none of this would be important. [*Clasping his
hands.*] Why don't we try to love each other, *please,*
Madeleine? Love puts everything right, you know, it
changes life. Do you believe me, can you understand?
(*A*, 52–53)

But that the world of *Amédée* belongs not to the quick,
but to the dead, is evident as Madeleine, pointing to the
corpse, exclaims: "It's *his* world, not ours" (*A*, 53).
As in *Victims of Duty,* love is prescribed as the *sine qua
non* of paradise, but such human communion is beyond
attainment.

No character of Ionesco's is more given to nostalgic
memories than the Bérenger of *The Killer.* Nor does
any one express more fully than he, particularly in the
first act of that play, an awareness of the staggering
contrast between past and present. Bérenger, moreover,
senses not only a difference between past and present
but also a dissonance between his own being and the
total physical and social universe in which he lives. He

feels no correspondence between the seemingly joyous possibilities of his inner being and the indifferent or hostile outside world. He feels too that such a potential burst of inner life needs some kind of compatible, sympathetic environment in order to realize itself. It is as if a human being contains a seed which can come to growth only through some fructifying outer climate. His first vision of the Radiant City is misleading and causes him to believe that he has found again an outer world capable of nurturing the spark within. And so he unfolds his dream to the Architect who has been his guide:

. . . to project this universe within, some outside help is needed: some kind of material, physical light, a world that is objectively new. Gardens, blue sky, or the spring, which corresponds to the universe inside and offers a chance of recognition, which is like a translation or an anticipation of that universe, or a mirror in which its own smile could be reflected . . . in which it can find itself again and say: that's what I am in reality and I'd forgotten, a smiling being in a smiling world. . . . (K, 19)

Bérenger's sense of laceration springs from his feeling of alienation, of being cut off from and bearing no relationship to the whole outer world. And his sense of death-in-life—"I felt I couldn't go on living, and yet I couldn't die" (K, 19)—springs from the juxtaposed consciousness of a deathlike present and remembrance of a vital past. His treasured memories he describes in images similar to those used by Choubert and Amédée: figures of spring, warmth, light, and joy characterize feelings experienced in his earlier life. Such experiences occurred only rarely even then—perhaps five or ten times, he tells the Architect—yet frequently enough to bequeath a memory capable, for a time, of overcoming some later gloomy mood of the moment and of giving "fresh life to the force within . . . [him], to those reasonless reasons for living and loving . . ." (K, 21).

Even memories, however, grow dim with time and cease to serve as sufficient bulwark against the ravagement of the present. As Bérenger remarks, "My supplies of light have run out" (K, 22). The last feeling of

euphoria, experienced some two decades or more ago
when Bérenger was in his late teens, bore as one of its
distinguishing marks the sense that inner and outer
worlds were in perfect accord. Neither, on the one hand,
was the phenomenal world simply an emptiness which
could in no way be apprehended or grasped or re-
sponded to, a mere vacuum in which Bérenger was
adrift; nor, on the other hand, was it so oppressive, so
full of dark and lifeless matter, that he felt bound fast
and immobile, in no way able to penetrate its density.
Bérenger poetically describes that utopian condition in
which the human being finds his home in the created
universe. "My own peace and light spread in their turn
throughout the world, I was filling the universe with a
kind of ethereal energy. Not an empty corner, everything was a mingling of airiness and plenitude, perfectly
balanced." (*K,* 23) It is the memory of this perfect
balance which had sustained Bérenger for a time, but
which has since been almost completely absorbed by the
chilled darkness of the fallen world.

Bérenger's memories differ from those of Choubert
and Amédée in being no way tied to a past experience
of love for a younger Madeleine. Yet Ionesco empha-
sizes once again the interdependence of joy and love.
Before Bérenger comes to understand the deadly nature of the Radiant City and while he still interprets it
as the realization of his fondest dreams, he relates the
change in feeling which his false optimism has triggered:
"I'm as young as I was a hundred years ago. I can fall
in love again. . . ." And even before Dany, the Architect's blonde secretary, appears on stage, Bérenger enthusiastically calls toward the wings: "Mademoiselle,
oh, Mademoiselle, will you marry me?" (*K,* 26)

It is through attention to the memories of Choubert,
Amédée, and Bérenger that we may come most fully
to an understanding of the hopes and goals underlying
Ionesco's works. Without the expression of these memories, it would be difficult to find in most of Ionesco's
plays the desired alternatives to the chaotic worlds in
which his characters live. Moreover, the nightmarish

present of his plays would not so fully convey the tragic frustration of contemporary life, were this present not seen in its bewildering contrast to what man dimly remembers as a joyous past, to what he may hope to recapture out of the welter of his engulfing chaos. Nostalgic dreams find an important place in Ionesco's generally dyspeptic vision.

It is easier to describe the nature of Ionesco's lost paradise, even if only in the most general terms, than to account for its loss. The plays to which we must look for such an account are those involving some metamorphosis, some unfolding of the process of the fall. Such plays may be contrasted to the more static ones, which portray a world already fallen and depict the ensuing emptiness. This is not to imply that each play is a compartmentalized presentation of one segment of Ionesco's thought, that each can be classified under some such single rubric as memory, metamorphosis, stasis. Important as the factor of memory is to the three plays just discussed, it is by no means of exclusive, or perhaps even of predominating, importance. Most of the plays touch upon more than one of the themes we have enumerated. At the same time it is clear that *The Lesson,* for example, is a drama involving a vast metamorphosis and that *The Bald Soprano* is a conspicuously static play. The works which show best the process of man's disintegration are *The Lesson;* the companion plays *Jack, or The Submission* and *The Future Is in Eggs, or It Takes All Sorts to Make a World;* and *Rhinoceros.* The first three are early in the Ionesco canon, all written in 1950 or 1951; *Rhinoceros* was written in 1958.

The first critical problem should be the attempt to isolate the common denominators of these plays. Are there within them certain prevailing characteristics which may help account for the fall from the radiant world remembered by a Choubert, an Amédée, a Bérenger, to the present frustrating emptiness? This is not to say that the protagonists of what we are designating as

metamorphic plays actually begin in a worldly paradise, but they do begin with enviable characteristics which
are undermined in the course of their dramas.

We may initiate our study of these plays and our
search for common denominators by reference to
another play, *Victims of Duty,* whose Madeleine declares that the process of change *can* be described:
"Now the modern world's in a state of decay, you can
always report on the process!" (*VD,* 162) And we
need turn only to the play's beginning to learn the
broad outlines of the process. Choubert, lamenting that
men no longer possess the peace of mind of a bygone
day, describes to Madeleine an official announcement
which has just come into his hands:

CHOUBERT.   It's quite interesting. The Government's urging all the citizens of the big towns to cultivate detachment. According to this, it's our last hope of finding an
answer to the economic crisis, the confusion of the spirit
and the problems of existence.
MADELEINE.   We've tried everything else, and it hasn't
done any good, but I don't suppose it's anyone's fault.
CHOUBERT.   For the time being the Government's merely
recommending this ultimate solution in a friendly manner. They can't fool us; we know how a recommenda-
tion has a way of turning into an order.
MADELEINE.   You're always so anxious to generalize!
CHOUBERT.   We know how suggestions suddenly come to
look like rules, like strict laws.
MADELEINE.   Well, my dear, you know, the law *is* necessary, and what's necessary and indispensable is *good,*
and everything that's good is *nice.* And it really is very
nice indeed to be a good, law-abiding citizen and do
one's duty and have a clear conscience! (*VD,* 118)

Experience has taught Choubert and Madeleine that
the governing process is an inevitable series of steps
moving from suggestions to rules to strict laws, and that
goodness is somehow equated with a person's renunciation of his own individuality, with his turning away from
the path along which his own nature and will and desire
would lead. One's duty becomes an abiding by the law,
without consideration of the nature of either the law
itself or the law-makers who have decreed it. The fact

that blind obedience to such law is equated with duty and considered as prerequisite to a clear conscience is to Ionesco one of the bitter ironies of the world he inhabits. The characters of this play are, after all, *victims* of duty. The majestic legislative forces of which they are victims are not identified, but their delegate quite obviously is the cruel, arrogant, tyrannical Detective, who clearly defines *his* duty: "My duty, you know . . . is simply to apply the system" (*VD,* 156). And his spectacular success is well symbolized at the end of the play when all the characters, declaring themselves victims of duty, are mechanically stuffing Choubert with bread to the rhythmical chant of "Chew! Swallow! Chew! Swallow!" (*VD,* 166) The bread is not the bread of life but the pap which was at first merely *suggested* but later became the *strict law* of undernourishment. Moreover, Choubert has, finally, become so resigned to his imposed fate that he not only chews and swallows but also joins in the commanding choral chant.

Those Ionesco characters whose falls are most explicitly chronicled—the Pupil of *The Lesson,* Jack of both *Jack, or The Submission,* and *The Future Is in Eggs,* and Jean, Botard, Dudard, and Daisy of *Rhinoceros*—share the common plight of being victims of duty. The Pupil alone refuses to resign herself to victimization, only to be murdered for her resistance. It is she to whom we may first turn in our search both for those external malignant forces which would dehumanize the whole world of man and for that inner struggle, often in vain, of a human being to maintain the individuality which distinguishes him from his neighbor.

The Lesson opens on a bright, vivacious, eighteen-year-old girl arriving for a tutoring lesson at the home of a seemingly decorous, timid professor. In the brief course of their study, they gradually exchange some of their originally predominating characteristics, the student becoming progressively more withdrawn, the instructor more extroverted and aggressive. As the play moves toward its end, the girl falls victim to various bodily pains and finds it increasingly difficult to speak coherently. Finally the Professor plunges a knife into the body of the Pupil, symbolically raping her and actually murdering her. This young lady, we discover, is the murderer's fortieth victim and, just before the curtain, the forty-first pupil arrives for her lesson.

The lesson, ostensibly undertaken in order that the student may work her way to the "total doctorate," has three main stages: arithmetic, philology, calamity. It is difficult to distinguish between sense and nonsense in the play, to differentiate between remarks and attitudes which illuminate the process of an individual's fall to tyrannic forces and those which are simply wonderfully and ridiculously comic. In fact, the dialogue and action are for the most part simultaneously serious and comic. For example, the young lady shows a fine skill in addition but cannot subtract three from four. Such foolishness is indeed comic, yet the Professor's response to it is also a seriously ironic comment on the course of life: "You always have a tendency to add. But one must be able to subtract too. It's not enough to integrate, you must also disintegrate. That's the way life is. That's philosophy. That's science. That's progress, civilization." (L, 55) And the Professor is, of course, highly skilled in the art of disintegrating.

Of great significance in The Lesson is the exercise in philology. As the Professor moves from arithmetic to philological instruction, his maid, who has observed the sequence of his pedagogy on thirty-nine previous occasions, tries to dissuade him from going on, cautioning him with a twice-repeated "philology leads to calamity" (L, 60). Certainly there is no conviction Ionesco expresses more frequently than that of the failure of language to serve as a communicating agent. The lesson in philology is therefore appropriately marked, from beginning to end, by a thick obfuscation. The apex of philological art is reached when nothing is communicated. This thesis, ironically, is expressed clearly:

PROFESSOR. . . . If you utter several sounds at an accelerated speed, they will automatically cling to each

other, constituting thus syllables, words, even sentences,
that is to say groupings of various importance, purely
irrational assemblages of sounds, denuded of all sense,
but for that very reason the more capable of maintaining themselves without danger at a high altitude in the
air. By themselves, words charged with significance will
fall, weighted down by their meaning, and in the end
they always collapse, fall . . .
PUPIL.   . . . On deaf ears. (*L,* 62–63)

The Professor's art of teaching, based on the principles of disintegration and obscuration, gradually takes
its toll. The Pupil is no longer the confident young girl
of the beginning of the play, the Professor no longer
the timid pedagogue who would lead his student by
gentle persuasion through a course of studies toward the
total doctorate. He would now force upon her the strict
and dehumanizing laws of his frightening world. The
student's sickened physical response to his power begins with a toothache, a pain which increases in severity
and then spreads to the whole of her body. The ultimate
aim of the Professor is power over all students who seek
from him the means of understanding. And the ultimate expression of power is rape and murder—as both
Green Eyes and Lefranc of Genet's *Deathwatch* also
make clear. The Professor's knife, the symbol of both
kinds of power, is the instrument which carries to their
inevitable conclusions both the lewd gleam in his eye
and the insatiable craving of his tyrannical impulse.
The girl, knifed by her instructor, slumps, as the stage
directions inform us, *"in an immodest position onto a
chair . . . her legs spread wide and hanging over both
sides"* (*L,* 75).

When the Maid rebukes the Professor for his action,
he is quick to account for its cause: "It wasn't my fault!
She didn't want to learn! She was disobedient! She was
a bad pupil! She didn't want to learn!" (*L,* 76) Whatever the Pupil did not want to learn—perhaps the art
of disintegration or the art of directing collapsed words
to deaf ears—her disobedience was her unwillingness to
resign herself to the Professor's power. And her unhappy fate is so common that it will go unnoticed—as

the Maid remarks: ". . . people won't ask questions, they're used to it" (L, 77). If the Pupil, as well as her predecessors and successors, is a victim of disobedience, the Professor, like the Detective of *Victims of Duty,* is the person whose duty "is simply to apply the system." As the play nears its end the Maid takes an arm band, which Ionesco suggests may appropriately be a Nazi swastika, and says to the Professor: "Wait, if you're afraid, wear this, then you won't have anything more to be afraid of" (L, 78). The Professor can work most safely and comfortably under the umbrella of an oppressive political system; embodying all the characteristics of a gigantic, dehumanizing force, he gives full allegiance to the power which offers the alternatives of resignation or death. And in so doing, he takes his place with the Detective of *Victims of Duty* as an obedient servant to all those forces which have led men from that nearly forgotten paradise to the present inferno.

Jack, or The Submission and *The Future Is in Eggs* are companion plays, the second a sequel to the first. As the first title suggests, Jack does submit, though only after a manly struggle, and he submits to a coercion from people who have nothing of value to offer him as replacement for what he surrenders—his individuality. The plays, again, are a blend of the ridiculous and the serious. Nothing is more comically ridiculous than the opening episode, in which Jack is being severely upbraided by his sister, parents, and grandparents. His father is so disenchanted by his son's behavior that he threatens to leave home. It is sister Jacqueline who is entrusted with the final attempt to effect that submissive change in Jack which would make him acceptable. She speaks to him words which accord well with the murderous Professor's description of "purely irrational assemblages of sounds, denuded of all sense." And Jack, after wrestling with his collapsing conscience, submits: "Oh well, yes, yes, na, I adore hashed brown potatoes!" (J, 87) That such issue should be made of so trivial a matter as one's culinary taste bears a fine ridiculousness. The serious implication is that, for would-be oppressors, no matter is so trivial as to be left to the discretion and choice of the individual.

Jack's family further insists that he submit not only to the adoration of hashed brown potatoes but to marriage as well; that is, to the convention of marriage for its own sake, not for any love which might encourage it. To facilitate such a liaison, the Jack family (Jack excepted) has agreed with the Robert family to the marriage of Jack and Roberta I. The young lady is summarily rejected by Jack because, though charmingly graced with "green pimples on her beige skin, red breasts on a mauve background, an illuminated navel, a tongue the color of tomato sauce, pan-browned square shoulders, and all the meat needed to merit the highest commendation" (*J*, 91–92), she is, alas, endowed with only two noses. But not all is lost. The three-nosed Roberta II steps forward and, though first refused by Jack, embarks on a passionate pursuit and finally wins her man.

The last section of the play chronicles Roberta II's successful seduction of Jack. It is a macabre and terrifying episode as Roberta II, early identifying herself as "the gaiety of death in life" (*J*, 101), first recites a surrealistic story which equates birth with the production of cancerous cells. Jack, in turn, tells of his birth (he was almost fourteen years old at the time), which he had at first refused to accept. Every enticement was made in an effort to persuade him to acquiesce to both his own birth and the world into which he was born. The more he struggled against his condition, the more he became trapped:

I had wanted to protest: there was no longer anyone . . . except those people there that you know, who do not count. They deceived me . . . And how to escape? They've boarded up the doors, the windows with nothing, they've taken away the stairs . . . Anything is preferable to my present situation. Even a new one. (*J*, 104)

Roberta II, quite ready to furnish this new situation and blessed with indisputable narrative powers, turns to a story designed to draw Jack to her. The story is about

horses—though spiced with remarks about a miller's in-
fanticidal, uxoricidal, and suicidal accomplishments—
and culminates in the action of a galloping, whinnying
stallion with beautiful and literally blazing mane. He becomes "a living torch," then "only a handful of cinders"
(*J, 107*), and the conveyed sense of fire and dryness
creates in Jack a thirst which, in erotic and nauseating
imagery, Roberta II offers to satisfy.

Jack, through his submissiveness, is now abased to
a subhuman level at which language ceases to be of any
importance. The dialogue having fallen into utter nonsense, Roberta suggests that the one word, *cat*, may be
conveniently used to designate anything under the sun.
Jack, intrigued by the ease with which he can now talk
and enchanted by his discovery that Roberta II has nine
fingers on her left hand, makes his second major submission—this time to marriage. The last brief sequence
of the play shows Jack and Roberta II in awkward embrace, the other characters circling about them in postures calculated to *"produce in the audience a feeling of
embarrassment, awkwardness, and shame."* Finally,
Roberta II alone is left on stage, her *"three noses quiver-
ing, and her nine fingers moving like snakes"* (*J, 110*).
The triumph of the Jack and Robert families over Jack
is complete. Though with reluctance, he has submitted
to a taste for hashed brown potatoes and to a coupling
with an extraordinary woman; in so doing he has lost
all traces of individuality, becoming obedient to forces
as disintegrating as those espoused by the Professor in
The Lesson.

Three years later the curtain rises on *The Future Is
in Eggs,* with Jack and Roberta linked in the same
awkward embrace of the end of the earlier play. As
they murmur lewd endearments to each other, we learn
of their families' keen disappointment that the marriage
has remained unfruitful. Jacqueline speaks for both
families when she chides the lovers: "You're neglecting
production! Why don't you get on with it? After all, it
is your main duty." And immediately from the other
relatives comes the choral chant: "It's your duty!" (*FE,*

123) We thus again have victims of duty, the duty this time being that of following the dictate that subjects produce new subjects. It is Jack who must submit himself to the continuing propagation of a race of unpersons. To Roberta's extravagantly suggestive postures and to the cheering section of doting and observing relatives, Jack and his wife finally achieve the devoutly wished consummation, conception, and production. The result is an endless retinue of baskets of eggs, which both Mother-Robert and Grandmother-Jack insist are the spitting images of their own respective kin. To the frantic ejaculations of "Production! Production! Production!" and "Eggs! Eggs! Eggs! Eggs!" (*FE,* 137), the blessed events are glorified.

Attention is then turned to what may most hopefully be the future aspirations and roles of the offspring, and after many imaginative speculations, most of the characters agree that "omelettes, lots of omelettes" (*FE,* 140) is the best prophecy. When Jack demurs, stating his preference for a progeny of pessimists, anarchists, and nihilists, his father asks him, first, if he has lost his faith, and then, what it is he really wants. Jack's reply, it seems, must spring from the depths of a long-buried memory: "I want a fountain of light, incandescent water, fire of ice, snows of fire." But Grandfather-Jack, who, though deceased, speaks from his portrait on the wall, is more realistic: "As it was in the past, the future lies in eggs!" (*FE,* 141) Two peas in a pod, two eggs in a basket, two men on this earth—they are all alike—subtle distinctions are things of a past which stretches beyond Grandfather-Jack's memory.

Rhinoceros is, of course, a work of far greater scope than *The Lesson* or the two Jack plays. Four of its main characters—Jean, Botard, Dudard, and Daisy—are victims of rhinoceritis, that tendency to surrender oneself to whatever seems at the moment life's easiest course. Only Bérenger maintains his individual integrity; he will be more fully discussed later in this chapter. At this point let us examine the other characters and note the nature of their respective falls from humanity.

The action opens on a square in a small town where Jean and Bérenger meet and sit on a cafe terrace. The apathetic, disheveled, generally irresponsible Bérenger is being chided by the eminently respectable Jean, who, urging his friend to mend his ways and improve his condition, defines the "superior man . . . [as] the man who fulfils his duty" (*R,* 7), a proposition of considerable relevance to the play as a whole. The Sunday morning quiet is abruptly broken by the panting, trumpeting sound of a rhinoceros galloping through the town. Only Bérenger remains calm amid the startled responses of those around him. A little later, when a second (or the same) rhinoceros rushes noisily by, Bérenger reacts with more feeling than he had evinced earlier, and the other characters show less immediate response. As the play progresses, Bérenger moves steadily from his original lethargy to an extremely strong response toward rhinoceroses, whereas the others move in the reverse direction and, finally, become metamorphosed into the very beasts which had at first so upset them. Jean, Botard, Dudard, and Daisy, though differing from one another in many ways, have in common a disposition toward rhinoceritis.

Jean, always more intent on keeping up appearances (whether human or rhinoceritic) than in abiding by principles, is perhaps the most hypocritical and self-righteous of the four. He is fastidious, boastful of his imagined superiority over Bérenger, more than ready to offer his friend advice, sensitive of his dignity—"I can't bear people to try and make fun of me!" (*R,* 15)—vaunting his "moral strength" (*R,* 18), and quite unwilling to practice what he preaches. He has strongly preconceived ideas about the way things are and should be; thus he gives a physical description of the galloping rhinoceroses, though, as Bérenger points out, he could not possibly have seen them so clearly as to give the details which he offers.

Jean, the first of the major characters to surrender his humanity, shows signs of disintegration early in Act Two. His sense of his own impending change is reflected in an unwillingness even to talk with Bérenger about those rhinoceroses which they had both viewed earlier as enemies of mankind; such a conversational topic would now be of acute embarrassment to him. And when Bérenger expresses affectionate concern at the initial evidences of his companion's metamorphosis—a change in voice, a lump on the head, a greenish epidermal tint—and goes on to affirm his friendship, Jean denies the possibility of such a human bond: "There's no such thing as friendship. I don't believe in your friendship." (*R*, 63) He goes beyond denying a relationship generally thought to reflect man's capacity for unselfish devotion and argues that there are really no significant differences in quality between the life of a human being and that of a rhinoceros. Jean's outer change is, in fact, the direct reflection of his inner disposition, and his disease is correctly defined by Bérenger as a "moral crisis" (*R*, 64). Jean, who once described the superior man as one who fulfills his duty, now asks Bérenger, concerning rhinoceroses and men: "Are you under the impression that our way of life is superior?" (*R*, 67) And when Bérenger urges that men possess moral standards unknown in the animal kingdom, Jean makes clear his own inhumanity:

JEAN. Moral standards! I'm sick of moral standards! We need to go beyond moral standards!
BÉRENGER. What would you put in their place?
JEAN. . . . Nature!
BÉRENGER. Nature!
JEAN. Nature has its own laws. Morality's against Nature.
BÉRENGER. Are you suggesting we replace our moral laws by the law of the jungle?
JEAN. It would suit me, suit me fine. (*R*, 67)

And shortly after this philosophic exchange, Jean, his metamorphosis complete, adopts the law of the jungle as he trumpets at Bérenger: "I'll trample you, I'll trample you down!" (*R*, 69) Jean, a man of no convictions, will follow the least resistant path, which, in the context of this play, is the road of rhinoceritis.

Botard is the most arrogant, stubborn, and unreason-

able of the four. He at first categorically rejects the
story of the rhinoceroses, insists that he believes only
what he sees with his own eyes, and proudly asserts his
scorn, characterizing the whole matter as an "example
of collective psychosis. . . . Just like religion—the
opiate of the people!" (*R*, 45) When he does witness
the phenomenon himself, he changes his position but
remains as rigidly convinced of the correctness of his
new view of things as he was of his old. He now de-
nounces the presence of rhinoceroses as a nefarious plot
against the "little people" (*R*, 50), among whom he
numbers himself, and he determines to go to his union
to protest. But in spite of such a protest, Botard shares
with most Ionesco characters a strong sense of duty, a
duty, once again, to adhere to whatever or whoever is
in power, a duty which fluctuates with each revision of
the power structure. Upon learning that a Mrs. Boeuf
is going to follow her husband into a rhinoceritic metamorphosis, he approvingly proclaims: "It's no more
than her duty" (*R*, 52). And later in the play, when
his own metamorphosis is reported, we are informed of
his last words: ". . . we must move with the times!"
(*R*, 89) It is Dudard who describes most accurately the
motivations behind Botard's fall from humanity: ". . . it
was a case of community spirit triumphing over his
anarchic impulses." (*R*, 89) Failure of spirit is translated as community spirit, and impulse toward individuality as anarchy. The truth is that all impulses,
except Bérenger's, quickly surrender to the spineless
moving along with the times. Botard, like Jean, lacks
the inner strength to resist whatever prevailing breeze
of convention may blow.

If Jean is a hypocrite and Botard, at least initially,
a swaggerer, Dudard is a relativist. He responds calmly
both to the original story of the appearance of the rhinoceroses and to the news of Jean's metamorphosis. He
is disposed to take Jean's case lightly, arguing that it
was an isolated phenomenon to be explained by Jean's
excitable and eccentric nature. Late in the play, as
Bérenger becomes increasingly upset by the succession

of events, it is Dudard who tries to calm him, urging that the best course is simply to ignore the beasts and acclimatize oneself to the changing times. Unimpressed by Bérenger's insistence that the new state of affairs is an evil one, Dudard evinces his own thoroughgoing relativism:

Who knows what is evil and what is good? It's just a question of personal preferences. You're worried about your own skin—that's the truth of the matter. But you'll never become a rhinoceros, really you won't . . . you haven't got the vocation! (*R,* 80)

And Dudard proceeds to argue for impartiality, tolerance, and an unemotional, realistic facing of the facts as they are. Moreover, he comes close to Jean's sentiments in the assertion that, after all, to turn into a rhinoceros is perfectly *natural*. He also echoes most of the other persons of Ionesco's world when, shortly before his submission to rhinoceritis, he exclaims: "I feel it's my duty to stick by my employers and my friends, through thick and thin"—and, a few lines later: "It's my duty to stick by them; I have to do my duty." (*R,* 93) What Jack remarked in a different context, we may now repeat: "Oh words, what crimes are committed in your name!" (*J,* 86)

Bérenger's beloved Daisy is the last to go, and it seems for a while that she might remain firm against the intensifying pressures of her brutalizing society. She, with Dudard, urges Bérenger to try to accustom himself to the situation and avers that they have no right to interfere with the lives of other persons; yet, close to the end of the play, she does promise Bérenger that she will never leave him alone again. But she becomes increasingly resigned to the compulsions of the times, and even Bérenger's hopeful plea that they be fruitful and regenerate the human race is of no avail. Daisy, like those who fell before her, shows scant respect for the life infused with some moral or ethical fiber and opts for the "natural" life, calling the rhinoceroses "real people" and observing that they "look very natural" (*R,* 103). When Bérenger tries to hold Daisy by apotheosizing their love, she shows how cheaply she holds that human bond: "I feel a bit ashamed of what you call love—this morbid feeling, this male weakness. And female, too. It just doesn't compare with the ardour and the tremendous energy emanating from all those creatures around us." (*R,* 103) Even after the expression of this sentiment, Daisy continues to vacillate briefly, but, finally, she departs for the world of tough hides and green skins. Bérenger is left alone.

The Lesson, the Jack plays, and *Rhinoceros* portray the process whereby victim falls to victimizer. In the three earlier plays, the victimizers have in common a lust for power. They covet the power to subdue all men, diminishing them to ciphers and quelling their slightest tendency to individuality. The Professor does not seek to dominate his Pupil in order to rechannel her efforts toward some specific end or purpose but in order to accomplish the disintegration which strips her of all personhood. When she refuses obedient submission, she must be destroyed. The Jack family would make of their son only a copy of themselves, one who would share their every taste and who, through marriage and "production," would ensure a future of numberless, faceless eggs. For the Jacks, their son excepted, security lay in the perpetuation of a race of unpersons indistinguishable one from the other. And since Jack submitted, physical destruction—as in the case of the Pupil—was unnecessary.

The Pupil and Jack fall to explicitly external forces, to a dictatorship that levels all persons to its own thoughtless and empty routine. The characters of *Rhinoceros* are not seen in combat with specific antagonists —with a Professor or a smothering family—so much as in struggle with themselves. Jean, Botard, Dudard, and Daisy are enchanted by a life which is "natural" rather than moral, which calls for no decisions once the metamorphosis is accomplished, and which brings the sense of security generally attendant upon membership in a majority group. They need only observe the increasing number of rhinoceroses to be lured into their domain. And they are lured because they have no convictions of their own, because they wish only to "move with the times," because such words or conditions as *friendship* and *love* have ceased to hold any meaning. There are no values; there is no faith; the only motivation is the prevailing tide, and the better part of discretion is submission.

Ionesco's world is largely, almost exclusively, a world of victims. And if its inhabitants would salve their consciences by insisting on the priority of duty, it is perfectly clear that the duty to which they pledge themselves is that of surrendering everything that would distinguish them as human beings. It matters little whether the antagonist is drawn as an active force demanding allegiance, as in the three earlier plays, or as more subtle sirens parading in the guise of rhinoceroses. The constant factor is that man surrenders himself to a power which can offer only the falsest security—the annihilation of humanity.

Central to the plays of submission and metamorphosis is man's surrender of his humanity. The protagonists, though they never inhabit a paradisiacal world, do at first possess marks of individuality precious to Ionesco and do relinquish such characteristics in the course of their dramas. Such plays are dynamic in the sense that they record the process of change. *The Bald Soprano* and *The New Tenant,* on the other hand, are Ionesco's two most static compositions. They are devoted exclusively to the fallen state of mankind, presenting characters who are already devoid of humanity or personhood as the plays open, who do not possess even a memory of more propitious times, who are the same at the falling curtain as they were at the beginning, and who seem unconcerned with any possible release from their imprisoned circumstances—indeed, the characters of *The Bald Soprano* are unaware of any imprisonment, and the new tenant takes careful steps to make secure his own.

The Bald Soprano, Ionesco's first play, written in

1948, stresses, with a fine balance of tragedy and comedy, one of the most distinguishing attributes of the fallen world—the absence of communication among persons. The condition of the characters is metaphorically reflected in lines from one of Matthew Arnold's "Marguerite" poems: ". . . in the sea of life enisled, / With echoing straits between us thrown, / Dotting the shoreless watery wild, / We mortal millions live *alone*." Yet Ionesco's characters lack any tragic sense of their condition. They recall no time when life was different, when there might have been some measure of communication; consequently they seem oblivious to any possibility of those human ties which depend on communicability for their very existence. They are simply frozen in their present plight, with the play's action representing one particular time in their lives destined to be repeated again and again. The play ends as it began, representing an ever-recurring cycle.

The Bald Soprano is devoted in great part to conveying the inanity and futility of language or, more accurately, to portraying the poverty of the human *uses* of language and the failure of mankind to uncover and employ modes of discourse which would serve as vehicles for satisfying communication. At the beginning of the play, the language is perfectly intelligible, though, as Mr. Smith's irresponsiveness to his wife's chattering monologue suggests, it is too trite and irrelevant to be worth the saying. Nothing of significance is communicated as Mrs. Smith informs her husband that they have finished their dinner, that they both had three helpings of fish, and that they have a two-year-old daughter named Peggy, who is happy with her diet of milk and porridge. By the end of the play the characters have resorted to mouthing syllables and then letters, yet we somehow feel that they are hardly worse off than at the start.

Since the problems of communication underlie all of Ionesco's plays, and since *The Bald Soprano* is specifically designated by him as the "tragedy of language," this would seem an appropriate juncture to bring to-

gether his many dramatic observations on the fact of
incommunicability. There are to Ionesco three principal
reasons why persons do not, cannot, or will not effect a
mutually satisfying interchange of words, thoughts, or
feelings. First, man is entirely too confident in his belief that matters of consummate importance can be conveyed through logical, rational principles of discourse;
in ridiculing such principles—the long-accepted laws of
causality, of contradiction, and of syllogistic thought—
Ionesco gains some of his most comic effects. Second,
the power structure, usually tyrannic and dictatorial,
has deliberately manipulated words and twisted their
customary meanings in order to confuse and enchain
those whom it would oppress. Third, human beings
constantly take refuge behind the most banal commonplaces of speech in order to hide their own incapacity
to feel or to think.

We might examine first Ionesco's belittling of those
most commonly accepted modes—rational, empirical, or
a combination of the two—of coming to, or communicating, the truth. Deeply cherished by most men is the
law of causality, the seeming assurance that given a
particular cause, a particular effect is certain to ensue.
Nothing in Ionesco serves better to travesty the law of
causality than the doorbell-ringing episode at the home
of the Smiths in *The Bald Soprano*. The doorbell rings
four times. Upon each of the first three rings, Mrs.
Smith opens the door, to find no one there. When she
obstinately refuses to answer the fourth ring, Mr. Smith
does so, to be greeted by the Fire Chief. The Smiths,
the Martins, and the Fire Chief immediately turn their
attention to the possible relationships between a ringing
and a ringer. Mr. Smith, observing the law of causality,
affirms that a ringing requires a ringer. Mrs. Smith, insisting that facts are more reliable than theoretical laws,
argues from their recent experience that, "when one
hears the doorbell ring it is because there is never anyone there" (*BS*, 23), and that the fourth ring simply
does not count! The Fire Chief, testifying that he had
been standing outside the door for forty-five minutes,

asserts that neither he nor anyone else occasioned the first two rings and that he rang the third ring and then hid. To Mrs. Smith's insistence that no one is ever at the door when the bell rings and to Mr. Smith's that there is always someone at the door when the bell rings, the Fire Chief offers the perfect solution to a perplexing problem:

FIRE CHIEF. I am going to reconcile you. You both are partly right. When the doorbell rings, sometimes there is someone, other times there is no one.
MR. MARTIN. That seems logical to me.
MRS. MARTIN. I think so too.
FIRE CHIEF. Life is very simple, really. (*BS*, 26–27)

The episode, more than just comic nonsense, is a challenging of one of man's habitual ways of seeking to make sense of daily phenomena. More significantly and more implicitly, it intimates that even if certain effects are consequent upon certain causes, the law of causality at best can make sense only of the relatively trivial and is of little use in illuminating life's major problems and mysteries. In short, it is a law in which man has placed undue confidence.

In much the same tone and for much the same reason, the law of contradiction is frequently ridiculed. Thus Mr. Smith describes one of the innumerable Bobby Watsons: "She has regular features and yet one cannot say that she is pretty. She is too big and stout. Her features are not regular but still one can say that she is very pretty. She is a little too small and too thin." (*BS*, 12) And in *The Chairs*, the Old Woman speaks lovingly of her child, only to have her husband say that they never had children; and the Old Woman speaks of her husband's perfect fidelity to his parents, only to have him confess that he shamelessly abandoned his mother to die alone in a ditch. In more philosophical terms, the poet Nicolas in *Victims of Duty* boasts of his desire to "introduce contradiction where there is no contradiction, and no contradiction where there is what common-sense usually calls contradiction" (*VD*, 158). And in *Improvisation, or The Shepherd's Chameleon*, the character named Ionesco declares: "I'm all for contradiction, everything is nothing but contradiction, and yet any systematic exposition ought not to . . . should it . . . in words, confuse opposites" (*I*, 118).

Ionesco intimates, then, that the laws of causality and contradiction are of quite limited usefulness in the effort to clarify and make communicable matters of human concern. He also challenges, through derisive observations or farcical examples, the modes of logic, and their employment, on which our civilization proudly depends. As the Old Man of *The Chairs* says: ". . . pure logic does not exist . . . all we've got is an imitation" (*C*, 145). Two examples of such "imitation" will suffice. First let us note, in the following narration by the Fire Chief, the juxtaposition of the complete illogicality of the tale and the transitional words, italicized by us, which imply a tight logical structure:

A young calf had eaten too much ground glass. *As a result,* it was obliged to give birth. It brought forth a cow into the world. *However,* since the calf was male, the cow could not call him Mamma. Nor could she call him Papa, *because* the calf was too little. The calf was *then* obliged to get married and the registry office carried out all the details completely à la mode. (*BS*, 30)

Second, one of the dialogues between the Logician and the Old Gentleman in *Rhinoceros* strikes against the very heart of logic—the syllogism:

LOGICIAN. . . . Here is an example of a syllogism. The cat has four paws. Isidore and Fricot both have four paws. Therefore Isidore and Fricot are cats.

OLD GENTLEMAN. . . . My dog has got four paws.

LOGICIAN. . . . Then it's a cat. . . .

OLD GENTLEMAN [. . . *after deep reflection*]. So then logically speaking, my dog must be a cat?

LOGICIAN. . . . Logically, yes. But the contrary is also true. . . .

OLD GENTLEMAN. . . . Logic is a very beautiful thing.

LOGICIAN. . . . As long as it is not abused. . . .

LOGICIAN. . . . Another syllogism. All cats die. Socrates is dead. Therefore Socrates is a cat.

OLD GENTLEMAN. And he's got four paws. That's true. I've got a cat named Socrates. (*R*, 18–19)

It is evident that Ionesco is, in seriocomic tone, mocking either man's inherited tools for coming to some sense of phenomenal meaning or man's bungling attempts to use them. In either case, the inhabitants of this confused and confusing world can speak only nonsense in a framework that would pretend logic. And it would seem that man's only control over the medium of communication is the perverse one of twisting the customary meaning of words in order to mislead and trap other men. Mother Peep of *The Killer* is one of Ionesco's most clearly drawn tyrants, thoroughly imbued with the Newspeak of George Orwell's *1984*. Her harangues to a hypnotically admiring crowd are the perfect expression of the propagandistic and tyrannic rape of language:

I promise you I'll change everything. And changing everything means changing nothing. You can change the names, but the things remain the same. The old mystifications haven't stood up to psychological and sociological analysis. The new one will be foolproof and cause nothing but misunderstanding. We'll bring the lie to perfection. (*K*, 76)

We won't persecute, but we'll punish, and deal out justice. We won't colonize, we'll occupy the countries we liberate. We won't exploit men, we'll make them productive. We'll call compulsory work voluntary. War shall change its name to peace and everything will be altered, thanks to me and my geese. (*K*, 77)

Incommunicability, then, may be in part the result of basic fallacies within classical forms of logic or of the inept use of these forms; it may too be in part the consequence of a deliberate perversion of language so that bondage may henceforth be called freedom. But even more importantly and elementally, there is no communication because human beings no longer have anything of value to communicate. Consequently Mrs. Smith must spend the evening telling her husband of the dinner they have just eaten, and the most welcome news that Jack can convey to his family is that he loves hashed brown potatoes. To follow Roberta II's suggestion that all words be subsumed under the one word *cat* would, under the circumstances, entail no considerable loss.

One purpose of observing and communicating is to make distinctions, and the Ionesco world is one in which distinctions have been lost, in which there is no longer a dividing line between important and unimportant, or good and bad, or one person and another. Ionesco's most effective device for presenting this leveling process is the juxtaposition of disparates. Examples are many. In *Maid to Marry,* the Gentleman, enumerating various catastrophes of modern civilization, refers to the atom bomb. "Oh, *that thing!*" the Lady replies, and we await some description of its horror. She continues: "It appears it's changed the weather for us! We don't know where we are with our seasons now, it's upset everything!" (*MM,* 153) *Victims of Duty* opens with a discussion of the daily news, and Choubert mentions in the same breath "a cosmic disturbance" and the nuisances dogs commit on sidewalks (*VD,* 117). The Architect of *The Killer,* recounting "the misfortunes of mankind," mentions together "children with their throats cut . . . massacres, and floods, and dogs run over" (*K,* 36). As Amédée contemplates the possibility of removing the vast and growing corpse from his apartment out into the city streets, he remarks that he would, among other things, "be charged with obstructing the traffic . . ." (*A,* 69). And as Bérenger desperately tries to make his way to the Prefecture so that he may expose the Killer in the interests of public safety, one of the policemen directing the traffic retorts: "Public safety? *We* look after that. When we've the time. Traffic comes first!" (*K,* 92) Mother Jack berates her as yet unsubmissive son: "Then, you don't love your parents any more, you don't love your clothes, your sister, your grandparents!!!" (*J,* 81) And Amédée shows a similar tendency to incongruous juxtaposing: "Yes, you can get attached to almost anything . . . to a dog, a cat, a box, a child" (*A,* 57).

The Ionesco character shows no surprise at such incongruities, because for him everything is leveled and assumes an equal importance with everything else. He shows no surprise either as the most bizarre events take place before his eyes. He accepts with a remarkable degree of equanimity the fact of a three-nosed girl; the fact of a growing, mushroom-sprouting corpse (Amédée and Madeleine are frightened, but not amazed); the fact, in *Maid to Marry,* of a maiden who is a robust, moustached man. And if the characters are unmoved by the bizarre, they are beside themselves in the presence of the commonplace. In *The Bald Soprano,* a play in which the incredible elicits little surprise, the ordinary is greeted with incredulity:

MRS. MARTIN.   In the street, near a café, I saw a man, properly dressed, about fifty years old, or not even that, who . . .

MRS. SMITH.   . . . What was this man doing?

MRS. MARTIN.   Well, I'm sure you'll say that I'm making it up—he was down on one knee and he was bent over.

MR. MARTIN, MR. SMITH, MRS. SMITH.   Oh!

MRS. MARTIN.   Yes, bent over.

MR. SMITH.   Not possible.

MRS. MARTIN.   Yes, bent over. I went near him to see what he was doing . . .

MR. SMITH.   And?

MRS. MARTIN.   He was tying his shoe lace which had come undone.

MR. MARTIN, MR. SMITH, MRS. SMITH.   Fantastic!

MR. SMITH. If someone else had told me this, I'd not believed it.

MR. MARTIN.   Why not? One sees things even more extraordinary every day, when one walks around. For instance, today in the Underground I myself saw a man, quietly sitting on a seat, reading his newspaper.

MRS. SMITH.   What a character!

MR. SMITH.   Perhaps it was the same man! (*BS,* 21–22)

Unpredictable weather is as upsetting as the possibility of atomic holocaust, and a dirty sidewalk as worrisome as "a cosmic disturbance"; a dog's being run down by a car is a misfortune indistinguishable from that of a child's having his throat slit; traffic problems are of equal seriousness with maniacal murders; a man's attachment to his clothes or to his sister, to a box or to a child—it all comes to the same thing; and what is customarily thought to be extraordinary is seen as commonplace, and vice versa. Just as no distinctions are made among matters which strike us as being poles apart in degree of significance, no distinctions are made among human beings either: there is an indistinguishable merging of persons as there is of values. We learn in *The Bald Soprano* of a large family, each of whose members is named Bobby Watson. The first Bobby Watson mentioned is referred to by Mr. Smith as "the handsomest corpse in Great Britain." And to Mrs. Smith's "Poor Bobby," Mr. Smith asks, "Which Bobby do you mean?" Mrs. Smith replies:

It is his wife that I mean. She is called Bobby too, Bobby Watson. Since they both had the same name, you could never tell one from the other when you saw them together. It was only after his death that you could really tell which was which. And there are still people today who confuse her with the deceased and offer their condolences to him. Do you know her? (*BS*, 12)

And as it is virtually impossible to distinguish among persons, it is equally difficult to define the personality of any one person or to assume that a person has definitive characteristics. How, for example, can one describe or fix the character of the Old Woman in *The Chairs?* She is, by turns, wife to the Old Man, his compassionate mother, and a forward slut in the presence of the invisible guests. The Madeleine of *Victims of Duty* also undergoes various metamorphoses.

In a world in which most distinctions have been lost, and in which there has been a leveling both of values and of persons, the bonds of friendship and love are exceedingly difficult to attain. The kinds of distinctions that make communication possible and that would enable two persons to come to an exciting and rich knowledge of each other have all but vanished. In *The Bald Soprano* Ionesco carries to its ultimate point the thesis that one person does not really know another, an observation which gives either the reason for or the result of incommunicability. When we recall that both Choubert and Amédée had in earlier life seen marriage as their greatest hope, as the basis of a sharing of love and joy, it is particularly ironic that the marriage of Mr. and Mrs. Martin serves as insufficient basis for their even recognizing each other. They arrive together at the Smiths, sit eyeing each other, and then agree that they seem to have met before. Their memories are in some ways acute. Each remembers the precise train which he took from Manchester to London some five weeks earlier, as well as the class, coach, and compartment in which he traveled. Each recalls that he lives at 19 Brom- field Street, in flat 8 on the fifth floor; that his bedroom, located at the end of a corridor between a w.c. and a bookcase, contains a bed with a green eiderdown. Yet stocked as their minds are with memories of things, neither has any distinct memory of the other. Moved by the fact that they have so much in common, Mr. Martin remarks: "How bizarre, curious, strange! Then, madam, we live in the same room and we sleep in the same bed, dear lady. It is perhaps there that we have met!" To this Mrs. Martin replies: "How curious it is and what a coincidence! But I do not recall it, dear sir!" (*BS*, 18) Their assurance of being married to each other seems clinched when each discovers that he has a pretty two-year-old daughter named Alice, who has one white eye and one red eye. But even such seeming proof of their relationship fails, as all rational deduction must fail, when the maid Mary discloses that Mr. Martin's child has a white right eye and a red left eye, and Mrs. Martin's a red right eye and a white left eye. Mary's conclusion—"Thus all of Donald's [Mr. Martin's] sys- tem of deduction collapses when it comes up against this last obstacle which destroys his whole theory" (*BS*, 19) —is the perfect epitaph for a once esteemed order of logic. And marriage, presumably the closest of human relationships, has hardly served as a communicating medium between Donald and Elizabeth Martin.

The failure of logical thought, the perverse misuse of language, the absence of communicable matter resulting from blurred distinctions—such are the prevailing char- acteristics of Ionesco's less-than-human universe. And as we get ready to leave *The Bald Soprano,* we are reminded once again that any person is both *no* person and *every* person. The play ends as it began, with wife repeating to husband the same lines about the evening meal. But it is not Mrs. Smith speaking to Mr. Smith, but Mrs. Martin speaking to Mr. Martin. It is another example of a difference which makes no difference.

If we were to seek among Ionesco's writings the most depressing archetype of contemporary man's life and situation, we might well turn to *The New Tenant.* The curtain rises on a bare one-room apartment. The woman Caretaker enters, soon followed by the Gentleman who is the new tenant. The voluble Caretaker speaks at length of the old tenants, obsequiously offers to be of good service to the new one, and is offended when the taciturn Gentleman tells her she will not be needed. His single request for service, one about which he is quite firm, is that she close and keep closed the room's one window. With the Caretaker's angry departure, two furniture movers appear and, to the most precise instructions of the new tenant, put in place various articles of furniture. The Gentleman draws a small circle in the middle of the room and has an armchair placed within the circle, the many other pieces around it. The window is completely blocked off, affording no light. The only other object which may provide some view of or communication with the outside world, a radio, is given its place beside the armchair *because* it does not work. There is a profusion of movement and a growing silence as the Gentleman directs the movers by pointing to the proper place for the now seemingly innumerable objects. Finally the room is filled. Moreover, furniture crams the entire staircase up to the sixth-floor flat; it has brought traffic to a standstill through blocking the streets, has filtered into the underground and stopped all trains, and has, with its bulkiness, even dammed up the Thames River. The new tenant, invisible and seated in his armchair, is now completely enclosed by objects, as the curtain falls on silence and darkness.

Very early in the play the Caretaker had commented

to the Gentleman: ". . . you're at 'ome now, aren't you?"
(*NT,* 93) And just before the falling curtain one of the
furniture movers remarks: "Sir, you're really at home
now" (*NT,* 116). To be at home is clearly to be absolutely cut off from all persons by a proliferation of things.
It is the final dissolution of all communication, the final
preference for a safe, secure world of objects. And if
The New Tenant is a depressing play, even more dis-
couraging is the fact that the characters of *The Bald
Soprano* are no closer, one to another, than the new
tenant is to any other human being. Each character of
The Bald Soprano also has his carefully preserved circle
and lives without expressive sound or vitalizing air or
illuminating light.

If *The New Tenant* presents the archetypal and un-
ambiguous description of the way things are, the Radiant
City of *The Killer* exemplifies man's ingenious attempt
to make things appear other than they are. Like *The
Bald Soprano* and *The New Tenant, The Killer* offers
the landscape of a fallen world, but one in which attempts have been made to conceal the ruin. When
Bérenger first comes upon this seemingly remarkable
oasis, he interprets it as the realization of his fondest
dreams, as a city fulfilling in all ways that paradise
which lies deep in his memory. It is a city of bright
flowers and green leaves, of comforting warmth and
solacing peace. He contrasts this small pocket of beauty
to the rest of the town in which he lives, juxtaposing its
dreamlike springtime to the damp, barren winter which
has been his domain:

The leaves on the trees are small enough for the light to
filter through, but not too big, so as not to darken the
front of the houses. I must say it's amazing to think that
in all the rest of the town the sky's as grey as the hair on
an old woman's head, that there's dirty snow at the pavement's edge, and the wind blowing there. When I woke up
this morning I was cold. I was frozen. . . . I was saying . . .
oh yes . . . in my district, especially where I live, everything is damp; the coal, the bread, the wind, the wine, the
walls, the air, and even the fire. What a job I had this
morning, getting up, I had to make a big effort. It was

really painful. I'd never have made up my mind if the
sheets hadn't been damp too. I never imagined that, suddenly, as if by magic, I should find myself in the midst of
spring, in the middle of April, the April of my dreams . . .
my earliest dreams. . . . (*K*, 13–14)

Closer scrutiny shows, however, that the seeming
oasis is but a mirage. All building construction has been
suspended; excepting Bérenger and the Architect, not
a soul walks the streets. The inhabitants, actually eager
to leave this seemingly perfect city, keep within the confines of their homes in constant terror of some devastating force, having no place else to which they can go
in any case. The Ornamental Pool of the city, which at a
distance had promised beauty, holds in fact three corpses
—a woman's, a man's, and a child's. And as Bérenger
comes to a sense of the stillness and death that lie beneath
the dazzling exterior, he realizes that the Radiant City is
the falsest of imitations of the city of his memory. The
sudden evaporation of what had seemed his return to
paradise is devastating, and he reverts to the unhappy
condition which had characterized his morning's awakening: "There are no radiant ones! . . . It's even worse
than the other districts, in ours, the busy crowded ones!
. . . I feel so upset about it. I feel shattered, stunned . . .
My tiredness has come on again . . . There's no point in
living!" (*K*, 34)

The Radiant City represents the specious and empty
products of modern technology. The Architect, who
presides over the city, early makes clear the principles
on which it was built: "It's all calculated, all intentional.
Nothing was to be left to chance in this district" (*K*,
12). Any modern-day paradise, it is implied, is only
the carefully calculated imitation of what lies in Bérenger's memory and is the ground of his hope. The
peace he seeks must come, if at all, not from calculated
deception but from a loving heart; and the loving heart
has given way to the occasionally ingenious mind. What
man can now create has but the thinnest veneer of what
once was paradise. Even a hasty glance beneath the sur-

face reveals not life and love but death and either hate or indifference.

The outlines of Ionesco's world are evident. Man is a tired, isolated creature inhabiting a gray universe. He is occasionally haunted by memories of a distant and far different past. He is a victim, sometimes of an outer tyranny, but perhaps even more often of his own emptiness. And the occasional solace that modern gadgets and technology may seem to offer proves both illusory and frightening. Unable to communicate because he is unable to love—and unable to love because he is unable to communicate—he is either apathetically indifferent or defensively hostile. The poet Nicolas of *Victims of Duty,* in announcing his hopes for the contemporary theatre, offers ground rules which reflect well Ionesco's sense of the way things are: "We'll get rid of the principle of identity and unity of character. . . . We are not ourselves . . . Personality doesn't exist." (*VD,* 158) In short, man is dead. The remaining question is whether Ionesco believes that man may live again and, if so, by what means he may regain the paradise of life.

The plays of Ionesco concerned most explicitly with the question of some kind of human redemption are *The Chairs* and the four Bérenger plays: *The Killer, Rhinoceros, A Stroll in the Air,* and *Exit the King.*

We have already discussed how the great gap between aspirations and achievement is shown in *The Chairs.* The almost unrestrained optimism of the ninety-five-year-old lighthouse keeper sees his life's work, devoted to a painstakingly formulated redemptive message, as culminating in the salvation of the whole world. He— like Choubert, Amédée, and Bérenger—has memories of a loveliness long lost. He recalls a beautiful place, situated at the end of a garden and named Paris. And when his wife insists that such a place never existed, he replies: "That city must have existed because it collapsed . . . It was the city of light, but it has been extinguished, extinguished, for four hundred thousand years . . . Nothing remains of it today, except a song."

(*C,* 116) His saving message, in which he and his wife express such confidence, will lead man back, if not to that utopia then to some other one. Yet even before the Orator's arrival, a prophetically ominous shadow is cast over the earlier sanguine tone of the play; it comes through an echoed dialogue between man and wife:

OLD MAN.   We'll save the world! . . .
OLD WOMAN [*echo*].   Saving his own soul by saving the world! . . .
OLD MAN.   One truth for all!
OLD WOMAN [*echo*].   One truth for all!
OLD MAN.   Follow me! . . .
OLD WOMAN [*echo*].   Follow him! . . .
OLD MAN.   For I have absolute certainty! . . .
OLD WOMAN [*echo*].   He has absolute certainty!
OLD MAN.   *Never* . . . [our italics]
OLD WOMAN [*echo*].   Ever and ever . . . (*C,* 146–147)

The Old Man's "Never" may be for him an unconscious slip of the tongue. But its implication does not escape the play's spectators who, once the Orator has arrived, may question the Old Man's enthusiastic entreaty to his wife that, their work done, they "withdraw . . . immediately, in order to make the supreme sacrifice which no one demands of us but which we will carry out even so" (*C,* 157–158). The Orator advances the cause not at all. If the Old Man even so much as had a message, it is, at this place and at this time, incommunicable.

The Chairs, one of Ionesco's relatively early plays, does not chart the way to paradise. Perhaps of even more significance than the depressing conclusion is the nature of the protagonist himself. For the Old Man is presented not as a person whom we can take with great seriousness or as one with whom we feel a particular empathy. Ionesco, with Olympian detachment and ironic condescension, draws for us a ludicrous, crazed figure, and we are inclined to write the Old Man off as at best a well-meaning but ineffectual fool. Or are we conceivably meant to interpret him as a pretentious and potentially dangerous meddler, a type of the would-be savior whom Ionesco, in his critical comments, strongly derides?

If our planet is today in mortal danger, it is because we have had too many saviors: saviors hate humanity, because they cannot accept it. (*NCN,* 123)

And while we debate whether Ionesco himself accepts humanity, we may note an even stronger statement.

It seems to me that in our own time and at all times religions and ideologies are not and never have been anything but alibis, pretexts that mask the murderous will, the destructive instinct, the fundamental aggressiveness and the profound hatred that man employs against man. . . . The saviors of mankind have founded inquisitions, invented concentration camps, constructed crematory ovens, established tyrannies. (*NCN,* 161)

The Old Man in the context of his play seems hardly so wicked, yet Ionesco's expository statements may suggest at least some part of his intentions in *The Chairs.*

It is in his two most impressive and satisfying plays, *The Killer* and *Rhinoceros,* that Ionesco turns most explicitly to the question of whether man, so close to a lifeless hell, may begin a turning back toward that paradise that lies now only deep in his memory. The plays are companion pieces, with Bérenger, the protagonist of both, confronted with rather similar antagonists symbolized by the Killer and rhinoceritis. That Bérenger is certainly defeated in one case and seemingly victorious in the other is an interesting paradox. But in defeat or in victory, Bérenger is a protagonist with whom we can identify ourselves more fully than we can with the Old Man, and a protagonist for whom we feel a strong respect.

Neither *The Killer* nor *Rhinoceros* speaks specifically, as does *The Chairs,* of a redemptive message for all mankind; Bérenger is not so ambitious as the lighthouse keeper. Yet Bérenger is, in both plays, the spokesman for whatever values may be attendant upon human life. The central theme of both plays comprises the question of whether life is worth living, whether there are any distinguishing human characteristics worth sustaining or reviving. It is as if Bérenger has by now wandered as far from paradise as a man can possibly go, short of the last step which is death. He is, then, at the point where he may either forsake what little life is left and die, or reverse his direction and move back toward a richness of life. He is Ionesco's most fully drawn character.

We have already characterized Bérenger's condition at the beginning of *The Killer,* particularly as he contrasts his habitual life with what at first glance seems to him to be the quality of life within the Radiant City. He thinks that he has moved from darkness and cold and ugliness into light and warmth and beauty, from a death-in-life into life itself. Perhaps the most precise epithet he can find for his customary condition is the "winter of the soul" (*K,* 20), that state just one step shy of death. The Bérenger of the beginning of *Rhinoceros* is much the same. He moves onto the stage in unkempt and fatigued condition. He confesses boredom and inability to become accustomed to life. And in conversation with the neat, confident, and well-adjusted Jean, he makes clear the winter of his soul. He speaks of being in fear and anguish, feelings which have led him to seek solace in alcohol. Jean is highly critical:

JEAN. You try to escape from yourself!
BÉRENGER. I'm so tired, I've been tired for years. It's exhausting to drag the weight of my own body about. . . .
JEAN. That's alcoholic neurasthenia, drinker's gloom. . . .
BÉRENGER. . . . I'm conscious of my body all the time, as if it were made of lead, or as if I were carrying another man around on my back. I can't seem to get used to myself. I don't even know if I *am* me. . . .
BÉRENGER. . . . I've barely got the strength to go on living. Maybe I don't even want to. (*R,* 17–18)

The question of both plays, answered each time in the last few pages, is whether Bérenger will succumb to a beckoning death or will begin the long road back to life. *The Killer* offers no hope. Victory will go to the Killer or—what comes to much the same thing—to the tyrannical, dehumanizing Mother Peep. The first character to take arms against the fatally oppressive forces is Mademoiselle Dany, who, coming to recognize the real nature of the Architect and telling him she can no longer support his cause, quits his service. Upon her consequent murder, the Architect argues the futility of opposing the power of death-in-life: "She was in the Civil Service! He [the Killer] doesn't attack the Service! But no, she wanted her 'liberty'! That'll teach her. She's found it now, her liberty. I was expecting this" (*K*, 41).

The other character who opposes the power structure, this time represented by Mother Peep, is designated simply as the Man. That he is presented, much like the Old Man of *The Chairs*, as a ludicrous figure, perhaps indicates Ionesco's view of the weakness of resistant forces. As Mother Peep calls for the goose step and for a perversion of all language, the Man, his drunkenness punctuated with hiccups, calls for a hero, a "man who dares to think against history and react against his times," who "fights his own age and creates a different one" (*K*, 79). He urges a revolution to overthrow the Architects, the Mother Peeps, and the Killers of the world. Noble as his proposals are, his clownlike quality prevents our taking him with full seriousness. And as the voices of the mob call for his downfall and Mother Peep engages him in combat, she finally exclaims: "*My geese have liquidated him. But only physically*" (*K*, 83). But the hope that her words might convey—that there are persons strong morally if not physically—is hardly borne out by the remainder of the play.

The last ten pages or so of *The Killer* present the climactic struggle between Bérenger and the Killer. It is important to note Ionesco's stage directions, printed prior to Act One, for the presenting of Bérenger's long and final dramatic monologue:

Bérenger's speech to the Killer at the end of the play is one short act in itself. The text should be interpreted in such a way as to bring out the gradual breaking-down of Bérenger, his falling apart and the vacuity of his own rather commonplace morality, which collapses like a leaking balloon. In fact Bérenger finds within himself, in spite of himself and against his own will, arguments in favour of the Killer. (*K*, 9)

And later, as Bérenger begins his monologue, the stage directions read: "*He speaks with an eloquence that should underline the tragically worthless and outdated commonplaces he is advancing*" (*K*, 99).

Bérenger advances virtually every argument that has ever been made for the preservation of what are generally considered human values. That the Killer is neither impressed nor stayed by any one of them suggests that *no* positive affirmation is strong enough to counter nihilism. The Killer is a monstrous, dwarflike creature whose only responses to Bérenger's nervous flow of words are a shrug of the shoulders and a chuckle. Bérenger first threatens him with his own superior physical strength and then assails him with a barrage of arguments and questions, all unanswered. He stresses the desirability of happiness, every possibility of which the Killer has thwarted. He asks the antagonist if he has killed out of a wanton, hate-motivated passion for destruction, or perhaps out of a merciful compassion for human suffering. He contrasts the Killer's seeming hate with the principle of the brotherhood of man and proclaims that Christ died for the Killer, that the saints weep for him, and that he, Bérenger, will comfort him in every way possible. He appeals to the Killer's reason, to the expedient insistence that crime does not pay, to common sense. Yet Bérenger is brought to confess his own doubts, his own uncertainty about every article of faith or reason that has been advanced for the intrinsic value of life. He is finally reduced to the purely relativistic position that "there's *no reason* to kill or not to kill" (*K*, 108). His own threat to kill the Killer dissolves "against the resistance of an infinitely stubborn will" (*K*, 108), and, at the curtain, Bérenger can only gasp, "Oh God! There's nothing we can do. What can we do . . . What can we do" (*K*, 109). The Bérenger of *The Killer*, finding no hope or solace in any argument which would posit the fundamental goodness of life, surrenders to death.

We have already mentioned that the Bérenger of *Rhinoceros* is, at the play's beginning, in a deep winter of the soul, with little energy, strength, or will to live. He is, at the first appearance of a rhinoceros, so apathetic as to remain unmoved. Of *all* Ionesco characters he undergoes the greatest change within the course of a play. Paradoxically, he experiences an even greater change than the physically metamorphosed characters of *Rhinoceros.* For Jean, Botard, Dudard, Daisy, and the rest, as they become great, green beasts, merely assume the physical characteristics of what has long been their spiritual condition. They typify all those persons who, having no convictions or faith, simply move with the times, falling to whatever may be most conventional at the moment. Their reflexes are perfectly attuned to the majority situation. Their condition is defined as rhinoceritis.

Bérenger, on the other hand, is finally awakened to life by his recognition of the disease of his fellows. His change is manifested, first, by his continually heightened response to the appearance of rhinoceroses. Whereas the first one went virtually unnoticed by him, the second did not. And he advances to the point where he alone is unwilling to take them for granted. His moving from apathy to engagement, and from near death to life, is charted as he debates with one character after another about the blandishments of rhinoceritis. As we have seen, it is with his friend Jean that he first argues. He recognizes that Jean is not only changing physically but "passing through a moral crisis" (*R,* 64). When Jean suggests that there is little to choose between being a man and being a rhinoceros, Bérenger insists that there is a difference in moral standards and that human beings "have a philosophy that animals don't share, and an irreplaceable set of values, which it's taken centuries of human civilization to build up" (*R,* 67). Bérenger does not join Jean in the flight from humanity or—to put it perhaps more accurately—Jean does not join Bérenger in his *return to* humanity.

Bérenger's next major verbal antagonist is Dudard. And though Bérenger has earlier confessed his uncertainty about who he himself is, it is clear by the time he engages Dudard that he knows whom he does not wish to become: "I'm frightened of becoming someone else" (*R, 73*). The extent of Bérenger's change from the beginning of the play to the time of his dialogue with Dudard is quite evident: "I feel responsible for everything that happens. I feel involved, I just can't be indifferent." (*R, 78*) Whatever arguments Dudard may advance that there is something quite natural about a man's becoming a rhinoceros, Bérenger remains unimpressed. If he cannot submit a clearly reasoned argument for the superiority of man, he nevertheless feels deeply the rightness of his position: "But I do feel you're in the wrong . . . I feel it instinctively—no, that's not what I mean, it's the rhinoceros which has instinct—I feel it intuitively, yes, that's the word, intuitively" (*R, 85*). Finally, Bérenger expresses a far different concept of the meaning of duty from that of the characters in this and other Ionesco plays. When Dudard argues that it is his duty to follow his friends into rhinoceritis, Bérenger, perhaps the sole major Ionesco character who is not a "victim of duty," states his own conviction about man's proper role: "No you're wrong, your duty is to . . . you don't see where your real duty lies . . . your duty is to oppose them, with a firm, clear mind" (*R, 93*).

Not even Daisy can persuade Bérenger to betray his humanity. When they find themselves the last human beings in a rhinoceros-filled world, he pleads with her to stay with him and save the world through the regeneration of the human race. But Daisy too must fall to the outer form which reflects the inner self, and she follows the others into the animal world.

The play ends with Bérenger's monologue, which, certainly at first reading, seems thoroughly ambiguous. Asking himself if the metamorphosis is reversible, he seems on the point of trying to persuade his former friends to become human again, only to realize that he and they share no common language of communication. He then wonders if perhaps *he* is the mistaken one and expresses regret that it is now too late to join his friends

in the kingdom of beasts. Are we to believe that Bérenger has lost all faith in human beingness and does not
now finally become a rhinoceros only because he cannot? We have already remarked that the stage directions
in *The Killer* define Ionesco's sense of Bérenger's moral
collapse in that play. In *Rhinoceros* the stage directions
are again helpful, perhaps even decisive, this time suggesting that Bérenger's expressed inclination to capitulation is but a momentary phase.

Immediately after he expresses regret for being
trapped in his humanity, the direction, "*He suddenly
snaps out of it,*" intimates movement from a passing
phase back to an abiding conviction. And his last lines
reaffirm his fidelity to humanity, even as a minority of
one: "Oh well, too bad! I'll take on the whole of
them! I'll put up a fight against the lot of them, the
whole lot of them! I'm the last man left, and I'm staying
that way until the end. I'm not capitulating!" (*R,* 107)
Dudard earlier remarked quite accurately to Bérenger:
"But you'll never become a rhinoceros, really you won't
. . . you haven't got the vocation!" (*R,* 80) Bérenger's
vocation is, in fact, to return to life. Even if the human
race must finally die with his death, it is gratifying that
at least one person will die a man.

In 1962 Ionesco wrote two additional Bérenger plays,
A Stroll in the Air and *Exit the King,* neither of which
is so impressive as the two earlier dramas with the same
protagonist. The later plays are, in terms of their ultimate views on man's destiny, closer to *The Killer* than
to *Rhinoceros.*

In *A Stroll in the Air* Herbert Bérenger, a dramatist
who finds that he can write no longer, is struck by the
sudden realization that he is going to die. Feeling at the
same time a mysterious joy, he tries to convey to his
wife Joséphine the peculiar sense he has of the beauty
and the freshness of this world: "Like some feeling of
joy that's been forgotten, forgotten yet still familiar, like
something that's belonged to me from the beginning of
time" (*SA,* 37). In his state of euphoria, symbolized
by his desire and ability to fly, he wishes to cross a

dazzlingly silver bridge and venture into the world of physical death, where, he hopes, he will find in their fullness the joys of which this world has furnished an intimation. Bérenger may have gone to school with Wordsworth's "Ode on the Intimations of Immortality."

His voyage made, his return is heralded by a graying landscape and a metamorphosis of the formerly lovely countryside into smoking ruins. His buoyancy destroyed by his vision of what lay beyond, he can now only hope —while convinced of his hope's utter vanity—that he has been dreaming. For the other world, far from possessing a consummate beauty of which this earth is but a reflection, is a desolate waste of bottomless pits, ravaged plains, ice, and fire. Only Bérenger's daughter Marthe, who has not made the epiphanal voyage, can at the play's end voice the faint hope that perhaps the fire will die, the ice melt, the gardens return. *A Stroll in the Air* suggests that the intimations of the world beyond death are to be found not in the occasional joys of this earth but in its griefs and sufferings; that the desert wastes of *this* world are but dim adumbrations of the full horror and nothingness which is to come; that to see face to face will reveal a terror, the clarity of which our present dark mirror gently obfuscates. We can only wonder how to assess the fact that the last lines of the play are Marthe's. Is she the one character in the play gifted with the love which may, *mirabile dictu,* nurse the wasted gardens back to bloom?

Exit the King, somewhat akin to the medieval morality play, does not look beyond the curtain of death so much as it heralds the death of the human race—and of God as well. King Bérenger the First appears to be an allegorical catchall, representing individual man, society in the form of the State, and God. His first wife, Queen Marguerite, is accurately convinced of the decay of all things and of the imminence of her husband's death; his second wife, Queen Marie, is mistakenly hopeful that the vitality of joy and love will save the King and the world. The physical and metaphysical climate of the play is Ionesco's familiar winter of the soul.

The central heating system of the palace has broken down; the clouded sky permits little light to break through. The palace is disintegrating, the mountains are sinking into the quaking earth, and the outer planets are colliding. The end of the world is at hand.

King Bérenger is, in true Renaissance fashion, the microcosm of both God and State: The King is, by divine right, god of his State; and as the King goes, in health or in sickness, so goes the State. We have mentioned earlier that Marie's twice-repeated "O God!" (*EK,* 22, 26) could be exclamatory or vocative. And Bérenger has, during his lifetime, possessed those powers of creation and miracle peculiar to God or the gods (*EK,* 34, 78), but these powers are no longer his. Twice his own state or personal condition is equated with the State which is the Kingdom (*EK,* 39, 46).

It is the fresh, lovely, and hopeful Marie (counterpart of Marthe) who would stay both the personal and the cosmic disintegrating forces. She senses, or thinks she senses, deep within Bérenger the wonder and power of life, and she apotheosizes the potentiality of the human will. "Open the floodgates of joy and light to dazzle and confound you," she urges her husband and King. "Illuminating waves of joy will fill your veins with wonder. If you want them to." And with that recourse to paradisiacal memories, which mark a large part of Ionesco's work, she continues:

I implore you to remember that morning in June we spent together by the sea, when happiness raced through you and inflamed you. You knew then what joy meant: rich, changeless and undying. If you knew it once, you can know it now. You found that fiery radiance within you. If it *was* there *once,* it is *still* there *now.* Find it again. Look for it, in yourself. (*EK,* 51)

Marie is the only woman in the entire Ionesco canon to celebrate the infinite possibilities of love. As she urges upon Bérenger the miracle of love, she reminds one of a Choubert or Amédée in search of a Madeleine's heart:

. . . if you love blindly, completely, death will steal away. If you love me, if you love everything, love will consume

your fear. Love lifts you up, you let yourself go and fear
lets go of you. The whole universe is one, everything lives
again and the cup that was drained is full. (*EK, 66*)

But it is too late, and it is Queen Marguerite who,
seeing things as they are, is the prophetess of doom. It
is she who controls the action of the play and the action
of its characters. She is the harbinger of death under
whose power Marie simply disappears. And although
King Bérenger, like King Lear on the heath, does come
to the knowledge of his long-standing selfish neglect of
others and also to a faint apprehension of the joy life
may hold, he has surrendered too much of his earlier
grace to survive the strength of death. Queen Marguerite, a Beatrice in reverse, disappears after she has
led the King to the demonic and destructive vision. And
man, society, and God—compacted within the symbol
of King Bérenger—fade away in the mist as the curtain
falls.

The Bérenger of *The Killer* and the Bérenger of *Rhinoceros,* except for their final decisions, are much the
same man. They both initially experience the winter of
the soul; they next encounter those forces which would
deprive them of the individuality that distinguishes one
man from another and would rob them of life itself;
then finally they use much the same arguments against
their assailants, seeking to reaffirm those values which
have traditionally been viewed as the life-giving sus-
tenance of their culture. Yet one capitulates to the
Killer, and the other holds out against rhinoceritis.
Herbert Bérenger sees the horror beyond physical death;
King Bérenger makes his exit with death. That Ionesco
seems or is inconsistent matters little, for he is not intent
upon defining the ultimate fate of sick men in a sick
society. In *Rhinoceros* Bérenger, after attending a long
disquisition on rhinoceroses by the Logician, says, rather
disappointedly: "That seems clear enough, but it doesn't
answer the question." The Logician replies: "Obviously,
my dear sir, but now the problem is correctly posed."
(*R, 37*) Ionesco too presents the problems but does
not try to offer definitive solutions. It is thus not surpris-

ing that, in his two most stunning and probing plays, *The Killer* and *Rhinoceros,* he gives his protagonists the same name, similar characteristics, and similar dilemmas and antagonists, and yet he provides each with a different outcome; nor is it surprising that *A Stroll in the Air* and *Exit the King* play still other variations on the same basic theme. Even with such variations, however, it is possible to make some general observations about Ionesco's view of man and society. To take into consideration his whole work is to conclude that he is hardly optimistic about our chances of regaining paradise. He makes of the Old Man of *The Chairs* something of a pathetic fool as he prophesies universal redemption; he derides and undercuts, through the stage directions of *The Killer,* the hopeful arguments Bérenger advances; he gives Herbert Bérenger a fearful wisdom and offers no hope to King Bérenger.

Yet there is implicit in his works a thin ray of light. At the least Ionesco is saying that we must learn to accept the inevitability of death with dignity and manliness. King Bérenger may be speaking for Ionesco and addressing all of us when he remarks: "All the rest of you, be me, come inside me, come beneath my skin. I'm dying, you hear, I'm trying to tell you. I'm dying, but I can't express it, unless I talk like a book and make literature of it." (*EK,* 53) And the King calls to those who died before him to teach him how to accept death. We may recall that the Bérenger of *Rhinoceros* was at least in a position to die a man, not a nonentity.

At the most Ionesco intimates that, if there is the possibility of a man's working his way out of this world's present foggy thicket, it lies in a stubborn, persistent, courageous conviction that he is different from the beasts of the field—and from every other man as well. If a man is to hold on to or return to life, he must be convinced, with Queen Marie and Marthe, of the potential power of love, of life's joys, of his own precious individuality. Only then does he have no vocation to fall to rhinoceritis or to a killer.

The Empty Reservoirs

I

As is the case with all genuinely creative writers, the total value of Ionesco's work cannot be contained within the arguments of his themes. In discussing with his critics the theories and presumptions on which his plays are founded, he has himself emphasized this fact. "If . . . [my plays] were to be completely exhausted by my arguments, entirely contained in them, they would not be of very great value" (*NCN,* 11). As is so often the case, the chief flaws in the body of Ionescan criticism are caused by the tenacity of the critic in pursuing his own theory, causing an imperceptible but gradually widening and fatal parting of his interpretation from the Ionesco text itself. Or, as Ionesco puts it: "The voice of the work itself can no longer be heard through the din of debate; while all kinds of points of view are being developed, it is always the work itself that is lost sight of" (*NCN,* 60).

No writer is more intransigent toward the effort to classify him than is Ionesco. His stormy and often contradictory altercations with his critics have largely been influenced by his resentment at being pressed into a mold—any mold whatsoever. His fear of even the threat of this process has occasionally led him into contradictions beyond those fluent and flexible contradictions which are a spontaneous part of the functioning of his art. He has himself seen this clearly, describing himself as ". . . a harassed author who, in trying to defend him-

73

self on all fronts at once, sometimes gets caught up in contradictions which will surely be noticed by his readers and for which he offers his apologies"; and he cites "the illogicalities that arise from emotional involvement in present-day problems, tangled affirmations and denials that cancel each other out." (*NCN,* 10) This statement of Ionesco's is crucial to an understanding of his work, for the deliberate contradictions in the plays, the "tangled affirmations and denials that cancel each other out," are the sort of fecundating cross-images to which Dylan Thomas refers in his well-known statement on the poetic process: "I let . . . an image be 'made' emotionally in me and then apply to it what intellectual and critical forces I possess—let it breed another, let that image contradict the first, make, of the third image bred out of the other two together, a fourth contradictory image, and let them all, within my imposed formal limits, conflict."[1]

There is another sort of contradiction, a profound and sterile one, which Ionesco repudiates. In *Improvisation, or The Shepherd's Chameleon* Ionesco, as himself, protests to his critics, Bartholomeus I, II, and III, "I'm all for contradiction, everything is nothing but contradiction, and yet any systematic exposition ought not to . . . should it . . . in words, confuse opposites" and finally cries, ". . . what's true is true and what's false is false," to which Bartholomeus I shouts: "Horror! Tautologies! Nothing but tautologies!" (*I,* 118–119)

If at times Ionesco's fundamental presumptions seem to have headed him toward a logical *cul-de-sac* from which there is no egress, it never quite happens. It never quite happens because at the final moment he eludes the entrance by an honest demonstration that the *cul-de-sac* is really not there, because it is irrelevant to his purpose and practice. It is, however, an escape which must later be discussed more fully.

Two basic assumptions must underlie the analysis of Ionesco's work: that the analyst must never for one

[1] Quoted by John Ackerman, *Dylan Thomas: His Life and Work* (London: Oxford University Press, 1964), p. 54.

instant stray from the dynamic material he is examining; and that it is possible—all evidence of contradiction notwithstanding—to examine the work in the light of Ionesco's own objectives. Ionesco himself feels strongly about these qualifications for the explorer's role: "If however we admit that the critic clearly has the right to exercise his judgment, he should only judge a work on its own terms, according to the laws that govern artistic expression, the mythological structure of each work, and so penetrate each new universe afresh. . . . For me, the theatre is the projection onto the stage of the world within: it is in my dreams, my anguish, my dark desires, my inner contradictions that I reserve the right to find the stuff of my plays." (*I, 150*) Whether this can be the ultimate word on the critical approach is doubtful. It is certainly, however, the ultimate and essential word for the preliminary approach—that of comprehending and evaluating, without desiccation, the writer's degree of success in implementing his own vision.

For the reader of Ionesco, there are three essential areas of exploration: Ionesco's sense of alienation, Ionesco's conception and use of humor, and Ionesco's sense of his own place, historically and in contemporary society.

II

Alienation has become such a fashionable catchword that its strict usage here must be defined. It is used in its most profound and powerful sense—that of a separation, the perception of an absence. To the Ionesco protagonist it is the recollection of the beatific vision, now lost, which has caused life to become intolerable. In *The Killer,* Bérenger explains his difficulties with the burden of daily life: "It weighs on you, it weighs on you terribly, especially when you think you've seen . . . when you've thought you could hope . . . Oh! . . . then you can't go on" (*K, 62*). Earlier Bérenger remarked: "There was a chaotic vacuum inside me, I was overcome with the immense sadness you feel at a moment of tragic and intolerable separation" (*K, 24*). This is no natural, healthy separation; no species of growth, no commencement of self-reliance or sense of freedom. It has two major characteristics. It is tragic; worse, it is intolerable. It is, specifically, none of the alienations debated by housing authorities and liberal-minded organizations. It is not national; it is not economic; it is not racial; it is not social—though all of these minor lonelinesses may be subsumed in its darkness. It is the absence of conviction, the absence of being sure, the absence of significance.

BÉRENGER. . . . For years I felt sure . . .
ARCHITECT. Sure of what?
BÉRENGER. Sure I'd been sure . . . (*K*, 25)

Later he adds: "The water in the well had dried up and I was dying of thirst" (*K*, 25). Bérenger's alienation is not from the condition of happiness—the product of events—but from the condition of joy, the sense of felicity, of being sure of the truth of his early vision of radiance, the radiance by virtue of which he knew himself to be alive: "Not happiness, I mean joy, felicity, which made it possible for me to live" (*K*, 20). In the vision of his childhood, the physical materials of life were translated into light by the power of a supreme luminance: "The houses I was passing were like immaterial shades ready to melt away in that mightier light which governed all" (*K*, 23).

This major alienation, from felicity and its revelation, manifests itself in Ionesco's work in four guises. First, in matter—the objects used and encountered in daily life. Second, in the spiritual alienation which produces an emotional atmosphere as comfortless as the weather —gray forever, half-sleet, half-snow: ". . . perpetual November, perpetual twilight, twilight in the morning, twilight at midnight, twilight at noon" (*K*, 25). Third, in the alienation of language, which, deprived of the dynamic and corrective inspiration of conviction, has run wild, in meaningless repetitions, proliferations, and distortions. And last, in the perpetual harassment caused by the sense that there must be both a source and an objective, coupled with the inability to recapture the one or conceive the other.

An adumbration of Ionesco's total sense of alienation has been achieved in the opening and closing scenes of *The Killer*. In the first scene Bérenger and the Architect are alone in the Radiant City; in the last one Bérenger faces the Killer. To trace the rise and fall of these two scenes is to see clearly, in its essence, the process of Ionesco's sense of dislocation, of being a displaced person. The monologue of Bérenger on stage alone with the Killer is carefully balanced against the opening action. In fact, the two scenes complement each other, on different planes—the motion of the first scene rising, then descending; and that in the last taking up where the first leaves off. The latter is punctuated by the Killer's inane and deadly chuckle of indifference; the former by the inane and deadly indifference of the Architect, talking into the phone whose wires end in his own pocket, while Bérenger pours out his crucial account of a paradise lost. Technically, the scenes balance beautifully. The Architect's supercilious contempt for Bérenger's distress and soul-searching is at one with the Killer's later attitude. While Bérenger speaks, the Architect talks into his phone, busies himself with his files, and acknowledges Bérenger's words in only the most condescending manner. The fact is that he *cannot* listen, *cannot* really concede the identity of Bérenger.

In these two scenes the whole motion of *The Killer* and, indeed, of Ionesco's entire work is graphed. In the beginning of the first act it rises, starting with Bérenger's euphoric reaction to his first glimpse of the Radiant City and progressing in an arc through his recapture of his own radiant vision—that sense of a significant luminance of sky, of earth, of his own identity, which was at once astonishing and deeply familiar—and through the consideration of that vision's loss, and finally, a few pages later, to the dissolution of the image of the Radiant City itself. The first stone falls in Bérenger's path; the Ornamental Pool, which he has instinctively feared, yields the weight of its dead; the arc descends to the

final point of his despair when, once more in the gray
and bitter air of his habitual streets beyond the gates,
he learns that the Killer has freshly killed and that the
new victim is Bérenger's blonde young "fiancée" Dany.
This first plane has the shape and proportion of the
latter, lower plane, as Bérenger and the Killer confront
each other. Begun in fear and courage, it rises to visions
of retribution and justice, and curves through the summoning of all Bérenger's values—those values by which
he had believed he believed life to be sustained; but
these values, empty and treacherous as the mirage of the
roses, as the blues and greens of the Radiant City, drop
steeply down to the final gray, shabby, pitiless death—
Bérenger's own.

In the early scene he is concerned with the recaptur-
ing of joy. In the later one, he is struggling to stave off
the death which will ensue now that felicity no longer
makes it possible for him to live. In between the two
scenes, he has come to discover how complete has been
his loss and how relentlessly he carries within himself
the principle of death that took seed in that loss. In the
first scene, he pursues life; in the last, within himself he
unwittingly prepares a welcome for the Killer. The play's
tragedy thus hovers, unannounced and undefined, over
even the first scene. Perhaps already the Killer has
arrived. Or rather, his first faint chuckle is given within
Bérenger himself: "There was a kind of chaotic vacuum
inside me" (K, 24).

For all his ecstatic reaction to the first lovely shock
of the Radiant City, Bérenger is not invulnerable to unwelcome perceptions, which begin to cloud over his
just-achieved light and warmth. At first, struck by the
resemblance of the shining scene before him to the lost
morning of his never-forgotten experience, he is lavish
with his enthusiasm: "A miracle, or, as I don't suppose
you're a religious man, you'd rather I called it a marvel!
I congratulate you most warmly, it's a marvel, really
quite marvelous, you're a marvelous architect!" (K, 10)
And so he is—an architect not of miracles, for which
Bérenger instinctively hopes, but of marvels. The Radi-

ant City is not only a moral illusion; it is also an illusion sensually speaking. Bérenger describes its beauties, as he touches its nonexistent edifices: "And with you it's not the unreal product of an overheated imagination. These are real houses and stones and bricks and cement. [*Touching empty space.*] It's concrete, solid, tangible." (*K,* 26)

But he already senses, without defining it, the danger and vulnerability of a calculated illusion. Already the print of death is subtly present, though invisible. Objects and facts change with the lighting; they rearrange themselves: where was first the greenhouse, apparently fostering growth, appears the Architect's office, fostering the pretense of growth; and close by, a few minutes later, will stand, outside the gates and close to the cemetery, the bistro, friend to the grave, where wreaths as well as aperitifs are sold. Before the first stone falls in his path, Bérenger has felt a strong though inexplicable disinclination to look into the Ornamental Pool he has admiringly noticed. Already he carries within himself the full-grown knowledge of death; and though there is nothing to indicate a content more sinister than lilies or goldfish, he intuitively fears the pool. The sad secret is available to him; but almost without allowing himself to notice that he does so, he defers facing it.

ARCHITECT. You want to have a closer look? [*He appears to hesitate.*] Very well. If you insist, I'll have to show it you.
BÉRENGER. Or instead . . . I don't know what to choose . . . it's all so beautiful . . . I like ornamental pools, but I rather like the look of the flowering hawthorn too. If you don't mind, we can look at the pool later . . .
ARCHITECT. As you like.
BÉRENGER. I love hawthorn bushes.
ARCHITECT. You've only to make up your mind.
BÉRENGER. Yes, yes, let's go over to the hawthorn.
ARCHITECT. I'm completely at your service.
BÉRENGER. One can't see everything at once.
ARCHITECT. True enough. [*The pool disappears. . . .*] (*K,* 18)

Exactly so will Édouard and the Old Man protest that they have not looked into their briefcases. And the pool's is not a true disappearance but a retreat; it is waiting all the while. Eventually, with inexplicable misgiving, Bérenger approaches the silently returned pool. In its small circumscription lie floating the bodies of a swollen officer of the Engineers, a woman whose long red hair undulates like water-weed, and a little drowned boy with his hoop. Man, woman, child—all members of the human race are represented in the foul, bloating water of the Ornamental Pool. The Killer has announced himself.

After presenting the bodies in the pool, the stone thrown, the distortion of the voices of playing children which sound like the yelping of dogs, the Radiant City clouds and lowers, and Bérenger, back once more in the characteristic dirty chill of his own sector beyond the gates, learns of a new murder—that of Dany. He is back in the heart of alienation in good earnest; now, indeed, he realizes that he has never left it, that the Architect-constructed Radiant City had neither air nor sun nor rain but only concealed ventilators, copied by the Architect from "those oases that crop up all over the place in the desert, where suddenly out of the dry sand you see amazing cities rising up, smothered with dewy roses, girdled with springs and rivers and lakes," of which Bérenger asks naively: "You mean those cities that are also called mirages?" (K, 17) From here on the play curves ferociously and precipitously downward.

Cut off from both the radiance of his early recollection and from its spuriously constructed semblance, Bérenger fights now merely to stave off the Killer himself, or at best to capture and convince him. His first thought is that the Authorities must be forced to act. His suggestion to the Architect, that a plain-clothes detective lie in wait for the Killer at his favorite spot, is rejected "for technical reasons" (K, 40)—an important point in the Ionesco canon. But when, during the visit to Bérenger of the deformed and sickly Édouard (that minion of death, in his pallor, black clothes, and mourning arm band), whose briefcase, accidentally flying open, reveals the equipment of the Killer, Bérenger conceives that both prevention and retribution are in his hands.

The subsequent events—up to Bérenger's actual encounter with the Killer—illustrate brilliantly a number of Ionesco's tenets. But it is in the encounter with the puny, evil, speechless Killer that the theme of alienation reaches its highest and deepest point. Disconnected from his radiant knowledge, unsure, Bérenger lacks all inner conviction for the cause he pleads. He helplessly carries inside himself the cold senseless chuckle which finds all things equally worthless. He has found in none of the pronouncements or apologetics of mankind that "background that would answer some profound need inside, which would be somehow . . . the projection, the continuation of the universe inside you" (*K*, 19). As each frantic argument goes down before the indifference of deafness, and the deafness of indifference, Bérenger continues desperately to protest that there *must* be a valid argument, there *must* be something which can be done to move the Killer. But the final lines, as the Killer moves in to strike, are their own answer: "What can we do . . . What can we do" (*K*, 109). For it is not an argument which could stop the Killer, but a belief. And in belief, as distinct from nostalgia, Bérenger is bankrupt.

In his book *The Theatre of Revolt,* Robert Brustein perceptively describes the long quest for faith in which "even the most materialistic programs are embraced as a form of metaphysical salvation. . . . The theatre of revolt fails to build its Church, and records this failure in a growing mood of despair. . . . The theatre of revolt, then, is the temple of a priest without a God, without an orthodoxy, without even much of a congregation, who conducts his service within the hideous architecture of the absurd."[2]

At the last Bérenger *can* no longer affirm anything; three times, in one of his final speeches, he cries, "I don't know!" ending with, "say what you believe, can't

[2] Robert Brustein, *The Theatre of Revolt* (Boston: Little, Brown & Company, 1964), pp. 12, 16.

you? *I* can't, *I* can't." (*K,* 107) And in the end it is the Killer's special triumph that he succeeds in provoking in Bérenger just that paroxysm of blind rage which has simmered perpetually among the citizens of the gray, sleety city—policemen, truck drivers, the concierge. Furiously, Bérenger cries: "You filthy dirty moronic imbecile! . . . I'm going to finish you, and then I'll stamp on you and squash you to a pulp, you stinking rotten carcass of a hyena! . . . I'll shoot and shoot, and then I'll hang you, I'll chop you into a thousand pieces, I'll throw your ashes into Hell with the excrement you came from, you vomit of Satan's mangy cur, criminal cretin" (*K,* 108).

Although *Frenzy for Two,* dolorously funny in spots, provides a minimum of new material for the Ionesco canon, it does heavily underline this atmosphere of querulous animosity. Within surroundings that make of the city streets a nightmare of danger, noise, violence, and death, petty hostilities and irascibility ferment sourly in beleaguered rooms, where the inhabitants interrupt their barricading of themselves against the threatening outside world only long enough to exchange insults and blows. The very pettiness and bad temper of the recrimination within the walls make its stale vindictiveness more frightening even than the alarums and disasters of the embattled streets. It is as though the frenzied two survive only by dint of and for the purpose of mutual vilification. As the Journalist in *A Stroll in the Air* succinctly puts it:

You see, friendship . . . friendship was a snare and a delusion. Besides it slowly sucks the life out of you. Loathing is better. It provides the most favourable background for life. It's the only thing can give us strength. Loathing means energy. It's energy itself. (*SA,* 59)

So—"imbecile . . . seducer . . . slug . . . moron . . . pig . . . liar," cries the mistress. "Slug!" cries the lover, both taking time out to exchange resounding slaps before they resume the blocking of windows and doors.

The spiritual alienation with which *The Killer* deals produces physical results, related and immediate. As the spiritual atmosphere produces the gray, sleety mists of Bérenger's city, so the bodies of those exposed to its miasmas show injury. Édouard has a twisted arm and a wracking cough; Roberta has three noses; the Killer lacks an eye; Amédée and Madeleine have a growing corpse filling their apartment; the Pupil develops first a toothache and then agonizing pains in all her body; in *Rhinoceros,* Bérenger's friends and associates develop greenish leathery skins and sprout horns; Amédée, Choubert, and Bérenger suffer from chronic fatigue, against which they must struggle with failing strength. In Ionesco's world, the outer cannot fail to manifest the inner.

As language, freed from convictions it wishes to communicate, suffers distortion and disintegration, so matter, uninhibited by spiritual control, proliferates in a senseless jumble. Chairs, a corpse, furniture, noses, teacups, it is all one. Objects breed madly, to block and stifle life. The interior dynamic energy that vitalized the human being has died out, has degenerated into the senseless energy of matter, gone wild like a sick cell. Sénart says of this: "Mais cette prolifération n'est pas anarchique. C'est une 'progression géométrique': elle obéit à sa loi, s'accomplit dans son ordre. Cancer abominable, elle est produit du monde du mal et de la mort, du monde matériel, du monde méchanique où rien n'est laissé aux inspirations de l'esprit et aux caprices du hasard, où tout est réglé par la volonté suprême d'un démiurge organisateur et destructeur."[3]

In *The Killer,* Bérenger has explained to the unlistening Architect: ". . . once upon a time there was a blazing fire inside me. The cold could do nothing against it, a youthfulness, a spring no autumn could touch; a

[3] Philippe Sénart, *Ionesco* (Paris: Editions Universitaires, 1964), p. 74. Translation: "But this proliferation is not that of anarchy. It is a 'geometrical progression': it is obedient to its law, is fulfilled in its own order. Abominable cancer, it is the product of the world of evil and death, of the material world, of the mechanical world where nothing is left to the spirit's inspirations, and to the caprices of chance, where all is ruled by the supreme will of a demiurge, organizing and destroying."

source of light, glowing wells of joy that seemed inexhaustible. . . . There was enormous energy there . . . it must have been the life force, mustn't it?" (*K,* 20) That energy has seeped from Bérenger, from Amédée, from Choubert, and appears in the corporate beast of Roberta's stallion, the Killer, and the rhinoceroses. Bérenger instinctively realizes this. Suddenly he says to Édouard: "After all, these terrible crimes in the radiant city might be the cause of your illness." (*K,* 65)

At its most acute, this disease and degeneration of the flesh, which is the outer and visible sign of an inward and spiritual disaster, results in the hideous wrecks of flesh common to existential theatre. Robert Brustein has remarked on this characteristic, common to Ionesco, Beckett, Genet, and many others: "One of the strongest identifying marks of the existential drama is its attitude towards the flesh, which is usually described in images of muck, mud, ashes, fecal matter, in a state of decomposition and decay."[4] We think instantly of Roberta, of Édouard, of the Killer, of the Corpse.

If matter, disconnected from spiritual energy, tends to mortify, in so doing it inevitably loses its distinctions. If a human being becomes an object, listing it among other objects is no longer bizarre. Floods, dogs run over, soiled sidewalks, and children with their throats cut are no longer unacceptable under a common heading. The owner of the bistro offers his customers a "first-class rabbit pâté, pure pork" (*K,* 38), much in the tone of Winnie's discovery, in *Happy Days,* that the purity of her toothbrush is guaranteed by its being genuine hog's bristles. *The Bald Soprano* is a perfect broth of dissolved personalities: the clock strikes seven and then three; in consecutive speeches, Bobby Watson's death is placed as having occurred two years ago, eighteen months ago, four years ago; Bobby Watson's wife, met "by chance" at Bobby Watson's movable burial, is unpretty, big, stout, thin, small, pretty. These contradictions, one of Ionesco's peculiar trademarks, spring from just this dislocation.

[4] *Op. cit.,* pp. 27–28.

Conviction, the understanding, can no longer confer identity. Everything becomes fluid; above all, nothing proceeds *from* conviction *to* a result. As Bérenger cannot draw from his belief any argument which will move the Killer, so material objects and physical characteristics, undirected, proceed not *from* a source and *to* an objective, but merely circle around and around. "Take a circle, caress it, and it will turn vicious" (*BS,* 38), says Mr. Smith to the Martins; and this same vicious circle changes the Smiths into the Martins, sets them forth again on the same orbit, brings a fresh Pupil to the Professor's door, confronts the critics Bartholomeus I, II, and III with Ionesco's pinwheel play. As we shall see, Genet repeatedly uses the concept of the vicious circle, and the circle is obsessive in Beckett's work, which is a nightmare of wheels.

Both the use of contradiction and the use of the static derive, in Ionesco, from the overmastering sense of a lapsed conviction, with a resulting tendency for the material manifestations which should stem from that conviction to circle meaninglessly and repetitively. A circle neither departs nor arrives; it, like a contradiction, is opposed to progress. As Genet's Queen, in *The Blacks,* who is simultaneously embroidering, sleeping, and washing dishes, ends by first paralyzing and then destroying her own image, the image of Bobby Watson's wife is destroyed for the reader.

The tricky thing about Ionesco's use of contradiction is that he employs it in at least two differing ways— and deplores its use by anyone in a third manner which is basically a corruption of the first. The static contradictions he employs to indicate that time, physical characteristics, or human identity have become meaningless, are at once a device of humor and of tragedy, a condition seen as sad, as ludicrously horrifying, and often as both of these at once. His characters confuse themselves and each other with contradictions because they have neither seen nor heard: they have become incapable of listening, or of vision.

The second kind of contradiction used approvingly

by Ionesco involves the living conflict of elements, the fecundating strife described by Dylan Thomas. This strife produces sparks like the light given off by those houses that were luminous but that glowed under a governing light. These are the healthy contradictions of flux and growth, the freedom of movement that Ionesco never stops promulgating as the essential condition of the artist: "I do not believe we need overcome and resolve contradictions. That would mean impoverishment. We must allow contradictions to develop freely; perhaps our conflicts will resolve themselves dynamically by counterbalancing each other." (*NCN*, 116)

The third manner of contradiction, used unsympathetically by Ionesco, is the contradiction masked as choice, for which Mother Peep speaks:

We won't persecute, but we'll punish and deal out justice. We won't colonize, we'll occupy the countries we liberate. We won't exploit men, we'll make them productive. We'll call compulsory work voluntary. War shall change its name to peace and everything will be altered, thanks to me and my geese. (*K*, 77)

The best will be chosen, and the worst will be delivered in its name. It is the understanding of this sort of contradiction that has caused Ionesco to assert to the Bartholomeuses: "I'm all for contradiction," but "what's true is true, and what's false is false." (*I*, 118–119) It is the same sort of contradiction which, ludicrous in the case of the amorphous Mrs. Bobby Watson, is so sinister in the Newspeak of Mother Peep—the "fair's foul, and foul's fair" of the manipulator.

The inability to see or to hear has become a disease, the ravening disease of indifference, and this indifference in even physical terms begins in injury and ends in murder. As the knowledge of, and indifference to, the Killer has made Édouard ill, eating away at his vitality, so his indifference, like that of the Architect, menaces Bérenger himself. Ionesco is not merely playing with words when Bérenger cries: "Your indifference makes me sick! And I don't mind saying it to your face." And when Édouard replies, "Well you know . . . I . . ." Bérenger says loudly, "Your indifference makes me sick!" (K, 64)

The indifference springs largely from lack of conviction, but partly also from fear. As Bérenger shrank from examining the pool, as he has never faced his own lack of conviction, so the Old Man says indignantly, of his empty briefcase: "That's nobody's business. I don't even ask myself. I'm not so inquisitive." (K, 81) And Édouard half guiltily protests: "I'm not always looking inside my briefcase!" (K, 39) Édouard's briefcase, is, actually, filled with a proliferation of objects (among them the enticements used by the Killer), and the stage directions read: *Much should be made of this scene: some of the objects can fly away on their own, others can be thrown by Bérenger to the four corners of the stage.* (K, 67) Oddly, Édouard uses the habitual tense: "I don't know. I never know what I've got in my briefcase, I never look inside." (K, 70) So the disconnected objects and physical characteristics proliferate, substituting eggs for babies, corpses for roommates, rhinoceroses for men.

The bodying forth of the "chaotic vacuum"—which resulted in cold, in grayness, in the perpetual sense of fatigue, debility, and ill-being, in the deathly touch implicit in Édouard's appearance and clothing, and in the concierge's grim and monotonous little song—manifests itself also in a peevish anger that rises to the pitch of hysterical rage in Bérenger's final confrontation with the Killer. This latent anger poisons the air like a noxious gas. There is everywhere evident a senseless animosity: in the abuse heaped by the concierge on Treasure, the dog she keeps on hand for the pleasure of mistreating it, in her attitude toward Columbine's visitor, in the exchange of insults between the drivers. It is indifference fretting itself to hostility. When Bérenger appeals to the police, the response is at first indifference. But it alters.

1ST POLICEMAN. Phew! They can talk themselves silly, some of them!
2ND POLICEMAN [*louder, turning to Bérenger again*]. It's not my racket, get it? I don't give a good goddam for

your story. If you're one of the boss's pals, go and see him and leave me in goddam peace. (*K*, 93)

It is not only the unexpectedness that makes us shiver when, before disappearing, the second policeman suddenly and intimately says to Bérenger: "I hate you." (*K*, 94)

This is the shadow cast by the meaningless murder, without robbery, in the deserted subway station, the senseless lethal beating of an old man never seen before and met on a midnight street. It is like the protagonist's attack on the old man in the forest, in Samuel Beckett's *Molloy;* like the gaze directed by the Lodger, in Harold Pinter's *The Birthday Party*. This is the material world seen by an alienated human being. At the moment in his childhood that perhaps marked the first chill of separation from the summer street of a country village, bright with the sureness of his own conviction of felicity, Ionesco observed a scene of violence, on a city pavement at twilight, which he was never able to forget. It became for him the dark base of his conviction that to be human was an insufferable condition:

I have no other pictures of the world apart from those which express evanescence and callousness, vanity and anger, emptiness, or hideous useless hate. Everything has merely confirmed what I had seen and understood in my childhood: futile and sordid fits of rage, cries suddenly blanketed by the silence, shadows swallowed up forever by the night. What else have I to say? (*NCN*, 154)

There are other physical manifestations of this "insufferable state." As the clock, striking at random, evidences the cessation of progressive time in *The Bald Soprano,* so the nightmare atmosphere of the static hangs over *The Killer*. Édouard says simply to Bérenger, who urges him to hurry on their way to the Prefecture to denounce the Killer: "Don't worry. You know perfectly well the time's the same as it was just now." (*K*, 76) The sense of the static is constant. As Bérenger hastens, in one place, to the never-nearer Prefecture, he mutters to himself: "Still a long way . . . Not getting any nearer . . . I'm not making any progress. It's as though

I wasn't moving at all." (*K,* 95) And the stage directions, just before the appearance of the Killer, read: ". . . *there is a still, timeless half-light*" (*K,* 94).

An alienation which is both spiritual and physical pre-eminently marks Ionesco's sexual themes. There is not a single instance of true rapport between a man and woman in all of Ionesco's writing. At one end is the fugitive and dream-ridden passion conceived by Bérenger for Dany—a pre-existent, romantic desire, inasmuch as he is already calling "Mademoiselle, oh, Mademoiselle, will you marry me?" (*K,* 26) when he first sees her; they never so much as talk together or touch each other, and she scarcely knows that he exists. At the other extreme is the ghoulish union of Jack with Roberta of the snaky fingers and the three noses, which will scarcely do as an instance of felicity either spiritual or fleshly.

In between lie the pathetic, foredoomed love affair of Daisy and the Bérenger of *Rhinoceros,* the fruitless efforts of Marie to protect and sustain the Bérenger of *Exit the King,* and the grim ménages of Choubert and Madeleine, the Old Man and the Old Woman, Amédée and his Madeleine. In every single case (with the exception of Marie, who is balanced by the savagely realistic Marguerite), it is the wife who is the destructive force —from the weakness, and ultimate defection of Daisy, to the bitter, loveless, domineering hostility of the two Madeleines. Even the Old Woman, reiterating "Darling, Darling," sweetly quavers to her husband all the things he *could* have been and *could* have done, and *is* not, and *did* not.

Nor, among his peers, is Ionesco alone in this. Concurrently with the demotion of the body to muck and ashes, love between the sexes has a difficult time. Leaving aside Genet's basically womanless world (for even Solange and Claire are boys in disguise) or Beckett's bone-chilling accounts of hags and moribund tramps coldly and clumsily repeating their masochistic rites, there is a singular absence of communication between the sexes on any level in avant-garde theatre. What

Leslie Fiedler wrote in *Love and Death in the American Novel* could even more fairly be spoken of contemporary drama. And Jacques Guicharnaud in *Modern French Theatre from Giraudoux to Beckett* notes of Anouilh: "There are no united and happy couples in Anouilh's theatre. All the mature couples who appear on stage are always plunged in a farcical situation and treated rather lightly or with an accent on the situation's sordid or bitter aspect."[5]

In Ionesco's work the male of the couple struggles at least to remain in touch with hope—a receding grace. As Bérenger comments to the Architect: "I was afraid to hope . . . hope, that's not a French word any more, or Turkish, or Polish . . . Belgian perhaps . . . and even then . . ." (*K*, 11). The husbands or lovers are afraid to hope, but consistently they long to do so. The wives, who from the beginning have despised hope as an unrealistic and subversive attitude, predict and ensure darkness, cold, obstruction, submission. Love is thus rendered an impossibility in these marriages, and to the loss of the conviction of a divine love is added the intolerable burden of human loneliness at the precise point where it could best be comforted. Bérenger in *The Killer* has hopes, unrealistic as they may be, of Dany; the Bérenger of *Rhinoceros* has hopes, futile as they prove, of Daisy. Marie, who clings to hope for the Bérenger of *Exit the King,* cannot reach him and is rendered powerless by the cold and deadly pessimism of Marguerite. The men and women who have committed themselves to each other exist in the abyss of a loneliness unbroken by the slightest genuine contact.

This is a loneliness quite different from solitude, a loneliness possible only to intimacy without communication. Ionesco stresses that contemplative solitude is opposed to, not identical with, loneliness: "Several times I have said that it is in our fundamental solitude that we rediscover ourselves and that the more I am alone, the

---

[5] Jacques Guicharnaud (in collaboration with June Beckelman), *Modern French Theatre from Giraudoux to Beckett* (New Haven: Yale University Press, 1961), p. 117.

more I am in communion with others . . ." (*NCN,* 78).
Elsewhere he writes: "For solitude is not *separation* but
meditation, and we know that social groups, it has
been said already, are most often a collection of solitary
human beings. No one ever talked of incommunicability
at a time when men were able to isolate themselves; incommunicability and isolation are paradoxically the
tragic themes of the modern world, where everything is
done collectively" (*NCN,* 151). The fact remains that
love is irreplaceable and that Ionesco's characters, like
those of Genet and Beckett, living with their sense of
absence, of being cut off, are incapable of love and live
in the hell of a perpetual thirst perpetually denied.

If man is disconnected from the slightest element of
the eternal, he knows himself to be a walking death;
he is born, as Beckett's Vladimir puts it, "Astride of a
grave"; and, like Molloy's mother, he finally dies—
"enough to bury." It is this sense of transience, this
terrible taint of the ephemeral, which more than all else
haunts Ionesco's pages and which forms the entire ambiance of his latest play, *Exit the King.* One is reminded
of the Street-Sweepers in *Camino Real,* those familiar
yet sinister, white-coated figures that catch up the dead
as trash and trundle them away to grim yet commonplace disposal. It is exactly the calibre of death which
haunts Beckett, with his hovering abattoirs, holes in the
ground, and ash cans. The dog, as the image of physical
degradation, both in intercourse and in death, recurs
constantly in Beckett. In *The Killer,* the grim concierge,
who keeps her dog for the satisfaction of abusing a living thing, speaks in answer to the Man's Voice: "Ah
yes, Monsieur. It's a dog's life, and we all end up in the
same place, a hole in the ground." (*K,* 45)

The theme of Bérenger's alienation is re-explored in
A Stroll in the Air, which provides a lucid summation
of some of Ionesco's major themes. The sentence of
death, with the reaction of despair and revolt it always
induces in Bérenger, is here set simply against his innate sense of joy. This joy—known of old, lost, and
desperately sought—is reflected here in the familiar

view of the radiant street, the familiar image of the white walls of houses, and the gentle, luminous sky. But for Bérenger, as for Ionesco, this does not remain sufficient. Bérenger is driven to explore, to go beyond the limits of this world—hopefully to discover the joy and beauty which may lie on the other side and of which the radiance in the city street is an intimation. The vision, however, is one of horror, an apocalyptic compendium of all the physical, social, moral, and emotional ravages sustained by life, the whole raised to the pitch of an inferno.

Bérenger's sense of alienation from all that could sustain him is acute. Upon his return, his wife Joséphine cries: "Well, what are you waiting for? Take us [wife and daughter] one under each arm, now you've proved you can do it, and fly us away. . . . Fly us away, much further away, far on to the other side of Hell." And then comes Bérenger's appalling answer, the acknowledgment of the Killer's shrug and chuckle: "I'm afraid I can't my darlings. . . . After that, there's nothing, nothing but abysmal space . . . abysmal space." (*SA*, 77) But unlike Bérenger's curtain lines from *The Killer*, "What can we do . . . What can we do," the lines just quoted from *A Stroll in the Air* are not the final ones. The curtain lines are spoken by Marthe, the daughter who has represented the faith of hope throughout the play, who has counteracted her mother's distrust, hostility, and cynicism with a buoyant, and up to that point justified, faith in her father. Now suddenly she tentatively offers a variant vision, which is no more than a ghost of a hope: "Perhaps it will all come right in the end . . . Perhaps the flames will die down, perhaps the ice will melt, perhaps the depths will rise. Perhaps the . . . the gardens . . . the gardens . . ." (*SA*, 77).

It is certainly not much. Its only support comes from its source in Marthe's general perceptiveness and strength and from its position at the end of the play's climax. It is as though Ionesco only refused to lock a door he had closed behind him. But the echo that remains differs in tone from the final echoes of *The Killer,* or even of *Rhinoceros.*

Of all the outward expressions of an inner loss, in Ionesco's world, the most dangerous and important is that of language, and it is this especial chaos which he has dazzlingly exploited. He has the air of having taken on the overwhelming and vital task of restoring language—because, as we shall see, when Ionesco thinks of the practice of any art, he thinks in terms of revelation by refreshment, never of avant-garde invention. In his attack upon the fallen state of language, he sees himself as having two separate and related tasks. The first and less difficult—or certainly the not impossible— is the restoration of freshness and significance to language. He is battling not only against the second and major ill, that of the want of conviction, the crisis in thought that has produced a crisis in communication, but more hopefully against the natural tendency of words to wear thin, to wear out, in their debility to become hopelessly tangled in the meshes of the cliché, to remain in their initial stance when their life has gone forth in another direction.

It is like cleaning a room, or nourishing a body, or breathing: it can never be finished until the room or the life is closed. It is a constant struggle to renew life, to adjust expression to the living movements, to discard, weed, refresh, nourish, renew. Ionesco is extremely logical in his concept of the process of renewal. The outline of his credo of language follows truly the outline of his credo in regard to the artist's obligations and privileges, which we will examine when we discuss Ionesco's position in contemporary society. Bizarre as are some of his situations, he is never promoting bizarreness. The bizarre, indeed, is for him one of the signs of the breakdown, the crisis. The distortion of speech, the crack-up of the nuances of significance—which at its most drastic will cause Roberta to discover that "cat" is the only word necessary to communicate everything there is to communicate—are invariably signs of degeneration. It is Roberta, the Martins, the Smiths, the Orator, who mouth and gibber mangled syllables. When Ionesco, in the character of the Playwright, is reduced to braying (*I*, 144), it is because Bartholomeus I, II, and III, his venal critics, have brought him to this ignominy by their callous, overbearing, and pompous pressure.

Ionesco profoundly resents the attempts of moralists, teachers, scientists, and journalists, to pre-empt the artist's role in his use of language. When Choubert discusses his theories as playwright with Madeleine, she concedes that his ideas are original and perhaps have some content: "Still, you ought to get an expert opinion on the subject." "Who from?" asks Choubert. And Madeleine replies: "Oh, there's bound to be someone, among the cinema enthusiasts, or the professors at the *Collège de France,* the influential members of the Agricultural School, the Norwegians, or some of those veterinary surgeons . . . A vet. Now there's someone who should have lots of ideas." (*VD,* 120)

Language is to clothe and transmit human ideas and emotions; when sterile forms are forced upon it, the stuffed man, victim of anorexia, gags and can only mouth: "Heu . . . glu . . . you . . . clem . . . neeg . . . erls. . . ." Then Choubert suddenly spews into his hand what has been forced into his mouth, and at once cries, "I wonder if you know? How lovely the columns of the temples are, and the knees of the young girls!" (*VD,* 161)

A good number of Ionesco's readers have been misled by bizarre dialogue and situation into placing him among those dismantlers who feel that nothing good can come from language until all previous premises have been destroyed, or even among those who feel, as does Richard Schechner, that in the world of the theatre the value of words will be increasingly debased, perhaps to the point of nonexistence in the theatre of the future. It is, on the contrary, Ionesco's tenet that words must be reunited to the truth of the human being and the artist. He sees language as menaced on all fronts—by the pomposity and ignorance of incompetent fiats from those who use it for other purposes than its proper one;

by the special pleading of Newspeak, which will subvert meaning to ends; by the omnipresent barbarism of the mindless and degraded, as with the single, meaningless syllable of Roberta and the nonsense of the Orator. Where language is abandoned, life is shut out.

The language employed by Ionesco's characters in those moments when they do attempt to reveal or restore their lost inner vision of happiness is of great simplicity. It is a language of stars, of sunlight, of warmth. It is, overwhelmingly, a language of youth—not of youth in chronological terms but of the youth associated with beginnings, with an Edenlike freshness and clarity. Ionesco has, on a number of occasions, pointed out that inasmuch as "the true temper of drama . . . lies in frenzy" (*NCN,* 29), language, used in the drama quite differently from its habitual uses in other forms, must share that sense of tempo on which he heavily relies for his changes in mood.

At its most destructive, language is driven into the victim like a knife. It is, indeed, the Professor's second knife in *The Lesson,* and it is Madeleine and the Detective's joint weapon against Choubert as they cry, "Chew! Swallow! Chew! Swallow!" (*VD,* 166); but in both cases it is the debased and distorted form of language that serves the offensive. Recognizing clearly the pitfall into which many a fine playwright has blundered (O'Neill at his worst is a fine example), that of using language in the theatre as it might well be used in an essay or in fiction, Ionesco has concentrated on the *motion* of words. His are in perpetual conflict and counterplay; they shift colors as his characters shift identity, displaying properties of which they could never have been suspected. They must be *listened* to; a moment's inattention and an unnoticed premise has been insinuated.

This special gift for forcing us to examine language, to watch it as one watches the movements of a strange and possibly dangerous animal, is one of Ionesco's most rewarding characteristics. He knows that if language tends to wear thin, to become inaudible from repetition, it is also fluid, and that once it is not held by a powerful grip of intention and belief, it will easily slip into another shape, unobserved. The audience or reader of an Ionesco play is perpetually and personally engaged with language, contesting it, rectifying it, watching it maneuver, seeing it disprove what it started to prove, and evidence what it seemed to hide. It is used as what it is: live material. We watch the author bring it pitilessly back to his service, break up its associations, free its contradictions.

It is strange that a number of perceptive critics have referred to Ionesco's contempt for language, seeing him as a writer who paradoxically believes words to be meaningless and communication between human beings to be impossible. Ionesco's work demonstrates, on the contrary, the conviction that language is the servant of belief (crisis in belief equals crisis in language); that when language is false to its beliefs, or indifferent to them, it loses touch with them altogether and becomes constricted, vacant, and ultimately unintelligible. As Ionesco has pointed out, if he truly believed in incommunicability, the profession of writer would be a curious choice.

It is significant that whereas Beckett, Pinter, Ionesco, and the like are still under attack from some quarters and are called defeatists, the voices of despair which will crumble the human image, and the apostles of disintegration and meaninglessness, from other quarters they have simultaneously been hailed as the apostles of surviving human identity. By a process so rapid, and still so limited as to be largely irrelevant to the general public, the entire idea of human identity and its ability to communicate through language has been discarded by a new wave of dramatists who substitute for the human being the object and for whose practical purposes the human being has indeed become an object. This viewpoint has complex ramifications, and it has been sustained by astute and intelligent argument. Its justifications and its purposes have no place in this book. But the point at which it becomes strictly relevant is where language, as practiced by Ionesco, Genet, and Beckett, comes to be regarded as an echo of the dead past. This is not only of crucial importance to any consideration of these writers; it is perhaps the crux of the entire question of the indicated direction of serious contemporary theatre.

Limiting discussion here to that of Ionesco's relations with language, a gulf is immediately revealed between the Happening school of drama and the drama of the Absurd—a gulf that makes the difference between an Ionesco and a Beckett, however ascertainable and deep, seem almost nonexistent.

Ionesco has never at any time taken the stand that it is impossible for human beings to communicate, if their belief that they wish to do so is genuine, nor has he even settled for the idea that they have nothing to communicate. His very strictures on the vacuity and incomprehensibility of human speech are a corrective anger of dismay. It is the misuse of language, the debility of desire and conviction that allows language to become at once rigid and flaccid, which Ionesco attacks. The characters' language springs from their vision, and rectification can ensue only from a vision fundamentally altered. The vocabulary of the young Amédée is that of spring: "Wake up . . . the room is flooded with sunshine . . . a glorious light . . . a gentle warmth! . . . The green valley where the lilies bloom . . . a blaze of joy . . . The light's gone mad . . . Mad with happiness . . . Blaze up, joy, blaze up! . . . a limpid lake . . . Our boat a bed of flowers . . . White churches! . . . Bells pealing! . . . Children's voices! . . . voices of fountains . . . voices of spring!" (A, 47–49) Madeleine (that foreseer of mushrooms) has her own vocabulary: ". . . night and rain and mud! . . . oh, the cold! . . . dark, dark, dark! . . . You're blind . . . Mushrooms! . . . mushrooms! . . . mushrooms! . . . mushrooms! . . . Boats bogged in the mud, in the desert sand . . . oaths and toads! . . . Forests of slime, nights in the hulks!" (A, 48–49)

From the point of view of language, the important

thing is not how the vocabularies of the young Amédée and the young Madeleine differ, but how they agree. Each represents a human identity, seeking to describe in accurate terms the world presented to his vision. The visions have nothing in common; what is shared is the conviction that the words used correspond to a vision of life, a belief rightly or wrongly held. If the belief changes, the language will change with it. This is, or is not, distorted vision, but this is also language functioning properly. The colloquy between the Martins and the Smiths is language out of control. In both instances the playwright's assumption is the same—that human identity exists, that language, properly used, can express and communicate that identity, and that a language that can do neither is a language robbed of its function.

Language is the sound of humanity. When the value of language is questioned, it is because the identity of the human being himself is being questioned. When in the story "Pretty Mouth and Green My Eyes," J. D. Salinger's psychiatrist, lying with faint embarrassment in bed with the wife of his unseen and unapprised interlocutor at the other end of the phone, says soothingly, "We're all animals. . . . Basically, we're all animals," the badgered and not altogether sober husband shouts defiantly, "Like hell we are. I'm no goddam animal. I may be a stupid, fouled-up twentieth-century son of a bitch, but I'm no animal."[6] But even the psychiatrist is on Ionesco's side of the gulf. Animals have no speech, no alphabet; they are dumb. But they communicate. They have a language of hunger, of desire, of emotions, of fear, even of joy. But an object cannot communicate with another object.

Communication, set back millennia when speech is discarded, is reduced to rock and to mud with no murmur when the human being becomes an object. It is the very tension between object and human which haunts Beckett's moribund and rigidifying morsels of humanity

[6] J. D. Salinger, "Pretty Mouth and Green My Eyes," *Nine Stories* (Boston: Little, Brown & Company, 1953), p. 182.

and makes them so powerfully moving. In their ash cans, Nagg and Nell remember faintly the blue of Lake Como; the three bodiless heads of *Play* rehearse the past fears, passions, and griefs of involved human beings; Winnie in her sand heap implores Willie to raise the finger which will signify that he has heard her. Perhaps the most moving line in *Waiting for Godot* is that in which Gogo implores the Messenger to take, as well as bring a message: "Tell him . . . [*he hesitates*] . . . tell him you saw me and that . . . [*he hesitates*] . . . that you saw me." These go straight back to the Psalmist's "Out of the depths have I cried unto thee, O Lord. Lord, hear my voice."

Roberta has reduced language to a single sound, thus annihilating it. Once defined and utilized as an object, the human being acquiesces in that annihilation. Between the sort of incommunicability which infuriates Ionesco and tortures Beckett, and the silence of the object, there lies a narrowing but still unbridgeable gap— as the apostles of the theatre of objects are the first to acknowledge. Discussion of that gap, however tempting, belongs elsewhere.

Another aspect of the whole problem extremely tempting to the critic is the allied question of whether writers such as Ionesco represent an open door, a reassessment, with an implied future direction, or are only the last whispered syllables before the silence— that silence which is the prelude to the rise of the curtain on the stage of the object.

As we have already noted, in Ionesco's world there is the ever-present danger of invasion by the object. Usurping the place of the human being, its proliferation is always sinister: chairs, noses, coffee cups, furniture, eggs—they are the enemy. They are the enemy because they have escaped from their proper position of subservience to the now-threatened human values. It is as though Ionesco has seen them massing for the attack. They are, all of them, necessarily, silent.

It has been noted that the dual compulsion motivating the Beckett protagonist is both the compulsion to

endure—the sheer act of physically continuing to exist
—and, on another level, the artist's compulsion to
speak. Nonexistence and silence, cohorts and doubles,
are what is forbidden, however desired. Ionesco has
more concrete hopes. He feels that art, and the language used to clothe its vision of life, are inseparable,
and that this vision has only to renew and refresh itself
in order for language to be renewed and refreshed, always providing that the vision itself has not been totally lost. This is what he means when he describes the
classical vision as his own. Revealingly, he says that
Beckett is a great playwright, not because he holds up
to a mirror the face of twentieth-century man but because his work is so close to the Book of Job:

> The importance of Beckett's *Endgame,* for example, con-
> sists in the fact that it is closer to the Book of Job than to
> the plays of the boulevards or to the *chansonniers.* Across
> the ages and the ephemeral fashions of History this work
> has rediscovered a less ephemeral type-history, a primordial
> situation which all the rest follow.
>   What is called "avant-garde" is interesting only if it is a
> return to sources, if it rejoins a living traditionalism that
> has been rejected. . . .
>   The freshest and newest works of art can easily be recog-
> nized, they speak to every age. Yes, the leader I follow is
> King Solomon; and Job, that contemporary of Beckett.
> (*NCN,* 156)

There can be few statements more uncompromising
than two made on this point by Ionesco. In speaking
of the relation between past and future, in life as in art,
he writes: "And yet all this will have existed. Nothing
can stop existence from having existed, from being in-
scribed somewhere, or from being assimilated material
of all future transformations." (*NCN,* 245) And, "In
the long run, I am all for classicism: that is what the
'avant-garde' is. The discovery of forgotten archetypes,
changeless but expressed in a new way: any true creative artist is classical . . . the petit bourgeois is the person who has forgotten the archetype and is absorbed in
the stereotype. The archetype is always young." (*NCN,*
131)

It is not coincidental that Ionesco should ascribe his introduction into the profession of playwright as having taken place because of his encounter with the amazing truths of the language of an English-French Conversational Manual for Beginners, a conversation of truisms, expressed as though for the first time, by a tongue, English, which came to him unburdened by habit and association. When truths become truisms and sounds no longer contain information or even true meaning, speech becomes a noise, the sound of those "talking because there is nothing personal to say . . . man sunk in his social background, no longer able to distinguish himself from it" (*NCN*, 180). Ionesco says he thought of *The Bald Soprano* as a tragedy and that when it was acted, he "was almost surprised to hear the laughter of the audience, who took it all (and still take it) quite happily, considering it as a comedy all right, even a sort of joke" (*NCN*, 179).

III

We have now, by consideration of Ionesco's use of language, come squarely upon his use of humor. Ionesco's sense of comedy is so intimately bound up with his sense of tragedy that he crosses and recrosses the line between the two with rapidity and frequency; consequently, he creates an atmosphere in which it is not only possible but proper to watch a single thing simultaneously from two points of view. Ionesco has said something about his own work which is equally applicable to the work of Beckett, and even to those relatively minor aspects of Genet's work which involve irony or wit—his modes of humor: "Push burlesque to its extreme limits, then, with a flick of the finger, an imperceptible transition, you are back in tragedy" (*NCN*, 182).

The thinness of the barrier between tragedy and comedy is a peculiarly contemporary phenomenon. As Richard Gilman has pointed out, the masks of tragedy and comedy were always the two masks of a single face.[7] For hundreds of years, tragedy and comedy have existed side by side in a single work. But the two modes have tended to be separated within the work, and the work as a whole has had a predominant tone, however that tone might be interrupted. In a comedy, even dismal events had about them an aura of ultimate well-being, whereas horseplay in a tragedy served as a breathing spell, to permit fuller reception of the tragic impact.

But simultaneity of tragedy and comedy is the earmark of our best contemporary playwrights (it is, incidentally, a supremely difficult task, and failure results in monstrosity). The sinister is never totally absent from Genet's mockeries. In Ionesco, tragedy and comedy share one breath; and if Beckett's grimmer sections are almost never without sudden levity, his burlesque is absolutely never without distress.

Our contemporary sense of vulnerability, so acutely developed, has merged the tragic and the comic to a degree inconceivable to the day of more solid assumptions. Ionesco's reputation has been made by a series of plays whose techniques have been largely those of comedy but whose insistent undertones are those of tragedy. In a typical mélange of approaches, Ionesco has himself classified his plays as Comedy (*Amédée*), Naturalistic Comedy (*Jack, or The Submission*), Comic Drama (*The Lesson*), Tragic Farce (*The Chairs*), Pseudo-Drama (*Victims of Duty*), and Anti-play (*The Bald Soprano*); he has classified simply as plays *Rhinoceros, The New Tenant,* and *The Killer.* Curiously enough, it is by way of a devotion to the "obsessive truths" that Ionesco comes to his use of comedy to convey the import of the tragic. Farce divorces itself from realism, and it is realism in its most limited sense which Ionesco wishes to escape: "Realism, socialist or not, never looks beyond reality. It narrows it down, diminishes it, falsifies it, and leaves out of account the

[7] Richard Gilman, "End of Season: A Love Letter," *Commonweal,* Vol. LXXVI (June 29, 1962), p. 352.

obsessive truths that are most fundamental to us: love, death and wonder." (*NCN,* 16)

In Ionesco's conception of comedy, two tensions play constantly against each other, bouncing events and people off into the air in dazzling or grotesque gyrations. One of these is his sense of the strangeness, the mystery, within all things; the second is his sense of the imminent danger of the hardening of all things into immobility. The former is the principle of life; the latter, of death. People constantly forget how amazing, how mysterious it is to be alive, how inexplicable are the simplest things. People abandon this realization and pursue instead an empty, rigidifying form, originally conceived to express an inner, dynamic motion. At some point, human beings must "find themselves naked, like a body stretched out on the sand, amazed to be there and amazed at their own amazement, amazed at their own awareness as they are confronted with the immense ocean of the infinite, alone in the brilliant, and inconceivable and indisputable sunlight of existence" (*NCN,* 108).

The moments of joy—actually exceedingly rare in Ionesco—come invariably from an ephemeral return to a confrontation with the freshness and beauty of beginnings. To this category belong young Amédée's ecstasy and the remembered felicity of Bérenger in *The Killer.* One is also reminded of Ionesco's nostalgia for his own early childhood. When these moments disappear, as they almost instantly do, we are thrown back to the robotlike reflexes whose *raison d'être* has departed. Bergson's dictum that *"The attitudes, gestures and movements of the human body are laughable in exact proportion as that body reminds us of a mere machine"*[8] is totally applicable to Ionesco. The Smiths and the Martins, wound up and set going in one direction, are like sinister toys, and provoke that peculiar

[8] Henri Bergson, "Laughter," in *Comedy,* ed. Wylie Sypher (Garden City, New York: Doubleday Anchor Books, 1956), p. 79.

malaise occasioned by a toy too like a human being, or a human being too like a toy. Bergson has added another definition to the underlying assumptions of Beckett, as well as of Genet and Ionesco, when he says: "The rigid mechanism which we occasionally detect, as a foreign body, in the living continuity of human affairs is of peculiar interest to us as being a kind of *absentmindedness* on the part of life."[9] The application of this sense of absence is important. It is as though the life force has absented its attention, and the puppet figures continue along the path of inertia. It is the same perception, that of the absent *raison d'être,* which causes Bergson to comment: "It is enough for us to stop our ears to the sound of music in a room, where dancing is going on, for the dancers at once to appear ridiculous."[10]

The absence of the essential music takes a number of forms in Ionesco: Madeleine's activity with her grounded switchboard in *Amédée;* the application, to the rhinoceroses, those savage intruders, of the values they depose; the Architect's telephone, the wires of which end in his own pocket; the "Chew! Swallow! Chew! Swallow!" of Madeleine and the Detective, as Choubert painfully masticates the tough and unnourishing shards of debris. The action has continuity, but the sense and spirit alike have departed.

Examining Ionesco's comic sense, one finally realizes that all of its various aspects stem from a central preoccupation with rigidity as the enemy of life and truth. Saint Paul, whose dicta Ionesco shows small signs of accepting, spoke of rigidity, in contrasting the killing power of the letter with the quickening power of the spirit. Almost all the manifestations of Ionesco's comic sense—that of tempo-frenzy, that of disparity, that of insertion of the meaningless into the form of the meaningful, that of the dually applicable conversation—refer to this initial concept of rigidity.

Anyone who has in the past been moved and impressed by a film which is later run off with rapidity

9 *Ibid.,* p. 117.
10 *Ibid.,* p. 63.

that makes frenzied automata of its actors has seen an example of what mechanized speed, unrelated to situation or emotional content, can do to turn drama or tragedy into farce. The same process on a turntable will transform the accents of a Gielgud or an Olivier into the squeaks of chipmunks. This is only another form of rigidity—the mechanically set speed dominating the particular, flexible needs and demands of the life portrayed. It has often been noted, in the broadest of generalizations, that the quick gestures are those of comedy and farce; the slow, those of drama and tragedy. Ionesco frequently employs the speedup. Random examples are the egg-production scene of *The Future Is in Eggs,* the chair-bringing scene in *The Chairs,* Jean's transformation scene in *Rhinoceros,* the forced-feeding scene in *Victims of Duty,* and the increasing tempo of the Professor's sinister instruction in *The Lesson.* It is a singularly effective device, largely because it implies a machine, running increasingly out of control in its own mathematical acceleration, influenced by no living and unpredictable consideration. One has only to think of an oath administered, a Mass celebrated, or any act of invocation or dedication, to feel how sharply great speed undercuts the sense of serious involvement.

As for the sense of rigidity implicit in Ionesco's use of the cliché form that is filled with surprising and inappropriate content, Bergson has observed: *"A comic meaning is invariably obtained when an absurd idea is fitted into a well-established phrase-form."*[11] And concerning the trick of the dually applicable conversation, he has said: *"A situation is invariably comic when it belongs simultaneously to two altogether independent series of events and is capable of being interpreted in two entirely different meanings at the same time."*[12] In both cases, the word "invariably" is a bit of optimism: once the formula comes to sound like a formula, the jest is dead. It is Ionesco's own ability to have both

11 *Ibid.,* p. 133.
12 *Ibid.,* p. 123.

the crossed conversations and the unexpected contents in the cliché form seem moments of spontaneity. Indeed, the entire discussion of humor is much like the attempt to dissect a living thing, uncongenial and essentially self-defeating. To perceive that two music-hall jokes, one naive, one scatological, with differing dialects, characters, and events, both function according to the rules of the formula "ignore the important, accent the unimportant," gives an accurate glimpse of how the joke functions and how it is allied to all other jokes of its kind—but by then the small surprise is as dead as the jest. (Two vintage chestnuts: Girl in bordello to visitor: "I've got to get out of here! I can't stand this life another minute! These stairs are killing me!" And: Johnny: "Mr. Smith ain't nothing but a stinking old bastard!" Mother: "Johnny, how many times do I have to tell you not to say 'ain't'?")

Apart from the dismal difficulty inherent in cold-blooded discussion of what is funny and why, in Ionesco's case the matter is complicated by the fact that his humor, while frequently frenetic, is seldom truly exuberant. The exhilarated speeches of his characters are for the most part uttered in deadly earnest; they deal with the glimpses, or recollection, of felicity, or the excitement of escape. There is always, in the latter, a harried undertone, as though pursuit were a hairsbreadth behind.

The absurdity-loaded cliché is a fine example of rigidity in action. The form is so familiar to us, as having always previously contained a long-established axiom to which we mechanically assent, that there is a delayed reaction: for a moment we feel we must have heard what we expected to hear, so that for a moment our rigidity of concept is added to the rigidity of the cliché form, and it is the "now, wait a minute . . ." reflex which amuses us. It is the same when the form of logic is evoked without its content, when words such as "since," "because," or "as a result," are followed by a complete *non sequitur*. But this formula-approach would rapidly become tiresome in the extreme were

Ionesco not able to illuminate it by the dismaying light of our realization that the process applies to innumerable reactions common to ourselves. These implications, inserted by the sentences' structure, these conclusions forced upon us by the same device—the form would have us accept them as natural to intelligence and logic. Once we attend and notice where we have been carried by the habit of accepting the rigidity of form as substitute for the living content of communication, perhaps we will look more closely at our own assumptions.

In *The Bald Soprano* Mr. Martin remarks: "You know, even though I'm not a maid, I also read poems before the mirror" (*BS,* 36). We can easily discern the implication that the reading of poems before the mirror is the earmark of a maid. But implications nearly as baseless do ride on common forms of speech, and Ionesco's ridiculous line is here, as always, a little frightening. So is the irrelevant, smuggled in by the relevant. The sequence goes: partially true; untrue, but associated; totally untrue. Mr. Martin says: "Paper is for writing, the cat's for the rat. Cheese is for scratching." (*BS,* 39) How close to political oratory this reads. Closely allied is the apparent rebuttal, another fine political device: Mr. Martin's "One doesn't polish spectacles with black wax" elicits from Mrs. Smith the response, "Yes, but with money one can buy anything." (*BS,* 39)

Here rigidity is again the method. To the degree that the mental rigidity of the hearer answers to this established form, "Yes, but . . . ," the hearer is bamboozled. And as frenzied tempo can alter drama to farce, so Ionesco's exaggeration of the *non sequiturs* he inserts into the rigid forms of speech habits can turn silliness into the taint of deceit. If rigidity rules, if sentence structure can carry us along like express trains out of control, so can sounds. Disassociated from flexible attention to meaning, they can career ahead, uniting utterly irrelevant things and ideas because it is the sound which hurtles straight ahead, uncontrolled by distinctions or individuals.

MR. SMITH.   The Pope elopes! The Pope's got no horo-
scope. The horoscope's bespoke.
MRS. MARTIN.   Bazaar, Balzac, bazooka!
MR. MARTIN.   Bizarre, beaux-arts, brassieres! (*BS,* 41)

This rigidity, succeeding in proportion to its speed,
inclusiveness, and the docility of the listener, makes a
senseless rigamarole, protected by the speech form of
instruction, *sound* like instruction:

> *That which distinguishes* the neo-Spanish languages from
> each other and their idioms from the other *linguistic
> groups, such as* the group of languages called Austrian and
> neo-Austrian or Hapsburgian, *as well as* the Esperanto,
> Helvetian, Monacan, Swiss, Andorran, Basque and jai alai
> groups, *and also* the groups of diplomatic and technical
> languages—*that which* distinguishes them, I repeat, is their
> striking resemblance *which* makes it so hard *to distinguish
> them from each other*—I'm speaking of the neo-Spanish
> languages *which one is able* to distinguish from each other,
> however, only *thanks to* their distinctive characteristics,
> absolutely *indisputable proofs* of their extraordinary re-
> semblance, *which renders* indisputable their common origin,
> and which, *at the same* time, differentiates them profoundly
> —*through the continuation* of the distinctive traits *which*
> I've just *cited.* (*L,* 61; italics ours)

The cumulative effect of all this is an uneasy sense
that perhaps the truly illogical, contradictory, untrue, is
being smuggled constantly into our brains by the rigidity
of our habitual assumptions. Like Pavlov's dogs, sali-
vating to the sound of the dinner bell, we are responding to the *sound* of sense.

The cross-conversations similarly function to subdue sense to rigidity. As has been noted, Bergson and
Ionesco suggest that a situation is always comic when
it belongs simultaneously to two altogether independent
series of events and is capable of being interpreted in
two entirely different meanings at the same time; this
tends to occur when a remark launched toward one
human being has *inadvertently* struck another to whom
it equally applies; that is, not because it was intended
for him, or has been formed for, or adapted to, his individual peculiarities, but *accidentally,* because he happened to be in its path at the appropriate moment.

The comic and horrifying rigidity of the jargon of pseudo-science (or of true science misapplied), of the habitual forms of speech, of the accidentally applicable comment which does not represent an intended communication from a fellow human all contribute to the stagnating of language. If we take a fresh look and shake ourselves free from the grooved habit patterns of hearing and seeing, we will find, Ionesco's humor announces, that we must assess each thing particularly and attentively. There is indeed, he feels, much strangeness in the sentences which tell us that the ceiling is solidly overhead and the floor solidly underfoot (especially when our eyes tell us this, and our brain tells us that we are clinging, half of the time upside down, by our feet, while whirling at incredible speed). His humor tells us that once we lose our sense of the strangeness of all things, and fail to test and retest our patterns of speech and thought for traces of ossification, we are mummies, or—more dangerous—automata.

There is one far more subtle sense of the danger inherent in rigidity implicit in Ionesco's plays, of which a prime example is the conversation between Jean and Bérenger, in the first act of *Rhinoceros*. Jean belongs to that company which accepts unquestioningly the *status quo*—anything conflicting with it or undermining it is intolerable. If the upheaval becomes too potent, then the upheaval itself must become the new *status quo,* so that everything can be fitted neatly into it. Of the two men, it is Jean who is initially far more upset by the appearance of the first rhinoceros. Having in mind a firm pattern of what the Sunday street of a town looks like, he is incredulous and outraged when an improbable rhinoceros charges into sight. Bérenger, whose convictions as to the *status quo* are far more uncertain, is not unduly upset, or indeed especially interested. It is only when the rhinoceros, through Jean's inaccurate and foolish assertions, impinges on Bérenger's sense of human reason, that he becomes genuinely concerned. As the play progresses, it is Jean who happily renounces one static conviction—that rhinoceroses are different

from, and inferior to, human beings and do not freely
rush through the streets of a town on a Sunday morning—in favor of another cut-and-dried *status quo:* that
in which rhinocerosdom is established, as the norm,
and all objections come from deviators who are debilitated eccentrics. Bérenger, on the other hand, using
his human mind to examine a new situation, and his
human moral sense to assess it, refuses to accept the
packaged reaction, and remains horrified by, and inimi-
cal to, the new *modus vivendi.*

This same apprehension, that of the rigidity his
humor pillories, is allied to Ionesco's apprehensive re-
jection of all dogmas—social, political, or religious.
Like everyone who, in public, "defends himself on all
sides," Ionesco has tripped himself with unintentional
contradictions, and, more importantly, in his haste to
keep his art mobile and free, has occasionally involved
himself in basic inconsistencies. But if, where such contradictions appear, we take his work (as he recom-
mends), rather than his statements, as the basis for all
comment, we shall find, in considering Ionesco in relation to his time, that the inconsistencies are those of a
few scattered comments and are not inherent, in any
basic sense, in his work.

There is another aspect of Ionesco's humor: the
heavy reliance on irony. As the line between burlesque
and tragedy is a thin one, so the line between what is
and what is desired is constantly breached. Irony can
become so savage that it scarcely strikes us as humor—
it is no longer funny but frightening. And then we may
realize that it is both savage and funny. From irony in
its simplest forms—such as the name of Treasure for
the concierge's luckless dog—to irony at its grimmest,
the element is constant in the plays. It is the Ornamental Pool in which the corpses float; it is the professional Orator who can only mouth syllables; it is the
alcoholic, depressed, ineffectual Bérenger who is the
solitary holdout from the trampling herd.

Ionesco's own somber outlook on life tends to make
the irony grim, the high jinks frenetic. We laugh be-

cause the latter are so brilliantly ridiculous; but the sense of hysteria is never far from the laughter. Unquestionably some scenes are, simply and truly, terribly funny—that, for example, in which Mrs. Boeuf leaps from the office landing down onto the back of her rhinoceros mate.

BÉRENGER.   I couldn't hold her back.

  [*The rhinoceros is heard from below, tenderly trumpeting.*]

VOICE OF MRS. BOEUF.   Here I am, my sweet. I'm here now.

DUDARD.   She's landed on his back in the saddle.

BOTARD.   She's a good rider.

VOICE OF MRS. BOEUF.   Home now, dear, let's go home.

DUDARD.   They're off at a gallop.

  [*Dudard, Botard, Bérenger, Papillon come back onstage and go to the window*.]

BOTARD.   They're moving fast.

DUDARD [*to Papillon*].   Ever done any riding? (*R*, 52)

But even here, in spite of the hilarity of the scene (with its perfect illustration of the rigidly banal used to point up the impossibility of adequate comment), the *frisson* is certainly only as far as the nearest analysis.

  There is one final aspect of Ionesco's humor, one which may seem curiously out of place but which is in reality an extremely important approach to his comedy. It is the omnipresent consciousness of death. In his trinity of love, death, and wonder (*NCN*, 16), it is the second which makes the third so strong and the first so powerful. For the man without a specific belief in the soul's immortality, or without the blinders of the professional optimist, the fact of death must tinge everything. If he sees the world in the same colors as Ionesco and is unable to persuade himself that there must be, somewhere, some sort of redress for its conditions and for its victims—some permanent significance —then the artist's humor is apt to have a bitter flavor. *"Nous sommes tous condamnés à la mort"*—and this fact sways all of Ionesco's thinking: "I mistrust pacifist plays, which seem to be showing us that it is war that destroys mankind and that we only die in wartime. . . . Most of us die in wartime: topical truth. We die: permanent truth. . . ." (*NCN, 56–57*)

It is partly due to this terrifying sense of the evanescence of all things, and the sense of solitude and suffering which this conviction brings, that Ionesco is so impatient of political panaceas as the solution to all of life's ills. "It seems to me that solitude and anguish especially characterize the fundamental conditions of man. This teacher, who believes that an economic and political revolution will automatically resolve all man's problems, is a utopian. My parrot is more intelligent." (*NCN, 78*)

If the pictures of the world a man holds in his heart and mind are "those which express evanescence and callousness, vanity and anger, emptiness, or hideous, useles hate," if everything has merely confirmed what he has seen and understood in childhood, "futile and sordid fits of rage, cries suddenly blanketed by the silence, shadows swallowed up forever by the night" (*NCN,* 154), and if this same man constantly conceives of death as at once the end and seal to this tragic chaos, then his comedy will necessarily be illuminated by a searing and ironic light. Evil deeds become futile and senseless as well as evil, and joy does indeed have his hand at his lips bidding adieu. If the farce often has a desperate air, it is because this is the comedy of desperation. Only an occasional brief glimpse of something like a lovely recollection, or the sense that the dismay with which he regards the scene around him must mean that he is not in his natural element, disrupts the pessimism. Comedy of Ionesco's sort is true gallows humor. It is interesting that Bérenger—obviously the protofigure of Ionesco's humanity—is the protagonist alike of the most optimistic as well as of three of the most pessimistic of Ionesco's plays. As the curtain falls on *Rhinoceros,* Bérenger's situation could not be grimmer, but his state of defiant insistence on his human entity, as the great beasts ramp and trumpet below him, is at the far end of the spectrum from the King, dissolving

into the chaos of death; from Herbert Bérenger, with his
ghastly vision of the nether world; or from Bérenger on
his knees before the Killer, mumbling not even a question: "What can we do . . . What can we do." All of
Ionesco's comedy has basically posed that question.
And, to date, the most optimistic reply seems to be:
"Hold out. Preserve your sense of the mystery and
wonder of things."

Like Proust before him, Ionesco finds in art one of
life's rare ameliorations. He has been sweeping, perhaps too sweeping, in his claims for the artist, as opposed to the teacher, the man of science, the statesman.
As he believes art to be "the realm of passion, not of
pedagogy" (NCN, 32), so he repeats that the teacher
and critic have everything to learn from and nothing to
teach the artist. Yet all comedy is necessarily value-
comment, and it is primarily through his use of the
comic that Ionesco attempts to instruct our sense of
values—deny himself the role of exhorter as he may.
He would, at the minimum, instruct it by correcting its
more blatant vagaries. And he chooses to correct these
by a mockery brilliant, uproarious, frenetic, and often
bitter.

IV

Controlled by his somber vision of life, Ionesco attempts by his use of comic drama and tragic farce to
renew and refresh language, to reveal through comedy
the forces of distortion, and to show that it is the artist,
unindoctrinated and uncommitted, who speaks most
clearly for life. What is his artistic position among his
contemporaries, and in his own eyes? "For my part, I
have never understood the difference people make between the comic and the tragic. As the 'comic' is an in-
tuitive perception of the absurd, it seems to me more
hopeless than the 'tragic.' The comic offers no escape."
(NCN, 27)

Illuminated by his attitude toward the relationship
of the "tragic" and the "comic," the question of Ionesco's
position as artist has at least three implied subquestions.

What line does Ionesco draw between the experimental and the destructive? What, if any, conflicts ensue between his theory and his work? To what extent does Ionesco fulfill the role which he conceives to be that of the contemporary artist?

Since, as we have seen, Ionesco allies himself with what he has defined, according to his special definition, as classicism and has seen the avant-garde as classical (*NCN,* 131), we may ask where, within the context of his argument, the line between the free, flexible, and daring innovation, and the rigidification of that innovation into a new kind of shibboleth, is passed. His answer: when innovation itself becomes an ideology— a dogma—and when resistance to *petit bourgeois* concepts becomes enshrined as an *anti-petit-bourgeois* mystique. His watchword is, "Test"; his anathema, "Formularize."

The experiment must be a true experiment, never an indoctrination. Some of his bitterest words have been saved for those who constitute themselves Public Prosecutor of the *petit bourgeois.* The trouble is that with angry hisses of "théâtre du boulevard!" and "conformist!" filling the air, definitions become as flexible as those flamingos with which Alice attempted to play croquet. Ionesco himself, less logical in his comments than in his comedy, has used *petit bourgeois* in varying senses in different discussions; it is fruitless to discuss his ideas of valid innovation or the deification of novelty, until we can gather what he really feels about the *petit-bourgeois* controversy. He has laid down one law on the subject, which seems illustrated by the body of his work, and it is this definition we accept as his steadfast belief:

. . . the petite bourgeoisie I had in mind was not a class belonging to any particular society, for the petit bourgeois was for me a type of being that exists in all societies, whether they be called revolutionary or reactionary; for me the petit bourgeois is just a man of slogans, who no longer thinks for himself but repeats the truths that others have imposed upon him, ready-made and therefore lifeless.

In short the petit bourgeois is a manipulated man. (*NCN*, 66)

Ionesco worries this *petit-bourgeois* theme on a number of occasions; even though he has clearly defined the terms by which he can be considered *anti-petit-bourgeois*, he is still nervous of such a classification. He notes that the breakthrough into his childhood world of the sense of violence and the presence of death proposed to him the never-escaped question, "Is it not true that we are going to die?" To those who may say that "this view of the world and of death is petit bourgeois," he retorts with fierce irony: "I find this vision of the world in a great number of petits bourgeois throughout the centuries: in Solomon, that petit-bourgeois king; in Buddha, that petit-bourgeois prince; in those petits-bourgeois, Shakespeare and St. John of the Cross; and in a great many more petits-bourgeois, saints, peasants, townsfolk, philosophers, believers, atheists, etc." (*NCN*, 154–155)

His point is clear: What the pseudo-intellectuals, obsessed with fear of being called *petits bourgeois*, often label *petit bourgeois* is merely the simple and basic acknowledgment of suffering and of death—in which case Ionesco will gladly be classed among the *petits bourgeois*. Under his own definition of "the manipulated man," the *petit bourgeois* is Ionesco's enemy to the end.

The truly experimental, then, is that which investigates and re-establishes permanent themes and their truths, themes which will vary only in their expression: "My plays were never meant to express anything else: just that man is not simply a social animal, a pioneer of his time, but also and above all, at all times, different in his historical context, identical in his essence" (*NCN*, 78). The truly destructive, according to this canon, is what denies validity to eternal themes of the past, what codifies and establishes any particular approach to the artist's subject matter, and what causes degeneration in language by its own degenerative indifference, hypocrisy, and formalism. It is hence apropos, and indeed necessary, to employ shock tactics to demonstrate where deadwood has crept in, where ossification has taken place, where the entire imaginative structure is riddled by termites. But these shock tactics are never to become an end in themselves; thus the mouthings of the Orator, and the final syllable to which Roberta reduces language are the symptoms of a disease.

His belief that a conviction formulated, rather than continually tested, is the end of experiment and the beginning of the tyranny of the rigid has embroiled Ionesco and his critics most deeply in the question of ideologies. Ionesco is never weary of repeating that his refusal to support or oppose any political concept stems directly from his passionately held convictions—the first of these being that any form of political proselytizing, or indeed, adherence, is basically irrelevant to the function of the artist, and the second being that the artist must not concern himself with advice or judgment.

In the course of the exposition of these beliefs, Ionesco has allowed himself to be led into a number of demonstrably untenable statements—a predicament he disarmingly acknowledges in his statement that he has, as "harassed author who, in trying to defend himself on all fronts at once" got sometimes "caught up in contradictions which will surely be noticed by his readers and for which he offers his apologies." (*NCN,* 10)

The famous controversy between Ionesco and Kenneth Tynan suffered considerably from the opponents speaking so frequently at cross-purposes. Without entering into the fascinating ramifications of the "committed" versus the "uncommitted"—matter for many a volume—it can be noted that Ionesco's statement ". . . my plays make no claim to . . . prove that some men are better than others" (*NCN,* 195) is sufficiently contradicted by his work to render the argument futile. It is no use pretending that the Bérenger of *Rhinoceros* is not a more satisfactory human being than Jean, or Amédée than either of the Madeleines, or that Ionesco is not himself aware of this. He has repeatedly adjured the critic to stick to the author's works and to assess his expressed opinions in their light. Certainly it is necessary to take Ionesco's expressed opinions into account—often they are brilliantly illuminating of his beliefs and approaches —but it is true that his plays are good evidence of his belief that art itself generates perception and light. It is also true, as pointed out in *Notes and Counter Notes* by both Kenneth Tynan and Orson Welles, that Ionesco dismisses in a rather jejune oversimplification the service done mankind by committed men and women. Actually, Ionesco's own value-judgments (on the relations between men and women, humanity and authority, good and tyrannical men) are implicit in all his plays.

As Ionesco's faith in experiment, with its balancing mistrust of novelty *qua* novelty, is traceable to his belief in the timelessness of art, so is his reluctance to put art in the service of any ideology traceable to this same conviction of the timelessness of truth and the importance to the artist of the "extra-historical community" (*NCN,* 111). There is for the artist "one day of grace," and of this beleaguered moment of spiritual perception Ionesco says: "At this timeless moment in time philosopher and shoemaker, 'master' and 'slave,' priest and layman are reconciled and indistinguishable" (*NCN,* 30–31). If in the fury of the combat Ionesco's professions do not always hang together, it is true, and more important, that his long-range position has a general consistency.

If Ionesco belongs to those who unarguably believe in the identity of the human being, enduring over time and circumstance, he believes no less in the necessity for the artist who seeks to understand humanity to seek that understanding within himself. He believes that the truths of love, death, and wonder are unchanged and unchangeable. He believes that the alienation of man is close to absolute, abrogated briefly only by the recollection of his lost spring or of the moment of perception which reconciles the varied miseries of mankind. He believes that language will suffer the indignity of death if it is not constantly renewed and re-related to the convictions, perceptions, and emotions of human beings. He believes that humor is fundamentally sadder than its other face, tragedy, and that it is peculiarly adapted to convey the nuances of distress, bewilderment, apprehension, and disintegration. He believes in the importance of the artist's maintaining his independence from the functioning systems of belief. Aesthetically he believes in the omnipresence of death and, lacking an antidote, in the unendurable suffering this omnipresence brings.

Having realized in detail how far the totality of these convictions sets Ionesco apart from the theatre now rising to challenge what he believes, one is brought face to face with the question whether the theatre exemplified by the work of Genet, Beckett, Ionesco, Pinter, and the like, has led logically, if not inevitably, to the theatre of the Happening, of the Object.

So far apart in all true fundamentals are these two theatres that it would be sad indeed to think that *The Killer* had led to *What Can I Do in the Water?* or, worse, to *What Is Being Done to It in the Water?* Certainly the progression seems by no means inevitable. But there remains a doubt.

One fact tells heavily in favor of the argument that the former are the precursors of the latter. The theatre of Ionesco, like the theatre of Beckett, is still the theatre of the human being. It is still the theatre of suffering, the desire for joy, attempts at communication, the recollection of felicity; it is still the theatre in which speech is at once the privilege and the obligation of the human being. It is more difficult, however, to make it out to be the theatre of the human personality, the human individual. Genet's characters are the images of power and weakness; Beckett's, all a single prototype of human suffering and confusion, sustaining and inflicting pain; Pinter's, human manifestations of eccentric, mysterious, or obsessed energy; Ionesco's, living illustrations of predicaments. With the exception of Bérenger in *Rhinoceros,* it is difficult to feel that we *know* an Ionesco character in the sense, for example, that we know the characters in the plays of Eugene O'Neill or Tennessee Williams. This does not stem from a failure on the part of the playwright; it is a penalty—or at all events, a result—of his theatrical mores. Ionesco is more interested in showing us his concept of the strangeness, absurdity, and terror of life as he sees it than in delineating a particular human character. This is true because he feels it impossible to express that strangeness in terms of conventional character analysis. He believes that kind of analysis had ceased to reflect the dynamic revelations proper to the artist and, therefore, had to be abandoned in favor of some fresh way of expressing the unchanging essence, now unrecognizable in the rigidified form.

But what has actually occurred is a downgrading of human individuality, a shift of emphasis toward predicament rather than person. And inasmuch as it has been the person who has given significance to the predicament, a tough problem arises.

On the one hand, the theatre of the absurd could quite possibly be the prelude to a fresh understanding of the human being himself. The crux of the question is whether Choubert or Amédée are forerunners or, instead, the last of a defeated tribe, finally going down into the silence against which they have gallantly but hopelessly struggled. Because, if the Bérengers of *The Killer, A Stroll in the Air,* and *Exit the King* are to have the last word, there is indeed little we can do. The shift from Bérenger on his knees, silent at last before the wordless chuckle of the Killer, to the Object wrapped in canvas, or the Object sprayed with tar and chicken feathers, will not be great, certainly not great enough to cause true resistance. The Unnameable, propped in the restaurant showcase, in his untended sawdust, was still horrifying because he still sent out signals through the vast grayness and seething space of the Beckett universe and because it even seemed, cruelly, that from time to time there was a faint answering hail.

If, as Ionesco suggests, we are at the germination of a new beginning, and are able to commence only by virtue of having freed ourselves to circle back to the truth by a fresh route, we have in prospect the amelioration of the situation that Ionesco currently diagnoses:

"We cannot predict what forms poetry, creation and art will take. In any case, already at this very moment, literature is not measuring up to life: artistic expression is too feeble, imagination is too impoverished to simulate the horror and the wonder of this life, or of death, too inadequate even to take stock of it." (*NCN*, 12)

Genet is not concerned with the continuity of artistic expression. For him, art develops the power to cancel, to negate, to exorcise, in a sacred ritual, the shapes of reality. But Ionesco regards himself as a descendant of a long and august line. He is squarely on the side of the classic themes. (We will ignore the pun inferred by certain avant-garde readers.) He is the supporter of the themes of love, death, and wonder, and he looks toward, and hopes for, a new impetus and release of imagination which can reflect those themes through the appalling, or ludicrous, or baffling actions of human beings.

One of the dangers by which Kenneth Tynan felt Ionesco's work to be threatened was a kind of solipsism: "M. Ionesco, I fear, is on the brink of believing that his distortions are more valid and important than the external world it is their proper function to interpret" (*NCN*, 94). But both this warning and Orson Welles's trenchant remark that neutrality is the archenemy of art (*NCN*, 100) are tangential. Ionesco is no solipsist, and his shifts, and refusals to be incorporated in alignments, are never the result of neutrality. They are instead the constant realignments by which he attempts to rectify the difficult course toward artistic truth. He has asserted repeatedly that his urge toward solitude, his tendency to seek all truth within himself, is caused by his strongly held belief that it is in their reflective solitude that men are most closely united.

There are then a number of conflicts inherent between some of Ionesco's comments and the major tendency of his plays. These particular comments are infrequent and are contradicted by the bulk of his commentary. What is important is that the plays themselves evidence no such conflicts. Ionesco may not assert that he distinguishes men of good will from their negators and enemies and is "on their side," but his plays evidence that he does and is. In common with most good writers, he is less interested in arranging the code and procedure by which firemen cope with arson than he is in the deep source which produces the vital water. Let the firemen look to their hoses—the artist, as guardian of the spring, is no less responsible.

Again, Ionesco repudiates for the artist any connection with human authority that is spelled with a capital *A*. Yet it is the *failure* of authority, not its functioning, which the plays, in contradistinction to the type of comment we have been examining, indict. In *The Killer*, Bérenger, discovering in Édouard's briefcase the tell-tale possessions of the Killer (or ones like them, for in how many of the briefcases in this gray city do they lie concealed?), immediately rushes off to inform the authorities. The seat of authority is as inaccessible as Kafka's castle; Bérenger can neither reach it nor advance toward it, and its representatives, encountered en route, are brutal, stupid, and venal. They are, actually, indicted for failure to perform their proper function—that, for example, of trapping the Killer rather than directing, or grotesquely *seeming* to direct, traffic.

There is no use in denying that Choubert, Amédée, and the Bérengers of *Rhinoceros* and *The Killer*, with all their defects, are more satisfactory human beings than are the Detective, the Professor, and the two Madeleines, and that Ionesco implicitly instructs the reader that this is true. Often Ionesco *comments* that authority is by its nature evil; in his plays he *shows* that it is highly dangerous. In John Hersey's *A Bell for Adano*, old Tomaso was never tired of asserting that all the evils of the world stemmed from Men of Authority, but this was only the natural result of the observation of cases, which leads us back to the truisms on the nature of power. It is, as Orson Welles very justly observes, and as Ionesco's plays themselves inform us, indifference which is the villain. It is indifference which silently watches the uses of power subverted to evil and to tyranny. It is the Killer's indifference, the impossibility of reaching his mind or emotions, and above all, Bérenger's own lack of viable conviction, which results in death—or, more truly, in a kind of suicide. It is, all over again, Yeats's complaint: "The best lack all conviction, while the worst / Are full of passionate intensity."

It is then possible to dismiss the apparent contradictions in Ionesco's comments on his own work, not as nonexistent, but as irrelevant. He has asked that he be judged by his work, and even in the commentaries themselves, we find preponderant an attitude which corresponds to that of the plays. We have seen that he deliberately employs, as a device, those contradictions demonstrating a static or rigid state. In the most fundamental sense, he asserts a final belief: he is, as we have remarked before, "all for contradiction," but "the false is not the true, the true is not the false," and "what's true is true and what's false is false." (*I*, 118–119)

It develops that Ionesco's work *does,* in fact, show certain characters and certain courses of behavior as superior to others. And if he seems, in controversy, to echo H. L. Mencken's dictum that if A claims to be doing something to B for the benefit of C, A is a scoundrel, it is quite obvious by the touchstone Ionesco himself has chosen that the plays do not offer this view. In *Rhinoceros,* it is Dudard who espouses the cause of indifference, using a significant alteration of the verb in a famous proverb: "Everything is logical. To understand is to justify." (*R*, 83) And it is Bérenger, in *The Killer,* who cries to Édouard: ". . . we can't wait until tomorrow. Between now and then the killer might make off . . . or find some fresh victims!" (*K*, 75) He is only too eager to act against the Killer, to protect possible future victims or, indeed, to punish the Killer for those already sacrificed. That Bérenger fails, that his failure is inevitable because he carries within himself the germ of doubt as to the value of anything he can define, is just his tragic dilemma.

Ionesco has said that "no ideology has yet abolished fear, pain or sadness" (*NCN,* 96). And since these three come, and will always come, from within the human mind and heart, it is obvious, even to Ionesco's parrot, that none ever will. Tynan retorts that if no ideology has abolished them, neither has any work of art. The important word here is "abolished." Unabolished they remain. But what the work of art can do, has immemorially done, and will always do, is afford the momentary illumination and escape which makes them more bearable.

It is in this sense that Ionesco is true to his identification with classicism. And this identification with classicism, as demonstrated in his plays, is perhaps his most valuable contribution as playwright entering the ominous area of the literature of the twentieth century's second half. For this originality—firmly rooted in faith in the classic themes of love, death, wonder, and the enduring of the "extra-historical"—is a bridge that may shorten the road back to that "main road" of creative work Kenneth Tynan believes Ionesco has abandoned. Ionesco's work tells us that this main road is now blocked: fortunate information, for in his view it ultimately sheers off into an abyss, and those who fondly imagine that they negotiate the abyss on the old hardened truisms are in reality not crossing at all, but are in stasis on the brink, where they rapidly mark time, much as Bérenger, in place, hurries more and more rapidly on his way to an inaccessible Prefecture.

The detour proposed by Ionesco has not reached the other side of the abyss; perhaps this especial route never will. But its chances are worth examining. We have already found in Ionesco's work preliminary qualities which are useful and powerful tools for the construction of this detour. He has brilliantly defined for us our alienation—not in the jargon of the social worker, the analyst, or the judge but by an examination of what it has done to our relations with matter, to our spirit and emotions, and to our ability to use language for purposes of communication. He has shown that on the darkening street and among the shades of violence he describes, comedy—fragmented, frenetic, dangerous—is sadder than is the ordered form of tragedy.

He is brought up short at the point where faith becomes an essential ingredient—faith in humanity, or in the significance of life, or in that system of order of which Beckett has said that he can find no trace. For Ionesco, not one of these faiths is unarguably present, but what is present is a quality classically allied with faith—hope. Unquestionably, in his work it flickers most fitfully; for the Bérengers of *The Killer* and *Exit the King,* it has been extinguished. But it does manifest itself, in varied and often acute forms.

Since life, as conceived by the Ionesco protagonist, is largely repellent, frightening, and incomprehensible, there persists the hope that this cannot be the life intended for him, the life which his intuition assures him should exist: "Have we not the impression that the real is unreal, that it is not really for us? That this world is not our true world? If it were, why should we want to change things? We would not even know it was imperfect or be aware of evil." (*NCN,* 110)

There is the hope implied in the recollection of that lost township of which the Radiant City is the travesty, in whose luminous streets the houses were "immaterial shades ready to melt away in that mightier light which governed all." (*K,* 23)

Although these manifestations of hope are both painful and elusive, they are extremely tough. Tough and important. The enormous difficulty lies in the fact that the man in Ionesco's plays (with the possible exception of Bérenger in *Rhinoceros*) has been able to formulate no basis on which he can act, or think, or assert a belief in order to recapture the luminance, or to explain the disaffection. Even Bérenger, holding out among the trumpeting herd, is sustained, and that barely, by a sense of innate revulsion and a profound instinct for resistance, rather than by an alternate vision.

The reservoirs are indeed dry. If neither ingenuity, will, nor deep springs can replenish them, then certainly we are facing a *cul-de-sac* rather than a detour.

If it is a *cul-de-sac,* in it will be piled Objects; in it, Happenings will take place. If it be a detour, this is a

fact of importance for those who have seen stale literature and drama marking time as they pretend to march.
In any case, although Ionesco can truly say that he
writes, and wishes to write, only of love, death, and
wonder, or of those things which derive from them, his
import in regard to the "unendurable" fact of human
existence, is quite undeniable. There is, in the Radiant
City, only the Ornamental Pool, stagnant with death.
"Monsieur, the reservoirs are empty." (*K*, 22)

Jean Genet and the Ascent into Nothingness

JEAN-PAUL SARTRE'S *Saint Genet: Actor and Martyr* is one of the remarkable books of the twentieth century, not so much because of its indisputable intrinsic merit as because of its place in literary history. Of all authors, only Jean Genet has been celebrated during his lifetime by a biographical-critical study of such dimensions as Sartre's. It is surprising enough to find a three-hundred-thousand-word study of a writer in his early forties—and with a good part of his literary career lying ahead. But it is positively staggering that a man of Sartre's eminence—a man whose philosophic and literary achievements distinguish him as one of the great minds of our century—should devote such painstaking care to a relatively unknown author. In 1952, the year of *Saint Genet*'s publication, Genet *was* relatively unknown, certainly as a literary figure. Judgments on *Saint Genet* will be various: most readers probably find it, by turns, stunningly brilliant and tediously repetitious; some may feel that it reveals as much about Sartre as about Genet. But however a reader may assess its psychological and critical astuteness, he will recognize that it is as comprehensive a treatment of Genet's psychical life as James Boswell's biography was of Dr. Johnson's outer life. (A comparison of Boswell and Sartre will show in full measure the influence that the science of psychoanalysis has had on the art of biography.)

Whatever our judgment may be of Sartre's mammoth work, its effect on Genet's fame is considerable. It is impossible to say to what degree it may have affected Genet himself—perhaps very little, yet we may wonder if he found in the book suppositions about his inner life of which he had not dreamed. If so, it is conceivable that his life and works after 1952 may have been influenced by his seeing himself in the Sartrean image. However this may be, there is no doubt that Sartre's study has been of immense importance in the forming of Genet's public image, both for those who have read the book and for those who have not. Those who have read Sartre's study may then read Genet through Sartre's eyes, which may help to clarify or may prove distorting. And those who have not read Sartre's work but know of its existence will be more disposed to turn to Genet than they would otherwise have been; the testimony of over six hundred pages, whatever their content, is a strong endorsement when coming from Sartre. The publisher of Genet's complete works (up to 1953) took full advantage of the windfall: the first volume of *Genet's* works is devoted entirely to *Sartre's* extended essay.

Sartre's work has, as we suggested, served as both impetus and, at times, obstacle to a reading of Genet. It has helped swell the ranks of Genet theatregoers and armchair readers. But like many another critical work by an eminent hand, it has in some ways made more difficult an objective, disinterested study of its subject. An attentive reader of Sartre may thereafter have a hard time seeing Genet from another point of view and giving his own critical vision free latitude.

There is still another impetus to a reading of the plays, as well as another possible obstacle to a disinterested criticism of them—the life and legend of Jean Genet himself. The autobiographical *Thief's Journal,* published in 1959, is the most important single document to have drawn attention to the eccentricities of Genet's life. One must look far in the history of autobiography to find a more sensational book. A paean to its author's three most prized virtues—treason, theft, and homosexuality—it celebrates the pursuit of these practices and the inversion of all beliefs and values which have traditionally been thought of as the norm. Genet's ethic is consistently and precisely the reverse of the customarily avowed ethic: *The Thief's Journal* is a profession of the demonic.

One does not have to read *The Thief's Journal*—or some of the other nondramatic works of similar substance, *Our Lady of the Flowers* for example—to be duly impressed by the sensational nature of Genet's life and works. The brief notices appearing on the back covers of some of his publications are aimed at the more lurid tastes. The paperback edition of *Our Lady of the Flowers* uses both covers and three additional pages to titillate one's aliterary sensibilities. It is small wonder that a reader may approach the plays with mental images extraneous to the text.

The attempt of this chapter will be to analyze Genet's five plays as an autonomous unit, to forget for the moment the intricate subtleties of Sartre, as well as the life and the nondramatic writings of Genet. There is not the slightest doubt that a reading of Sartre and a knowledge of Genet's life and nondramatic work can be helpful in any final appraisal of the plays, and we will weigh these factors later. But for the time being we will try to put them aside and view the plays in innocence of such extrinsic data.

The five plays of Genet—*Deathwatch, The Maids, The Balcony, The Blacks,* and *The Screens*—reflect his obsession with values and his bitter hostility to the traditional assessment of them. He is as explicitly intent upon anatomizing man's nature as was his older contemporary T. S. Eliot. The plays of both writers are variations on the theme of redemption, though the respective concepts of redemption are antithetical. The Eliot protagonist is redeemed from a condition alien to what the biblical God would will for him. All five of Eliot's plays trace the movement of the protagonist from alienation to reconciliation, a movement presented in a less explicit theological framework and language from one drama to the next and yet one present in his last play, *The Elder Statesman,* as it is in his first, *Murder in the Cathedral.*

The goal of the Genet protagonist is the polar opposite from that of his counterpart in Eliot. It is a demonic goal—the divine goal turned upside down. Genet's protagonists seek to be redeemed, in a sense peculiar to their author, from their present condition, to be released from their stultifying bonds. The plays of Genet call their audiences and readers to a radical change in their sense of values and, consequently, in their behavior. He writes with a passion to subvert the entire structure of values considered normative to Western civilization. Thus one major task of Genet's critics is to define his ethic and objectives, his radical sense of what constitutes contemporary man's redemptive goal.

In Ionesco, as we have shown, the redemptive goal is presented primarily in his memory plays; although man now enjoys no paradise, he does possess that faint remembrance of things past, of a time when life was joyful. But such nostalgia is foreign to the temperament of Genet. It is clear that he despises the present, where the wretchedness of appearance is in constant oscillation with the wretchedness of reality, and where the despised possessors and the miserable dispossessed are locked in mutual interdependence—one feeding, and one being fed by, the other. Despising the present, he yearns for a future void of sound and motion, of space and time— a future which, the goal of all human endeavor, is Nothingness. *The Balcony* defines this unfelt ecstasy as "Absence" (*Bal,* 1, 69); and the Genet protagonist whose journey thereto is most painstakingly recorded is the treacherous, blessed Saïd of *The Screens.* Five French revolvers, fired at Saïd at the end of the play, bring the unhero to his richly deserved Absence. And from that state there is, happily, no place to go.

Filled with the present and reaching out toward a future, Genet's plays are oblivious to a past. There is not, as in Ionesco, any recollection of a Golden Age.

Although a reader might at first be disposed to think of Genet's dramatic world as a fallen one, a result of some cosmic catastrophe, some fierce battle among titanic ruling powers or some irreparable misjudgment or malefaction among men, he will look in vain for some explanatory cause—scientific or mythic—of the present frustration and torture. There is neither nostalgia for a past when things were different nor rage or grief that things *have come* to be as they are.

We have already seen that, to chronicle Ionesco's "history" of mankind's changing condition—to move thematically from observation of an early paradise, to man's fall, to his present condition, to speculation on his future—is not to follow the plays in their chronological sequence. A study of Genet's drama, on the other hand, may best be accomplished by attention to chronology. The main themes of his plays—the juxtaposition of appearance and reality, the reverse mirror image, the moving from a wretched condition in space and time to an ethereal, abstract Absence or Nothingness—are set early, in *Deathwatch* and *The Maids,* and then developed and played out in a series of variations which culminate in *The Screens* with the complete victory of that complete outcast, Saïd. To follow Genet's plays in order of their writing is to be led, in his view, from our present unendurable misery to a consummation devoutly to be wished: this journey we may characterize as the ascent into Nothingness.

II

Although *Deathwatch* was first performed and published in 1949, two years after the initial performance and publication of *The Maids,* it is Genet's first composed and least complex play. The setting is a prison cell; the three main characters are Green Eyes, Lefranc, and Maurice. Green Eyes is king of the cell and object of the mingled envy and admiration of his two companions. In the well-defined hierarchy among the inmates of the prison, Green Eyes is outranked only by Snowball, a Negro prisoner frequently mentioned but never on stage. The action immediately preceding the rising curtain, a violent fight between Lefranc and Maurice, is repeated immediately preceding the falling curtain. As the curtain rises, Green Eyes is holding Lefranc back from the frightened Maurice.

The enmity, constant throughout the play, between Lefranc and Maurice is engendered by their feelings about and toward Green Eyes. Lefranc desires above all to be, or at the very least to be thought, a great criminal. He is terribly envious of Green Eyes's high position in the prison hierarchy and, in an effort to equal or outdo his cellmate, he both boasts of deeds he never accomplished and seeks the deed which will bring him greater prestige. Whereas Lefranc envies the king of the cell more than he admires him, Maurice admires Green Eyes more than he envies him. Maurice is more envious, or jealous, of Green Eyes's girl (because of her relationship to Green Eyes) than he is of Green Eyes's deeds. Maurice detests Lefranc because of his seeking to equal or eclipse Green Eyes; Lefranc despises Maurice because of his affectionate subservience toward Green Eyes.

The main action of *Deathwatch* is Lefranc's attempt to raise himself by matching the crime for which Green Eyes has been imprisoned and is awaiting the death sentence. The crime was the strangling of a girl. Under the prevailing circumstances of the play, the closest parallel that Lefranc has at his disposal is the strangling of Maurice. This violent action Lefranc achieves toward the end of the play. But when he then turns to Green Eyes for the admiration he thinks his due, he is met only with contempt. Instead of finding a place in the ranks of glorious criminals, he is spurned. His last words, "I really am all alone!" (*D*, 163), attest to his recognition of utter failure. In the rules of the game of *Deathwatch*, to be an outcast among outcasts is a horrible and lonely fate. Lefranc does not through his deed join the elect company of Snowball and Green Eyes; he reduces himself to oblivion. It is evident that murder does not in itself suffice to bestow glory. One of the

major interpretive problems of the play, therefore, is
the question of why Lefranc failed where Green Eyes
succeeded. The question is answered through an analysis of the differing motivations for the two similar
deeds.

What led Green Eyes to the strangling of the girl?
Certainly it was no crime of passion. There was no
fiendish Iago at the ear of a jealous lover who suspected
infidelity; there is no evidence even that Green Eyes
knew the girl before the fatal meeting. In fact, there
was *no* motivation, in the usual sense of the word, for
the crime. The girl in no way induced the crime; indeed,
any girl would have served equally well as victim. Nor
was there any force *within* Green Eyes which led him
to the murder; he was in no way a conscious actor.
Quite the contrary, Green Eyes was called to the crime;
he was as resistant to it as Moses was to Jahweh's call
to lead his people out of bondage. He was simply over-
powered by a mysterious, unwelcome force against
which he vainly struggled.

The first identifiable condition which led to Green
Eyes's culminating act was the sense of being swept up
by what he speaks of as a peculiar, virtually undefinable,
sweetness. "It's by its sweetness," he explains, "that you
recognize catastrophe" (*D,* 130). Everything and everyone was, suddenly one day, polite to him. For no apparent reason, a man raised his hat to him. Thus began
a process which would not be stayed. As Green Eyes
puts it, ". . . everything began to move. There was
nothing more to be done. And that was why I had to
kill someone." (*D,* 131) Such sweetness, such consideration, was the unmistakable mark of his being called to
his destiny. Why the call came at that moment, and why
the call was to murder are matters inexplicable: the
forces which impelled Green Eyes are as far removed
from the realm of logic as were the forces which impelled Laius, Jocasta, and Oedipus to their respective
fates. And once the deed had been done, Green Eyes
made every conceivable effort to turn back history and
return to the self he had been before the murder. His

futile attempt to undo the deed he recounts in detail to Lefranc and Maurice:

And I was scared. I wanted to back up. Stop! No go! I tried hard. I ran in all directions. I shifted. I tried every form and shape so as not to be a murderer. Tried to be a dog, a cat, a horse, a tiger, a table, a stone! I even tried, me too, to be a rose! Don't laugh. I did what I could. I squirmed and twisted. People thought I had convulsions. I wanted to turn back the clock, to undo what I'd done, to live my life over until before the crime. It looks easy to go backwards—but my body couldn't do it. I tried again. Impossible. The people around me kidded me. They didn't suspect the danger, until the day they started getting anxious. My dance! You should have seen my dance! I danced, boys, I danced! (*D*, 131)

It is clear that Green Eyes's intrinsic aversion to the deed of murder was no match for the outer force that first announced and manifested itself in the sweetness of others and then drove him to the senseless crime. It is clear too that the course of history is irreversible. Even so, Green Eyes intuitively understands that there was a certain naturalness and appropriateness in the action which he had taken.

It was destiny that took the form of my hands. It would be only fair to cut *them* off instead of my head. And for me everything became simpler. The girl was already under me. All I had to do was put one hand delicately on her mouth and the other delicately on her neck. It was over. (*D*, 133)

In short, Green Eyes *had* to commit the murder. He was not man acting but man acted upon by those mysterious, invisible powers that play their game of chess with human counters.

Lefranc's act of committing murder is almost an exact replica of that of Green Eyes. The equation would read: Lefranc : Maurice : : Green Eyes : the girl. Both murders and both victims have much in common. The girl was led to her death under the magnetism of a very special characteristic of Green Eyes, his habit of bearing a flower or flowers—in this case, lilacs—between his teeth. Attracted by the lilacs, the girl went to his room where, her body under his, he strangled her. Maurice is also the victim of strangling. More than this, Maurice is much like the girl who was Green Eyes's victim, for his feminine characteristics are stressed throughout the play. Attention is more than once called to his "cute little yegg's mug" (D, 157). His repeated gesture of tossing back a lock of his hair, his puerile delight in being "accepted by all the men" (D, 127), his jealousy of Green Eyes's present girl—all point to his feminine nature. The dialogue and stage directions which climax in his strangling show him in the same physical position, though homosexually, as the murdered girl. And if Maurice is to be equated with the girl, Lefranc usurps the role of Green Eyes. Thus Maurice, just before his death, says to Lefranc: "Is the gentleman afraid I'll disturb his bunch of lilacs?" (D, 158) That the strangling is then cast in the form of a homosexual encounter, the text makes quite clear. Yet, the deed done, Lefranc is brought up short by the recognition that, far from winning him a cherished place in the prison hierarchy, his deed has been his total undoing, leaving him utterly alone.

To distinguish between Green Eyes's success and Lefranc's failure is to understand one of the principal themes of *Deathwatch*. The crimes of the two prisoners, as we have seen, are the same. But the men are led to their crimes by motivations that are polar opposites in the world of the play. Green Eyes is properly motivated: he does what he has to do. Lefranc, on the other hand, is constantly trying to be what he is not destined to be. He is, in short, a phony from beginning to end. He boasts of crimes he has never committed, boasts, for example, about the marks on his wrists and his ankles, marks he claims to be those of the galley slave he became in consequence of his crimes. But there is a suspicion approaching conviction that the marks were self-inflicted. Lefranc's "trademark" is counterfeit. It has not the authenticity of the lilacs between the teeth, lilacs which stained the strangling hands of Green Eyes and, left in the hair of the murdered girl, provided the

clue leading to his apprehension. It does not even have
the authenticity of Maurice's mug, which made him the
darling of the prisoners and was a factor leading appropriately to his own murder. Lefranc's attempts to emu-
late Green Eyes are pathetic. He wears the latter's
clothes; and his tatoo, in imitation of that of Green
Eyes, is the product of ink, not of needles. Seeking to
enjoy vicariously what he cannot enjoy in fact, he keeps
in his mattress photographs of murderers, taking a once-
removed pleasure in deeds which were properly theirs.

Lefranc's ambitions are fanned by the taunts of both
his cellmates. He smarts under Maurice's deriding remarks that he is not of the same nature as the other
prisoners and never will be. And he is not discouraged,
but driven on, by Green Eyes's perception of his basic
flaw, his attempt to assume a role foreign to his nature:
"You're the one who's trying to act like a man. You're
trying to strut. A man doesn't have to strut. He knows
he's a man and that's all that matters." (D, 143)
Lefranc simply cannot accept himself and wishes above
all to disprove the truth known by his companions. It
is Maurice who, after a long and bitter denunciation of
the extent of Lefranc's phoniness, speaks to him the
words which finally trigger him furiously to murder:
"I'm going to strip you. I want to leave you naked.
You feed on others. You dress yourself up, you deco-
rate yourself with our jewels, I accuse you! You steal
our crimes!" (D, 158) And with this, Lefranc, desperately anxious to possess a crime which is his own, enacts
the rape-murder of his feminine tormentor.

Lefranc learns too late the first rule of the *Deathwatch*
game: the genuine criminal never *chooses* his crime;
his crime is always *chosen* for him and thrust upon
him. Lefranc did not await that sweetness which cor-
rupts, if indeed it ever would have come to him. A man
who tampers with, or seeks to forge, his destiny is lost
—so argues Green Eyes, who is the spokesman for the
play's point of view. Green Eyes despises Lefranc for
killing "for nothing," for killing "for the glory of it,"
"for blow[ing] in casually and bump[ing] off a kid!" (D,

160–161) And when Lefranc protests that he did what he did "out of a yearning for misfortune," Green Eyes lays down carefully the rules of the game:

You don't know the first thing about misfortune if you think you can choose it. I didn't want mine. It chose me. It fell on my shoulders and clung to me. I tried everything to shake it off. I struggled, I boxed, I danced, I even sang, and odd as it may seem, I refused it at first. It was only when I saw that everything was irremediable that I quieted down. I've only just accepted it. It had to be total. (*D*, 162)

A man does not properly storm the gates of misfortune or corruption or murder or anything else. The perfect criminal is seized, resists, is overcome, seeks to move backwards and undo the crime, finally acquiesces, and then, as Green Eyes puts it, rejoices in "really settling down in misfortune and making it . . . [his] heaven" (*D*, 162). A man's freedom, paradoxically, thus lies in his accommodating himself to the destiny to which he has been called; it lies in his willing bondage to his fate.

Of the three cellmates, only Lefranc is clearly an initiator of his action, thus depriving it of the purity and beauty inherent in a crime graciously bestowed. Maurice, though eager for the affection of Green Eyes, is rather passively contented with his mug and the unspectacular place it wins for him. Green Eyes has learned to live gloriously and also rather passively with all the laurels his lilacs have made possible. Snowball, even above Green Eyes in the prison hierarchy, owes his lofty position, as Green Eyes remarks, to the fact that the Negro's crime was "a little more necessary" (*D*, 145) than that of Green Eyes, that the forces which laid hold of the Negro and carried him to his crime were even stronger than those which impelled Green Eyes. And it is, perhaps strangely, the misled Lefranc who most clearly recognizes Snowball's triumph: "His chains carry him" (*D*, 107), Lefranc says of Snowball. In other words, the very marks of Snowball's bondage, the very instruments of his punishment, have been metamorphosed into his slaves, serving him and moving him. The counterfeit marks on Lefranc's wrists and ankles and his ink-wrought tatoo are the foils to Maurice's mug, Green Eyes's lilacs, and Snowball's chains. Lefranc alone has sought to direct his destiny.

The last words of the play, Lefranc's "I really am all alone!" are ironic. It is Lefranc who has wished to isolate Green Eyes, to separate him from the girl who visits him in prison, from the police, and from the whole world. Lefranc wanted not to be alone but to be let alone, to be free of the insolent and irritable provocation of Maurice and of his deeply felt inferiority to Green Eyes. His highest aspiration was to enjoy the favor and esteem of Snowball and the other prisoners. And his anxiety for this status led him to the very act which irremediably cut him off from all he desired. Far from succeeding in isolating Green Eyes, he isolated only himself. And in *Deathwatch,* as we have said before, the men who pride themselves on being outcasts from normal society have no wish to be outcasts among outcasts.

Lefranc is the protagonist of *Deathwatch.* It is he alone who strives desperately to change his status. There is evidence that Green Eyes cleverly eggs him on, that he perceives well the fatal weakness of his challenger and traps him into his catastrophic blunder. Twice Green Eyes invites Lefranc to murder: "And to be my size, you've got to do as I do" (*D,* 145) and ". . . you need a murder with all the trimmings. Nothing else'll do." (*D,* 153) But within the context of the play it is only Lefranc who acts. Genet's first play is the dramatic narrative of a protagonist who, ignorant of the rules of the game, ironically chooses his doom.

III

The Maids, though written after *Deathwatch,* was produced and published two years earlier, in 1947. The theme of *Deathwatch*—that fulfillment comes only to him who yields to, and then glories in, the destiny to which he is called—would seem to be challenged in *The Maids.* In Genet's second play the two protagonists,

like Lefranc before them, seek to change their status.
And although the attempt issues in the death of one of
them and the imminent imprisonment of the other, the
spectator is left with the feeling that they have accomplished their end and acquitted themselves nobly. The
focus of *Deathwatch* was on an individual's relationship
to his calling, and his decision to accept or reject it. It
is true that there was interaction among the three main
characters, that the behavior of each influenced the
others. But the emphasis was not so much on the relationships among the characters as it was on the response
of each character to the roots of his being. But beginning with *The Maids* and extending through Genet's
later plays, there is not so extensive an emphasis on the
individual character's action or passion as on the relationship among the characters and the interdependence
among their roles. In *The Maids,* the roles of protagonist and antagonist are interrelated to the extent that
the very life of one is dependent upon that of the other.

With the rising curtain of *The Maids,* the spectator
views a luxurious boudoir in which a maid named
Claire is attending her lady at the dressing table. Madame is both domineering and insulting. She stresses
through her authoritative commands and her offensive
language the gap she draws between served and server.
Angered that her maid has brought her kitchen gloves
into the hallowed bedroom, she remarks, "Everything,
yes, everything that comes out of the kitchen is spit!"
(*M,* 35) And when the maid does spit on Madame's
patent-leather slippers in order to polish them, Madame
is moved to ask, "Do you think I find it pleasant to
know that my foot is shrouded by the veils of your
saliva? By the mists of your swamps?" (*M,* 37) The
imagery of excretion is matched by that of smell. "You
smell like an animal," Madame tells her servant.
"You've brought those odors from some foul attic"
(*M,* 40). And, somewhat later, the maid rancorously
acknowledges the insults: "I'm going back to my
kitchen, back to my gloves and the smell of my teeth.

To my belching sink." (*M*, 46) The tone of the play is well set.

In the first ten pages of the play, as the maid, amid the thesaurus of insult, is helping Madame dress, we note that tea is being prepared; that Madame, having betrayed her criminal lover to the police, is now ready to follow him from prison to prison and share in the "glory" which is the attribute of the Genet outcast; that the maid can match her mistress insult for insult; and, importantly, that the two are engaged in some as yet unfinished business: as Madame orders her out of the room, the maid advances and declares threateningly: "But before I go back, I'm going to finish the job" (*M*, 46).

The spectators, as well as the dramatic characters, are then brought up short by the ringing of an alarm clock. We have been viewing, as we soon learn, not the play itself but a play-within-a-play. She who played Madame is really Claire, a maid, and she who played Claire is really Solange, another maid and the sister of Claire. We have not been spectators of a play and thus once removed from reality, but spectators of a play-within-a-play and thus twice removed. And we have been introduced to a theme important to Genet: the hazy relationship of appearance to reality.

The alarm was to warn the maids of Madame's imminent return, for which they prepare in feverish haste, a preparation including the making of tea. The maids bitterly discuss their servile condition, their mutual enmity, and their hostility toward their mistress, a hostility so deep that Claire (not Madame herself) actually had betrayed Madame's loving Monsieur to the police in an anonymous letter leading to his arrest, and so deep that Solange had actually once attempted to murder Madame. The phone rings; it is Monsieur, free on bail and leaving word that Madame, on her return, should come to meet him. The maids, terrified that their betrayal of Monsieur will be exposed, return to a discussion of their miserable servantdom, and, as Madame returns, determine to effect her murder by poisoning her tea. Madame, unaware of Monsieur's freedom, announces her plans to follow him from prison to prison. But noticing that the telephone receiver is off its hook —the careless result of Solange's dazed response to Monsieur's call—Madame learns of her lover's freedom and dispatches Solange for a taxi. Despite Solange's purposeful dilatoriness in accomplishing her mission, she returns a moment too soon, just as Madame is about to drink the poisoned tea. Madame rushes out to her rendezvous without drinking it. Claire and Solange seek again to play out the masquerade which was the beginning of the play. Finally, after frantic action and a mad soliloquy by Solange, Claire, drinking the tea prepared for Madame, commits suicide, knowing that Solange will be accused of murdering her. Solange's curtain speech, to which we will return later, is an ecstatic expression of what she deems to be the complete victory won by her sister and herself. In what conceivable sense can the maids be claimed the victors?

Search for an answer raises the question of what relationships may exist, in terms of characters and goals, between *Deathwatch* and *The Maids*. Claire and Solange are protagonists in that they, like Lefranc, are seeking to change their status and are primarily responsible for the action of the play. Madame, like Green Eyes, is the protagonists' object of envy. She is also, in a very typical Genetian sense, the antagonist, her very being standing in the way of the protagonists' desires. The maids' goal is to be like Madame, as Lefranc's goal is to be like Green Eyes. In pursuit of their goal, the maids accomplish a suicide-murder; in pursuit of his goal, Lefranc murders Maurice. Solange's curtain lines imply victory; Lefranc's last line, defeat. Lefranc's defeat, apparently, is the result of his assuming a role not properly his. Interpreting the conclusion of *The Maids* is a more complex task. It would seem that the maids, like Lefranc, have assumed an undestined role. Have they in fact done so, and are they in fact victorious?

The response of the maids toward Madame is ambivalent, a compound of hate and affection, of envy and admiration, with hate and envy predominating. The masquerade which opens the play, a masquerade which has been repeated many times with each sister playing alternately the role of maid and Madame, is a partial accomplishment of the maids' goal. For in this make-believe, one of the maids can for the moment be like Madame, and, as a bonus, the other maid can ease a part of her discomforting animosity toward Madame by hurling insults at an imaginary Madame. That the maids relish such pretense is evidenced by the passion with which they cast themselves into it. It is also evident that the masquerade, which gives each at different times the opportunity to play Madame and to exchange insults, is not fully satisfying. They would also, within the play-within-the-play, try to accomplish the mock murder of Madame. We will recall that the maid's last words before the ringing of the alarm are threatening: "But before I go back, I'm going to finish the job." The "job" is the simulated murder, a goal which has always, for one reason or another, fallen short of accomplishment. Solange upbraids Claire for never being ready, and Claire argues that they always "waste too much time with the preliminaries" (*M,* 47). The masquerade thus affords a measure of vicarious satisfaction but does not bring them even to the appearance of their ultimate goal, the death of Madame. Solange has also attempted the actual murder of her mistress, but her efforts have been frustrated in that as well.

Is it not one thing, however, to wish to be like another person and a different one to wish to murder that person? Actually, in Genet's concept of human relationships, the wishes can be equated. This strange equation is not stressed in *Deathwatch,* although we should remember that Lefranc not only desired to be like Green Eyes in the sense of being equal to him but also desired to "isolate" his rival and then to usurp his place. The point is pushed further in *The Maids,* where the death of Madame is a necessary prerequisite to the maids' escaping their servile condition. This fact brings us to one of the most prevalent themes in Genet's dramatic works, namely, that each one of a pair of opposites is dependent for its condition on the other member of the pair. Madame owes her "madameness" to the servantdom of her servants; Claire and Solange owe their servantdom to the "madameness" of Madame. To do away with either condition would be to deprive the other of its life; or, in terms of *The Maids,* to deprive Madame of life would be to erase the servantdom of her maids. Each item of any pair is the reverse image of the other item. When Solange, speaking of Madame, exclaims to Claire, *"Her* joy feeds on *our* shame" (*M,* 81), she epitomizes the reverse-image analogy. And Claire, in the role of Madame speaking of her maids, calls attention to the "distorting mirrors" which opposites provide for opposites: "Your frightened guilty faces, your puckered elbows, your outmoded clothes, your wasted bodies, only fit for our castoffs! You're our distorting mirrors, our loathsome vent, our shame, our dregs!" (*M,* 86) It is the reverse mirror image.

A reader may argue logically that the murder of Madame by Claire and Solange would not in fact change the maids into Madame: if the maid next door murders her employer, she does not thereby become her employer. But Genet is not interested so much in presenting individual human beings, characters of a fullness of individuality which sets them off clearly from other characters, as he is in presenting metaphysical or allegorical types which represent the basic conditions of mankind. Neither Madame nor Monsieur is personalized by a name, and Claire and Solange might just as well be designated as First Maid and Second Maid. There are even specific references to their merged identity. Solange playing maid speaks for herself and her sister when she says to Claire playing Madame: "We're merged, enveloped in our fumes, in our revels, in our hatred of you" (*M,* 46). Solange later remarks to Claire, "I can't stand our being so alike" (*M,* 60). And Claire, speaking to Solange, plays a variation on the mirror image: ". . . I'm sick of seeing my image thrown back at me by a mirror, like a bad smell. You're my bad smell." (*M,* 61)

Thus the dramatic conflict in *The Maids* is between the condition, status, or role of servantdom and that of madamedom. As the play progresses, we find that the protagonistic servantdom has been unable, in reality or in appearance, to do away with the antagonistic madamedom. And when Madame, just short of drinking her tea, goes out into the night to meet Monsieur, Claire and Solange are fatigued, embittered, and near despair. They have been unable to bring themselves to either the reality or the appearance of murdering Madame. Had they followed the ground rules of *Deathwatch,* they would have returned to the spit of their kitchen and the odors of their foul attic and accepted the destined servility of maids. And by their acceptance they would, like Snowball and Green Eyes, have elevated their degradation to some sort of mystique. As Snowball triumphed over and controlled his chains, so would Claire and Solange have triumphed over their servantdom. But, in fact, they do nothing of the kind.

With the exit of Madame the maids try to alleviate their distress through another masquerade. But Claire, nauseated by her attempt, is helped offstage by Solange, who then returns to deliver a sustained, schizophrenic dramatic monologue (*M,* 91–95). Addressing in sequence a series of imaginary characters, Solange rhapsodizes on the possible resolutions of her plight.

Her first words reflect her deepest wish: "Madame. . . . At last! Madame is dead! . . . laid out on the linoleum . . . strangled by the dish-gloves." But no: Madame is present and alive; it is Claire who is dead, murdered by her sister. And Solange madly chronicles her own metamorphosis:

I've been a servant. Well and good. I've made the gestures a servant must make. I've smiled at Madame. I've bent down to make the bed, bent down to scrub the tiles, bent down to peel vegetables, to listen at doors, to glue my eye to keyholes! But now I stand upright. And firm. I'm the

strangler. Mademoiselle Solange, the one who strangled her
sister! . . . Me be still? Madame is delicate, really. But I
pity Madame. I pity Madame's whiteness, her satiny skin,
and her little ears, and little wrists. . . . Eh? I'm the black
crow. . . . Eh? Who am I? The monstrous soul of servantdom!

The answer is "no," for Solange can no longer be
taunted with the epithets of "black crow" and "soul of
servantdom." Her courageous, if imaginary, deed of
murder has made her a very queen, now led to the
gallows in pomp and splendor by a host of servants in
full and gorgeous regalia. She is no longer merely Solange but now Mademoiselle Solange Lemercier, who
speaks of herself in the first person plural which is the
attribute of monarchs: "Now we are Mademoiselle Solange Lemercier, that Lemercier woman. The famous
criminal. . . . I'm not a maid. I have a noble soul."
And then, with the reappearance of Claire, Solange,
recalled to reality, brings her monologue to an end. She
realizes that, despite her dreams and imaginings, all
remains the same: Madame is now blissfully in the arms
of her lover; Claire is alive and on stage; Solange is
still a servant.

Claire, the younger sister heretofore dominated by
Solange, now takes control of the action and, through
her ingenuity and courageous determination, devises
the formula for victory. The maids have been unable
really to murder Madame; neither maid has been able
even to simulate the murder of Madame through the
mock murder of the other maid. There is but one satisfying solution: one maid will *really* murder the other
maid who *appears* to be Madame. Well, not quite, for
even this complexity is not complex enough. There will
really be a suicide which will *appear* to be a murder!
And even more than this, the suicide-murder will effect
the ultimate merger of the two maids. "Solange," Claire
insists as she orders her sister to pour her a cup of the
poisoned tea, "you will contain me within you" (*M,*
96). And as Solange demurs, Claire continues: "Be
still. It will be your task, yours alone, to keep us both

alive. You must be very strong. In prison no one will know that I'm with you, secretly. On the sly." (*M*, 97) It is a masterstroke which frees them both from the "monstrous soul of servantdom," for it is the ritual enactment of the death of Madame. And if Madame will in fact continue to live, madameness is dead. The mirror is smashed, and Madame will now look in vain for the reverse image of herself on which her madameness must feed in order to live.

Following upon the suicide of Claire, Solange's curtain speech, as mad as her former monologue, is her victory chant, celebrating the death of madameness, the death of servantdom, and the resurrection of Claire and Solange in a disembodied form free from all the hated and despised encumbrances:

The orchestra is playing brilliantly. The attendant is raising the red velvet curtain. He bows. Madame is descending the stairs. Her furs brush against the green plants. Madame steps into the car. Monsieur is whispering sweet nothings in her ear. She would like to smile, but she is dead. She rings the bell. The porter yawns. He opens the door. Madame goes up the stairs. She enters her apartment—but, Madame is dead. Her two maids are alive: they've just risen up, free, from Madame's icy form. All the maids were present at her side—not they themselves, but rather the hellish agony of their names. And all that remains of them to float about Madame's airy corpse is the delicate perfume of the holy maidens which they were in secret. We are beautiful, joyous, drunk, and free! (*M*, 99–100)

Three major Genet themes issue from a reading of *The Maids*. There is, first, the confusion and near indistinguishability of appearance and reality. The artistic form of this theme is the play-within-the-play, with the opening masquerade at first appearing to be the real action of the play. And even more complexly, the later real suicide-murder of Claire is the apparent murder of Madame, which is the real death of madameness. Second, there is the reverse-image theme, expressing the absolute interdependence of opposites: servantdom and madameness, the polar opposite complements of each other, must live and die together. There is no such thing as an independent or absolute wretchedness or splendor, for each condition is both dependent upon and relative to the other.

The third theme involves the movement, on the part of Claire and Solange, from their wretchedness to their exaltation. At the end of the play they are no longer the animal smell of a foul attic, but "the delicate perfume of . . . holy maidens." They also become one, eternally together in their new being. We will recall the repeated reference in *The Maids* to the person who betrays a lover and then expresses a saintlike devotion by following him in his imprisonment to the end of the earth. At one point Claire exclaims to Solange: "We shall be that eternal couple, Solange, the two of us, the eternal couple of the criminal and the saint. We'll be saved, Solange, saved, I swear to you!" (*M*, 63) It is a prophetic utterance, for, finally, Solange is a criminal, a person accused of the murder of a sister who committed suicide and thus a person betrayed by a suicide. And Claire, with her promise to be secretly with her sister in prison, will display her saintlike devotion. Most importantly, they are freed of their earthly burdens, now distilled into a delicate perfume.

The constant vacillation between appearance and reality; the mirrored reverse image stressing the interdependence of polar opposites; the moving from a wretched condition into the beauty, joy, drunkenness, and freedom of an ethereal abstraction—these are the themes of *The Maids,* to be repeated in Genet's later plays.

IV

Following Genet's first two plays there was an appreciable interval before the appearance of *The Balcony,* the first version of which, in fifteen scenes, was published in 1956. The second version, the one of which we will speak, consists of nine scenes and was published in 1960. Not only is *The Balcony* twice as long as either of its predecessors; it is also considerably more ambitious and somewhat more complex. And though it must yield to *The Blacks* in terms of theatricality, of playability, it is for the armchair reader perhaps the most satisfying of Genet's works. Its dominant themes are the same as those in *The Maids,* though the scale on which they are played is larger and more various.

The Balcony celebrates two worlds, two conditions of man: one is Madame Irma's brothel, the world of illusions; the other the city outside the brothel, representing the real world of normal routine but at this time wasting itself in a devastating revolution. Madame Irma's establishment, the most ingenious of its kind in fact or fiction, is a place of escape for those who sense only frustration and tedium in their real lives. In the brothel a man can, for a price, play out in make-believe his fondest dreams. Irma has the actresses, settings, and props which enable a client to masquerade in absolutely *any* role of his choice. The revolutionists envisage themselves as fighting against, among other things, the attitude toward life which the brothel represents. They see themselves as champions of the practical, the real, and opposed to the brothel's carnival atmosphere so purposely withdrawn from the substantial life of the town. Antithetical as the two worlds are, there is a part of the fabric of each woven into every major character in the play; indeed, the path between the two is well worn.

The brief first scene contains the three major themes of the play, the same ones which characterized *The Maids.* The setting is a sacristy. We behold a bishop who has just confessed a woman recently fallen to six deadly sins. But we feel an eerie discomfort. The heavy make-up and scanty attire of the woman are implausible in the prevailing circumstances, and her tone is surprisingly disrespectful. Moreover, there is present another woman who persists in demanding from the Bishop money which she claims is her due. We soon learn, less abruptly than in *The Maids,* that we are witnessing a play-within-a-play, that the man who appears to be a bishop is really a client of the woman who demands his money, and that the confessing sinner is an employee of the woman. We are viewing not a real sacristy, but one of the elaborate sets of Irma's house of illusions. The theme of the relationship between appearance and reality is thus fixed at once.

Second, we are introduced briefly to another familiar theme, one more heavily stressed in ensuing scenes. When the Bishop remarks to the penitent, ". . . our holiness lies only in our being able to forgive you your sins" (*Bal,* 4), we recognize Genet's doctrine of mutual interdependence. There would be no role for a bishop if there were no sins to be forgiven; there would be no sinner if there were no ecclesiastical order to define that human condition which falls short of God's will.

Third, and more emphatically than in *The Maids,* there is the theme of distillation or abstraction. Claire and Solange, as we have seen, withdrew from the wretchedness of the real world and were happily reduced to "the delicate perfume of . . . holy maidens." This same theme of disembodiment, of abstraction toward nothingness, is clearly stated in the first speech of *The Balcony.* The Bishop, seeking to define "the mark of a prelate," observes: "It may be cruelty. And beyond that cruelty—and through it—a skilful, vigorous heading towards Absence. Towards Death." (*Bal,* 1) There is, throughout *The Balcony,* a shuttle movement between two basic conditions, each of which has various designations. One may be described as absence, death, immobility, invisibility, non-being, appearance; the other as presence, life, mobility, visibility, being, reality. Each condition is, of course, the reverse image of the other, and consequently each is dependent for its meaning upon the other. In *The Maids* the curtain falls at the moment Claire and Solange have moved from the condition of presence, life, and the like, to that of absence. *The Balcony,* on the other hand, enjoys no such resolution. Its thesis would seem to be that man is a perpetual shuttlecock in constant movement from one condition to the other.

The second and third scenes of the play repeat the first, with a would-be judge and a would-be general, respectively, in place of the would-be bishop. Each of the three men, by means of a play-within-the-play, exchanges the reality of his humdrum life for the appearance of the role which removes him from life's misery and tedium. And we have in the second scene the most explicit statement of the mutual interdependence of roles. The man playing judge pleads with the prostitute playing thief:

My being a judge is an emanation of your being a thief. You need only refuse—but you'd better not!—need only refuse to be who you are—what you are, therefore who you are—for me to cease to be . . . to vanish, evaporated. Burst. Volatized. Denied. Hence: good born of . . . What then? What then? But you won't refuse, will you? You won't refuse to be a thief? That would be wicked. It would be criminal. You'd deprive me of being! (*Bal,* 14–15)

And the third theme, that of the movement toward absence and death, is also repeated in the second and third scenes. The make-believe Judge, as he savors the passing of sentence on the make-believe thief, defines his removal from the real world into the illusory world as death itself, a condition he sees, with Solange, as "that region of exact freedom" (*Bal,* 13). The third pretender, the man who would be a general, develops the same concept by relating the condition of death to the multiplication of mirror images, emphasizing in this case the desire to exchange the reality of his being for a series of reflections on it. He sees himself as "close to death . . . where I shall be nothing, though reflected *ad infinitum* in these mirrors, nothing but my image" (*Bal,* 22). And then imagining himself as already dead, he addresses himself to the girl who plays his horse, and he describes more precisely his disembodiment, his reduction to an abstraction, his absence:

What is now speaking, and so beautifully, is Example. I am now only the image of my former self. Your turn, now. Lower your head and hide your eyes, for I want to be a general in solitude. Not even for myself, but for my image, and my image for its image, and so on. (*Bal,* 23)

The goal is the image within the image within the image on to infinity, with each image moving farther from the reality of life and more deeply into the nothingness of reflection and appearance.

The themes are thus firmly set in the very early stages of the play. And the significance of the brothel in the play's philosophical scheme is quite clear. As Irma's star protégée, Carmen, once put it, to enter the brothel is to reject the world (*Bal,* 42). Once there, a person may strip himself of all those personal and individual characteristics which are the freight of his real life and become absorbed in the attributes of the role he seeks. In one sense, it is as if the flesh-and-blood person of this world is metamorphosed into a kind of Platonic form or idea. For there are no bishops, judges, generals, *no real persons,* in the brothel. So great is Madame Irma's skill that her clients—or visitors, as she prefers to call them—become transformed to the very soul of bishopdom, judgedom, generaldom, or any other role for which they long. An interesting variation on the theme, and one taking full advantage of its comic potentialities, is played as the real Chief of Police of the war-torn city wishes to dissolve not into a role foreign to his real-life occupation but into its own abstraction. But he cannot do so until someone else has requested the role of police chiefdom in the brothel. He cannot *play* the part which *is in fact* his until the part is requested by another, and it is to his humiliation, throughout most of *The Balcony,* that no one has thought well enough of his occupation to request its role.

The visitors to the brothel, it is clear, seek to empty themselves of all those burdensome traits which have marked their real lives. Set off against them are the rebels, who wish to immerse themselves in the practical, the real, and to affirm the value of the things of this world. To the rebels, the brothel symbolizes the principal threat to the good life; consequently, if they are to remain true to the principles they affirm, they must eschew any compromise with make-believe. As the rebel leader, Roger, declares: "If we behave like those on the other side, then we *are* the other side. Instead of changing the world, all we'll achieve is a reflection of the one we want to destroy." (*Bal,* 56) Yet the rebels, who start off faithful to their code of pursuing the practical and useful life, soon discover that their ways and goals are too drab and commonplace to serve as inspiration to sustain their troops in battle. In order to stimulate their flagging ranks, the leaders know they must resort to the methods of the enemy.

They have at hand the very means to effect their change of strategy. For Roger has brought with him to the rebel camp the charming Chantal, formerly one of the brothel's most accomplished employees. Her painstaking attempts to adapt herself to the new and useful life of bandaging the wounded have fallen short of complete success. The rebel leaders, with the exception of the high-principled Roger, see in Chantal the means to rejuvenate their dispirited troops. She could serve as an inspiring symbol—the singing voice that would urge the rebels on, the face that would appear on a legion of posters and charm the troops into action. Roger alone knows that such a plan, transforming a breathing person into an abstract, if fetching, symbol, would be a betrayal of rebel principles:

If I yanked Chantal from the brothel, it wasn't to plant her in another—or in the same one—that's a mockery of the old one. Carnival! Carnival! You know well enough we ought to beware of it like the plague, since its logical conclusion is death. You know well enough that a carnival that goes to the limit is a suicide! (*Bal,* 59)

Rogers fights for a lost cause. Chantal is sent out in a carnival atmosphere to rally the people. But as the symbol Chantal is no longer the real Chantal, the real revolution has become only an apparent one, for the rebels have joined principles with the very force they would destroy. Roger's rebuke to Chantal expresses perfectly the rebel capitulation: "You'll be what you've always dreamt of being: an emblem forever escaping from her womanliness" (*Bal,* 65). Chantal's escape is complete; she is killed by a bullet from an unknown assailant.

The path between reality and appearance bears traffic in both directions. For if the rebels, who would immerse themselves in reality and destroy the make-believe, fall to the methods of the pretenders, so do the pretenders, who would abstract themselves from reality, fall to the methods of the rebels. In order to witness this latter phenomenon, we need turn now to the loyalists, who, at the same time that Roger and his colleagues debate the proper action for Chantal, are having their own problems.

The loyalists are, philosophically, of the same persuasion as those who glorify the brothel: they too are in love with absence. And it is to the brothel that the loyalist Court Envoy hastens when their cause seems most severely threatened. His ensuing dialogue with Irma and the Chief of Police is of considerable importance, for through it we gain a greater understanding of a difficult concept—that of the movement toward absence. When asked about the welfare and safety of his Queen, the Envoy replies that "she had to carry to an extreme the Royal prerogatives," and that such prerogatives are subsumed in one condition—"Absence" (*Bal,* 69). He announces that the Queen is moving toward immobility and invisibility, that she is embroidering and not embroidering, is snoring and not snoring. The contradictions make only for bewilderment until it is realized that they define the state of absence, of nothingness. Each member of each pair of contradictions cancels out the other member. To assert that the Queen is both embroidering and not embroidering, both snoring and not snoring—to both affirm and deny the same activity of the same person—is to describe the state of impossibility, which is to remove, to erase, the very person of whom the impossibility has been predicated. In short, the Queen, taking fullest advantage of her royal prerogatives, *is not!* She has penetrated the void, the condition of bliss. The real Queen is not; the real General has gone mad; the real Attorney General has died of fright; the real Bishop, rumor has it, is now represented by his "decapitated head . . . on the handle-bars of a bicycle" (*Bal,* 73).

The leadership of the loyalist cause now rests com-pletely in the hands of the Chief of Police. His strategy is the reverse of that of the rebels. Chantal was to in-spire the rebel troops by moving from a real wound-bandager to a carnival symbol. The would-be Bishop, Judge, and General of the brothel are persuaded by the Chief of Police to ride through the streets masquerading as the real Bishop, Attorney General, and General, thus persuading the people that the loyalist leadership is in-tact. And Irma is to play the Queen. So persuasive are they in their new roles that they are mistaken for the real people whom they represent. Masquerade now takes on the dimension of reality.

Thus three quite ordinary men, who had previously moved from their routine lives into the masquerade of the brothel, now carry back into the real world the roles they have been playing. So titillated are they by a sense of power hitherto unfelt that they would now solidify their positions in the world. The new Bishop re-marks to Irma: ". . . you think we're going to be satis-fied with make-believe to the end of our days?" (*Bal,* 91) A struggle for power, a contention between the Chief of Police and the three men he had unwittingly intoxicated, becomes a central issue. And the ensuing argument draws a nice distinction between the two worlds of the play:

THE BISHOP [*beside himself*]. . . . So long as we were in a room in a brothel, we belonged to our own fantasies. But once having exposed them, having named them, hav-ing proclaimed them, we're now tied up with human beings, tied to you, and forced to go on with this ad-venture according to the laws of visibility.
THE CHIEF OF POLICE. You have no power.
THE BISHOP. No one has power. But you want us to have power over the people. In order for us to have power over them, you must first recognize that we have power over you.
THE CHIEF OF POLICE. Never!

THE BISHOP. Very well. Then we shall go back to our
rooms and there continue the quest of an absolute dignity. We ought never to have left them. For we were
content there, and it was you who came and dragged us
away. For ours was a happy state. And absolutely safe.
In peace, in comfort, behind shutters, behind padded
curtains, protected by a police force that protects broth-
els, we were able to be a general, judge and bishop to the
point of perfection and to the point of rapture! You tore
us brutally from that delicious, enviable, untroubled
state, but we have since tasted other delights, the bitter
delights of action and responsibility. We were judge,
general and bishop in order to be bishop, judge and
general beneath a perfect, total, solitary and sterile appearance. You wanted us to be these dignitaries this evening in order to conspire in a revolution, or rather in an
order, and to round it off, to ground it, as it were. Our
public appearance was already a participation in the
adventure. (Bal, 94–95)

The shuttle movement predominates. Chantal goes
from the sterility of the brothel to the world of real
adventure, then back to the abstract "emblem forever
escaping from her womanliness," and ultimately to the
immobility of death. The three main pretenders move
from city to brothel to city. And wonderfully ironic is
the fact that even Roger, the most rebellious of the
rebels, finally surrenders to the lure of the brothel and
requests that role hitherto unsolicited: the role of Chief
of Police! It is the most "absent" of all roles, symboliz-
ing as it does the most precious of all states—death.
The Envoy has already described its setting: a vast
mausoleum hewn of the most precious materials, to be
placed at the very center of the universe and to provide
the haven of eternal death. The Envoy also promised
within it "a road that will lead, after many and many
a complication, to a room where mirrors will reflect
to infinity—I say to infinity!—the image of the dead
man. To infinity—and for eternity—in the depths of a
vault. . . ." (Bal, 76) Roger enters the mausoleum,
but his bliss is short-lived; the appearance of eternity
must come to an end. Carmen soon reminds him that
his time is up and that he, like all the other brothel visitors, must return to the city. But Roger, who has al-

ready experienced to the full the real world and knows its limitations and insufficiencies, protests: "If the brothel exists and if I've a right to go there, then I've a right to lead the character I've chosen to the very limit of his destiny . . . no, of mine . . . of merging his destiny with mine" (*Bal,* 112). Making *"the gesture of castrating himself"* (*Bal,* 112), Roger symbolizes the attempt to cut himself off from reality and to merge himself with the sterile, dead condition which he seeks. He must, nevertheless, leave, but the Chief of Police can now rejoice that his role has been immortalized—and by his greatest enemy. It is a nice comic interlude when the Chief of Police descends the steps to the mausoleum, affirming that he will there spend an eternity. But, in fact, he is well enough acquainted with the play's philosophical framework to know that appearance is as temporary as reality and that he will soon step out again into the now quieted city.

The Balcony approaches its end. The spectator has been moved to a condescending compassion for its characters, who, with the probable exception of Irma, have found nowhere to lay their heads. There is for them no rest, no satisfaction to be found. Their daily round of activities—what we would call their real life—is unfailingly ungratifying. Their frantic efforts to lose themselves in the appearance of a role which brings with it some solacing sense of power, achievement, or ecstasy unexperienced in real life brings only a fleeting release. The characters are helpless pawns moved by a cosmic force which would seem to delight in withholding any firm ground of rest. The pretenders of *The Balcony*'s world *will* be cut off from their pretensions, as will the Rogers be cut off from their both-feet-on-the-ground immersion in the useful life. The characters must despair of finding any ground of being, in appearance or in reality. But we have been viewing a *play,* an appearance in itself, and we grimly assure ourselves of our superiority to the characters and their circumstances. *We* may have our daydreams, but *we* at least have that measure of control which enables *us* to face the real world and to surmount its obstacles. We will soon leave the theatre, a metaphor of appearance, and return to the solid reality and truth of our own homes.

At this point, however, Genet is ready to spring his trap. We have not been witnessing the imaginary characters of a play. We have been gazing, with an innocence that bred our sense of superiority, into a mirror. As Nathan said to David (II Samuel 12:7), Genet says to each of us: "You are the man." Genet's spokesman is Irma. She alone in the play is the omniscient one, who, with her view-finder and earphone, instruments revealing every sight and sound in her multiroomed establishment, can see all and hear all with the eyes and ears of a god. And if the pretenders and the rebels are our reflections, Irma, so we must infer, is Genet's. He, through her, is the seer who would expose our pathetic self-ignorance. It is Irma-Genet who, just before the curtain, leaves the illusion of the play and addresses us directly: "You must now go home, where everything—you can be quite sure—will be even falser than here" (*Bal,* 115). But for the moment, at least, we find ourselves frozen to our seats.

V

Since the appearance of the first version of *The Balcony,* Genet has published two plays: *The Blacks: A Clown Show,* with a first edition in 1958 and a second in 1960; and *The Screens,* published in 1961. As in *The Maids,* the central characters of these two later plays are outcasts seen in their relationships to the persons who oppress them. But whereas the outcasts of *The Maids* represent an occupational group, those of *The Blacks* and *The Screens* represent whole racial or national groups—Negroes and Algerians, respectively. The two later plays are also philosophies of history, dramatic versions of the decline of the West. In apocalyptic fashion, the spectators are apprised of the approaching death knell of Western civilization, as the white race and the western European nations are seen moving toward their eclipse. In both *The Blacks* and *The Screens* the socio-political overtones are on a grander scale than in any of Genet's earlier plays.

The Blacks, to a greater extent than any other Genet play, pulls the spectator into its fabric. At the end of *The Balcony,* we recall, Irma puts aside her dramatic *persona* and addresses the audience directly. In viewing *The Blacks,* the audience—the white audience at least —is self-consciously aware of itself from the very beginning. In a prefatory note Genet observes that the play was written for a white audience; that, if the audience is black, at least one white person should be invited to attend, should be pointedly welcomed and ushered to a prominent seat, and should, with spotlight thrown on him, be played to by the cast; that, if no white person attends, white masks should be provided for the black spectators; and that, if the spectators refuse, then a white dummy should be used.

There are various devices within the play to increase audience self-consciousness. Quite effective is the fitting of five of the Negro actors with white masks, cut in such a way that black hair and black skins are prominent around the masks' edges. The white audience is thus lifted from the auditorium and placed, symbolically, within the play itself. The setting, too, is predominantly black and white. As the black curtains are drawn, the spectator views a multilayered stage, on the bottom level of which four Negroes and four Negresses are dancing to the music of a Mozart minuet around a catafalque covered with a white cloth. On a higher level is a gallery on which the five white-masked Negroes take their places. And because Whites have always judged and controlled the lives of Blacks, these five actors—representing a queen, her valet, a governor, a judge, a missionary—serve as members of a court, looking down upon and passing judgment on the eight Negroes who maintain their black roles throughout the play. The white-masked players also serve as spectators of the "play" enacted on the lower stage. We thus have another variation of a play-within-a-play. More than this, the white theatre audience is simultaneously watching *The Blacks,* the play as a whole, and, through their identification with the masked actors, being absorbed into their roles and responding to the play-within-the-play. Of all Genet's works, *The Blacks* is most powerful in its effect upon the audience.

The various themes of *The Blacks* will be familiar to a reader or viewer of Genet's earlier plays. There is the vacillation between appearance and reality, played, as we will see, in a number of ways. There is the mirrored reverse image, the interdependence of polar opposites. As Solange and Claire were the "monstrous soul of servantdom" to Madame's elevated soul of majesty, so are the Blacks the monstrous soul of blackness to the masked players', as well as the audience's, elevated soul of whiteness. Whether the Blacks, like Claire and Solange, win a victory and, within the confines of the play, escape their wretchedness is a matter of considerable ambiguity. In *The Blacks* the events that furnish the "plot" on which the themes are played are apparent and/or real deeds of murder.

First, there is the alleged murder whose alleged victim is allegedly at rest in the alleged catafalque. Second, because some of the Blacks are skeptical about the spirit in which that presumed murder was committed, the murderer, Village, re-enacts, in the course of the play, the murder which has taken place before its beginning. Third, we are led to believe, through a series of reports by Newport News, that a real murder has taken place in real life quite outside the confines of the play. Finally, all the members of the Court, representing the white audience, meet their deaths on stage. Genet is supremely obsessed by the concept of death.

As the play begins and the players are introduced by Archibald, we are told that Village has accomplished the rape-murder of a white woman. The principal question, and one that recalls the murderous deeds of Green Eyes and Lefranc in *Deathwatch,* is whether Village committed the murder from the right motivation and in the right spirit. Was his deed executed in a way that would do full justice to the very soul of blackness? For, as Archibald points out, the color *black* "must be earned" (*Bl,* 17). Village's main detractor is Snow, a Negress who caustically questions the purity of spirit in which he acted. "There was a touch of desire in your hatred of her," she venomously accuses, "which means a touch of love. But . . . we, the negro women, we had only our wrath and rage." (*Bl,* 17) And as Village continues to protest the fullness of his guilt—or innocence!—Snow returns more graphically to her accusation:

If I were sure that Village bumped the woman off in order to heighten the fact that he's a scarred, smelly, thick-lipped, snub-nosed Negro, an eater and guzzler of Whites and all other colors . . . if I were sure he killed her in order to merge with the night . . . But I know he loved her. (*Bl,* 27–28)

Accordingly, it becomes necessary for Village to re-enact the murder that it may be determined if he epitomized in its fulfillment the color *black.* The re-enactment is necessitated by still another demand. A black deed must evoke not only the joyous satisfaction of the Blacks but also the condemnation of the Whites. Otherwise it would not exemplify the soul of blackness. And so the Judge, speaking in behalf of a Court eager for a replaying of the deed, urges the players on: "You promised us a re-enactment of the crime so as to deserve your condemnation" (*Bl,* 25). And Archibald, directing his players in their roles, reminds them of the desired goal: "Bear one thing in mind: we must deserve their reprobation and get them to deliver the judgment that will condemn us" (*Bl,* 30).

Thus *The Blacks,* in one of its aspects, presents a race passionately intent upon living up to the expectations of their role. They must follow the example of Green Eyes (and Eliot's Archbishop Thomas à Becket!) by doing the right deed for the right reason and in the right spirit. They must live up to the definition of blackness, as Archibald so eloquently informs them just before the eagerly awaited re-enactment:

I order you to be black to your very veins. Pump black
blood through them. Let Africa circulate in them. Let
Negroes negrify themselves. Let them persist to the point
of madness in what they're condemned to be, in their
ebony, in their odor, in their yellow eyes, in their cannibal
tastes. . . . Negroes, if they change toward us, let it not
be out of indulgence, but terror. (*Bl*, 52)

A large portion of *The Blacks* is devoted, in comic
tone, to the re-enactment of the alleged crime. But beyond this, and in more serious tone, there are references
to a murder completely outside the framework of the
play, a murder which impinges directly on the real lives
of those who are playing roles within the play. Newport
News, who makes many exits and entrances, gives the
actors and the audience a running account of this crime,
as well as of the trial and execution which ensue. The
whole episode is of keen interest to all the players, not
as actors but as real persons who live out their dispossessed lives in a society which despises them. In this
way, Genet plays the appearance, which is always the
mark of drama, off against the reality, that of the world
outside the theatre. Furthermore, of supreme irony is
the fact that the very purpose of the play itself is to
divert the white audience from witnessing the real inci-
dent (the real murder) which, with others of its kind,
will undermine and overthrow their supremacy. As
Newport News reports on the murder, he makes clear
the Black strategy: "Our aim is not only to corrode and
dissolve the idea they'd like us to have of them, we
must also fight them in their actual persons in their
flesh and blood. As for you [he is addressing the play-
ers], you were present only for display. . . ." And the
man who played the valet, now unmasked, replies: "We
know. Thanks to us, they've [the white audience] sensed
nothing of what's going on elsewhere." (*Bl*, 112) The
soul of blackness, it would seem, is changing. Earlier
in the play the Blacks appeared to be seeking to live up
to the concept of blackness as defined by the Whites,
to respond to situations in accordance with the expectations of the Whites. But now the Blacks have moved

toward a greater initiative, becoming more the de-
terminers of their actions.

If Genet is affirming that Black freedom will issue not
from the black man's willing surrender to a role assigned him by forces outside himself and beyond his
control but from his setting of his own course, then the
rules of the game of *The Blacks* differ from those of
Deathwatch. Green Eyes's victory was his ultimately
gracious acceptance of a call over which he had no
control, a call which he initially resisted but to which
he finally surrendered enthusiastically; and Lefranc's
defeat lay in his defiance of his assigned role. But in
The Blacks Genet moves from the metaphysics of
Deathwatch to a different metaphysics and to a philosophy of history, a kind of apocalyptic prediction which
celebrates the virility of the black man and the debility
of the white. The grandeur and glory of Western civilization, represented by the audience and the masked
Court which mimics the audience, and compounded of
"angel of the flaming sword, virgins of the Parthenon,
stained-glass of Chartres, Lord Byron, Chopin, French
cooking, the Unknown Soldier, Tyrolean songs, Aris-
totelian principles, heroic couplets, poppies, sunflowers,
a touch of coquetry, vicarage gardens" (*Bl,* 47), has
seen its day. It will in time come to be no match for
"Africa with the bulging chest and oblong thigh," for
the Africa "wrought of iron, in the fire, Africa of the
millions of royal slaves, deported Africa, drifting continent" (*Bl,* 77). In other words, Africa will reject the
role to which it has been assigned.

The last quarter of the play in surrealistic fashion
acts out a dramatic version of the decline of the West.
The members of the Court, for some minutes offstage,
now return; they have become quite drunk in an effort
to achieve valor but remain in fact dissolved in terror.
And they represent, of course, all of the authority
which has habitually been White. They are no ordinary
people but rather a monarch, a governor who is also
military leader, a judge, and an ecclesiastic. They are
imaginatively wafted back into a dark jungle whose

sounds are terrifying and whose flowers are poisonous. They seek to keep their courage up not only by drink but also by reminding themselves of their condescendingly having borne the white man's burden. They tremblingly set up their court of justice which is to try the perpetrator of the catafalque murder. But when Newport News moves the cloth covering the catafalque, they note with further horror that there is no catafalque and consequently no corpse. The horror of the Whites springs not from the fact that they would delight in a real murder of one of their own. It is, rather, that they must have at the very least an appearance of murder in order to play out their role. In *The Balcony* the would-be Bishop owed his role to a make-believe penitent, and the would-be Judge to a make-believe thief. In *The Blacks,* the Judge of the Court, aghast that no murder has been committed, sees the evaporation of his role. "But no corpse at all," he exclaims to the Negroes, "why that could kill us." And turning to Archibald, he asks, "Do you want to be the death of us?" (*Bl,* 99)

It is a good question, one which, in Genet's scheme, polar opposites must always ask each other. A person who murders his opposite simultaneously commits suicide, for each member of an antipodal pair—maid and Madame, penitent and Bishop, Black and White—depends on his reverse and complementary image for the particular quality of his own life. And out of this concept of relationships grows a complexity typical of Genet. The possessed, to maintain a rationale for judging and condemning the dispossessed, must be able to charge them with the crime of murder, preferably an apparent one; and the dispossessed, to expunge their servile status, must murder (or appear to murder) the possessed. On the other hand, the possessed, though feeling compelled to visit every indignity upon the dispossessed, must stop short of murder, real or apparent, for to murder the dispossessed would deprive the possessed of possession. In a long dialogue between the Negress Felicity and the "white" Queen, this last point is well made. The Queen orders all the Negroes put to

the sword, whereupon Felicity points out the foolishness
of such a command: "You fool, just imagine how flat
you'd be without that shade to set you off in high relief"
(*Bl,* 104). The Queen is, in any case, powerless, for, as
Felicity then asserts, the power structure is changing,
and black will soon have to itself all the former attributes of white:

But everything is changing. Whatever is gentle and kind
and good and tender will be black. Milk will be black,
sugar, rice, the sky, doves, hope, will be black. So will the
opera to which we shall go, blacks that we are, in black
Rolls Royces to hail black kings, to hear brass bands beneath chandeliers of black crystal . . . (*Bl,* 106)

Within the play—or, rather, within the play-within-
the-play—the change has begun. The Court is at the
mercy of the Blacks. And the Blacks both do and do
not want the death of the Court. They *do* want it as a
manifestation of their power; they do *not* want it because their newly won power depends on the Court's
life. Thus Archibald both begs the Governor not to
die and yet sets off the cap which "kills" him. The
Judge is also shot. The Missionary, who has derided and
acted brutally toward the black sorcerers, is, with a fine
poetic justice, transformed by sorcery into a cow and
ordered to the slaughterhouse. The Valet dies in a
paroxysm of fear. Only the Queen now remains, knowing through the accumulated years of her white wisdom
that the dispossessed must *both* die *and* stay alive in
order to be killed: "I too shall descend to Hell. I shall
take with me my flock of corpses that you keep killing
so that they may stay alive and that you keep alive in
order to kill." (*Bl,* 123) Her dying confession is memo-
rable: "And now, I die—I must confess—choked by
my desire for a Big Black Buck. Black nakedness, thou
hast conquered me." (*Bl,* 124)

Yet every Genetian victory bears within itself the
seeds of its own defeat. The Blacks, at the height of the
power and majesty which would now seem to be theirs,
can sustain themselves only through the nourishment
which their reverse image provides. Black is now White,

and White Black. But the time will come when the
Blacks too will have exhausted themselves, when there
will be another play, entitled *The Whites: A Clown
Show*. The audience will be black; the players will be
white, with a black-masked Court, whose blond hair
and white skins will edge their masks. There will be an
apparent black corpse in an apparent catafalque covered
in black. It is this distant time and this new play that
the Queen of *The Blacks,* Hell-bound, prophesies:
"We're going, we're going, but keep in mind that we
shall lie torpid in the earth like larvae or moles, and if
some day . . . ten thousand years hence" (*Bl,* 126). In
short, if Black soon does become White, White will in
some distant day become Black. The shuttle which
moved between appearance and reality in *The Balcony*
also operates in *The Blacks,* its terminals marking there
the conditions of possession and dispossession.

But the last word has not yet been spoken of *The
Blacks*. The action of the play-within-the-play, the presentation of Black victory, is not a present fact. It is
revelatory only of what is to come. As the white-masked
Queen assembles her Court for the journey to Hell,
Archibald summons us back to the play itself. The
masks are removed, and Archibald addresses the unmasked black faces, making clear that their time of triumph has not yet come and that, until it does, the
Blacks will continue to *play,* to live up to White expectation:

The time has not yet come for presenting dramas about
noble matters. But perhaps they suspect what lies behind
this architecture of emptiness and words. We are what they
want us to be. We shall therefore be it to the very end,
absurdly. Put your masks on again before leaving. Have
them escorted to Hell. (*Bl,* 126)

As the play moves now to its end, the entire cast sur-
rounds a white-covered catafalque, and the minuet
measures from Mozart's *Don Giovanni* are sounded.
The white audience, or the white-masked black audience, or the white dummy, is dismissed. On the rather
likely assumption that it is a preponderantly white audi-

ence which will now make its way out into the night,
they may recall, uneasily, the real crime reported by
Newport News. The make-believe theatre recorded
only the appearance—or the appearance of an appearance—of a Black crime. But each white spectator may
well wonder if his life—or death—story may be woven
into the fabric of the next production of *The Blacks*.

VI

The Screens, Genet's most recent play (1961), runs
to approximately two hundred pages, contains seventeen
scenes, and presents almost one hundred characters. It
is of more epic than dramatic scope, a panoramic spec-
tacle whose structure is more episodic than tightly knit.
A successful full-length production of the play is difficult to imagine, as is a satisfying first reading; and for
a person unfamiliar with Genet's earlier plays, it is
questionable if an understanding of *The Screens* will
come even with several readings. The play calls, at
least, for prior knowledge of Genet and for patient persistence.

The Screens is not only the longest, loosest, most
prodigally cast, and most difficult of Genet's works. It
is also, with its multiplicity of screens and tiers, the
most abundantly set: the last scene, divided into nine
parts, is played on four levels, each with its appropriate
screens. It is also the most witty and most obscene of
the plays. The dialogue is, in places, richly comic. The
dialogue and situation are in other places revolting, certainly abrasive to most sensibilities, even sophisticated
ones. *The Screens* is, thematically, perhaps the most
generous of the plays. All of the now familiar themes
are played again. Is the total medley a potpourri, or is
there, beneath the at least initially apparent episodicity,
some tie that binds the whole?

If there is a unifying force, it is the remarkable Saïd,
whose unheroic life-and-death story spans the seventeen
scenes and two hundred pages. It is true that he does
not appear in eight of the scenes, but in seven of these

eight he is mentioned, and from them we learn something of his character and of the response he evokes from others. And even in the one scene where he is not mentioned—Scene Two, the village brothel—a sensitive reader may detect his aura, for to his wife Leila, whose features embody the world's ugliness, he has not been unfailingly faithful. Saïd is one of literature's more eminent unheroes, a man whose filial and marital devotion falls short of perfection and whose thievery and traitorousness are prominent. Not merely an outcast from society, or an outcast among outcasts, Saïd is the soul of outcastness. Unlike Lefranc, Saïd is more than happy to be alone.

That Saïd delights in his role, that he self-consciously and self-pityingly savors his misery, is evident from the very beginning. Early on the morning of his marriage day, he is fatiguingly walking the long way to the wedding. When his mother, accompanying him, suggests that he rest on a nearby rock pile, his answer characterizes well his response to life's pleasures: "No. The stones are too soft for my ass. I want everything to make me feel blue." (S, 12) It is not only his poverty, and consequently poor bargaining position, that has led him to settle for the hand of the ugliest woman within his geographical region: it is also his love of misery. So well does he play his life's role that he is, later in the play, received in the kingdom of the dead—or, more accurately, of the "dead alive" (S, 193)—as a conquering unhero. It is around Saïd's epic journey that the unity of the play must be sought.

We have already suggested that *The Screens* is, thematically, typical of Genet, and abundantly so. It expresses Genet's philosophy of history, though less explicitly and persistently than does *The Blacks*. The Court is replaced by white colonists, or caricatures of them, exemplified by Sir Harold and Mr. Blankensee. In larger terms, the Algerian Arabs are the oppressed and the French the oppressors. But the western Europeans of the play have obviously had their day and are now in a state of decline before the increasing strength, daring, and treachery of the far-flung Arabs. In the last scene, various representatives of France's past glory, whose costumes of the 1840's symbolize a period of colonial power, have been reduced to rags (*decorative* rags, of course). As they discourse nostalgically on the days beyond recall, the Missionary, this time a white one without a mask, ruminates in splendid rationalization on the Algerian revolt: "What *can* be said with a certain amount of justice is that we were a pretext for their revolting. If not for us, if not—let's not be afraid to say so—for our cruelty and injustice, they'd have gone under. In all honesty, I think we're the instruments of God. Of ours and theirs." (*S,* 179) But the oppressors' cruelty and injustice have not been extreme enough and, it might be added, probably neither so imaginative nor so complete as that now in the process of being visited upon them by those whom they formerly oppressed.

Besides Genet's philosophy of history, other themes common to the whole of his dramatic corpus are found in *The Screens.* The near indistinguishability between appearance and reality is mirrored in the settings themselves. To this end many devices are used, particularly in the multiplicity of props designed to suggest the omnipresence of illusion. Various objects are painted on the shifting screens, and near each screen is a real object to remind the spectators that appearance and reality, non-being and being, are two realms of their daily encounters. The characters use make-up, masks, false noses, false chins. There is one brief sequence in Scene Nine where Leila, having stolen a real clock, can produce the real clock only by drawing it on a screen; asked by her mother-in-law whether the drawing is made of real or imitation marble, she proudly replies that it is imitation. Shortly thereafter the clock chimes. The confusion of reality and appearance goes beyond the settings. As we move toward the end of the play, the merging of life and death—again, of being and non-being—is so perfect that Saïd, finding himself unable to determine if he is dead or alive, can conclude only that he must be "dead alive."

Of great prominence in *The Screens* is the reverse mirror image, stressing the complementary nature and interdependence of opposites. It is important not only that the Algerians try to be all of the things the French are not or do not wish to be but also that the Algerians pursue a standard of values antithetical to that of their oppressors. It thus becomes necessary for the Arabs to act out a stereotyped role, most of the qualities of which are subsumed within the term *outcast*. It is necessary that Saïd be distinguished for his poverty and Leila for her ugliness, and that the Mother be so despised that she is refused even the privilege of mourning the dead. It is necessary that thievery be a trait common to *all* Arabs, a fact enabling the colonist Sir Harold to make a subtle distinction: "If a Frenchman robs me, that Frenchman's a thief, but if an Arab robs me, he hasn't changed. He's an Arab who has robbed me, and nothing more." (*S,* 75) Even the Arab's chickens are thieves, and, as Leila discerningly observes, "the black one, she's more depraved than the others. If only she could teach the white chickens how to go about it!" (*S,* 37)

It is Kadidja, an energetic woman of about sixty years, who is most vocal in urging her people to make the most of their roles and to live up to every expectation. We are reminded of *The Blacks* when we hear her invoke evil to impregnate her people (*S,* 97). And we sit aghast at the immediately successful results of her plea: the demonic prayer is no sooner uttered than answered, as a series of Arabs come on stage to proclaim their most recent achievements. The exploits include the disemboweling of three of their oppressors' cows—with calf—and the disemboweling of one policeman, the plucking out of a heart, the gouging out of blue eyes, the cutting off of hands and feet, the raping of a girl, and a few more minor peccadilloes. Kadidja elatedly cheers them on: "And don't be ashamed, my sons! Merit the world's contempt. Slit throats, my sons."

(*S*, 101) Leila is of much the same persuasion as, out of the pit of her ugliness, she addresses Saïd:

I want you to plunge into irrevocable grief. I want you—it's my ugliness, earned minute by minute, that speaks—to be without hope. I want you to choose evil and always evil. I want you to know only hatred and never love. I want you —it's my ugliness, earned second by second, that speaks— to refuse the brilliance of darkness, the softness of flint, and the honey of thistles. (*S*, 108–109)

Although Saïd is not one always to listen attentively to his wife or to heed her wishes, his plunging into grief and choosing evil are carried out with a sure hand. He is offensive even to his own kind and steals even from a fellow worker. As we see from the early part of Scene Ten, he is an outcast even among outcasts, is ostracized even by the Arabs who, with him, are working for Sir Harold. No one else could furnish so complementary and complimentary a reverse image to and for the Europeans who tyrannize over Algeria. One of the "elevated" characters, in complete fidelity to Genet doctrine, remarks of the Arabs in general: "The fact is that the dirtier they are the cleaner I am. They take upon themselves all the lice of the world." (*S*, 180)

The Screens is permeated also with the movement toward the abstraction from reality, toward the receding image of an image of an image, toward that Absence which is the Royal prerogative. Time itself is defined as that which "filters the inessential" (*S*, 144), a description which encapsules so perfectly one of the main tenets of Genet's metaphysics. Examples of this filtering movement are many. For Leila, Saïd is reduced to an empty pair of trousers, better built than their customary occupant! Sir Harold is filtered to the abstraction which best epitomizes him: a pigskin glove. One of the Arabs becomes in death what was most essential to his life: a trembling. In an episode whose coarseness matches its philosophical teaching, the Sergeant empties himself and becomes "Emptiness" (*S*, 170). Si Slimane, one of the leaders of the revolt, is transformed into a mouth. The prostitute Warda loses the qualities which make her a creature of flesh and blood and dissolves into the gesture which she has so assiduously cultivated; she speaks proudly of her most repulsive habit: "A real whore should be able to attract by what she's reduced herself to being. I worked for years at my tooth cleaning with a hatpin. My style!" (*S,* 21) Later, as she feels herself slipping back again into a real existence, she senses failure: "I, Warda, who was to fade away and leave in my place only a perfect whore, a simple skeleton draped in gilded gowns, here am I becoming Warda again at top speed" (*S,* 131). The goal is to move from being a whore to becoming the soul of whoredom, a condition evolving from the filtering of the inessential and comprising a "wiggle without . . . [the] rump" (*S,* 173), or, to borrow a phrase from another context, "a skeleton of precise gestures" (*S,* 127)—in short, a whore without the customary, and generally cherished, appurtenances of flesh and blood! The women who later prepare the corpse of Warda pay her an ultimate and hard-won tribute by placing between her immobile, though not yet invisible, teeth *"seven very long hatpins"* (*S,* 168).

In the same vein is Si Slimane's remarkable accomplishment, which challenges that of *The Balcony*'s Queen; thus he is described: "On his horse, in sixteen villages at the same time. A Kabyl from Saada told me that he appeared on his horse in sixteen villages at the same time, but that in actual fact he was resting in the shade, at the side of a road." (*S,* 20) To be every place is to be no place, for being at any one place cancels out the possibility of being at any other. The disappearance is complete. And as Saïd's mother is making her way from the place of life to the no place of the abode of death, it is Si Slimane who can best answer the question of her whereabouts: "Nowhere. But not yet quite nowhere. She'll be there shortly, when she's with us." (*S,* 146)

It is a marked tribute to the sensitive discernment of the dead that they know a good man when they see him. As early as Scene Fifteen, with the dead Arab woman

Ommu's "Blessed be Saïd!" (*S*, 133), the true stature
of the play's unhero is recognized. Moreover, both his
wife and his mother gain greater renown because of
their relationship to him. Leila, forced to admit that
other women exceed her "in rattiness," sees as her own
distinction the fact that she is "the wife of a traitor"
and consequently "deserves consideration and an em-
press's couch" (*S*, 156). Saïd's mother also basks in
his reflected glory and is brought a beautiful armchair
by Kadidja, who offers it to her graciously: "Try it. . . .
You have to sit in comfort. And in state. It was from
your belly that Saïd came, your ass is entitled to velvet."
(*S*, 174)

Finally, the long-awaited "prodigal son" (*S*, 188)
arrives, to the joy of the dead Arabs—who recognize
that he, as well as Leila, has taught them how they must
lose themselves—and to the dismay of the dead Missionary, who recognizes that the oppressed will be organized and bound together more firmly than ever in
death. To Saïd and his family Ommu pays the most
perceptive and extravagant tribute:

The knowledge that his holy family was sinking into muck
gave us all goose flesh. . . . And even now, whatever skin
and bone I still have has goose flesh. . . . The lords of
yesterday will tell the lords of today that nothing must be
protected so much as a little heap of garbage. . . . Let
no one ever throw out all her sweepings. . . . (*S*, 191)

This being so, there remains for the Arabs only the final,
happy charge of "embalming . . . [Saïd's] sordidness"
(*S*, 192), of accomplishing the last abstraction.

But Saïd, to his credit and to the at least initial cha-
grin of his fellows in oppression, remains faithful to his
consistent principle of cooperation with no one. He is
infuriated that Ommu will have him both dead, as a
member of this nether kingdom, and alive, as the vital
essence of sordidness. He obscenely dismisses Ommu
and all the other dead and is about to depart in spite of
Ommu's protesting plea that it is "through him that . . .
[the dead Arabs] breathe" (*S*, 197). As one of the
French soldiers tries to stop him in the hope that they

may "wipe the slate clean and start all over" (*S*, 198),
Ommu, now recognizing that there is a condition to be
preferred to life or death, urges him to go. And at his
holy mother's insistence that he accommodate himself
to no one, Saïd, much to the approval of the emptied
Sergeant, leaves to the salute of five shots from five
French revolvers. His victory is complete: he has bowed
to no one.

VII

It is with the reading of *The Screens,* following upon
the reading of the four earlier plays, that the eager in-
terpreter of Genet's drama penetrates to the innermost
recess, the unholy of unholies, the unark of the un-
tabernacle, of the author's mind. There is but one ultimate theme in Genet, the journey toward which is made
slowly and onerously over the tortuous paths of penulti-
mate themes. It is a theme which was touched upon in
Solange's curtain speech in *The Maids* and carried to its
logical conclusion in the Bishop's first speech, as well
as in the Envoy's remarks about the Queen, in *The
Balcony*. It is the Royal prerogative of Absence, exemplified by the Queen—who simply was not—but not really
demonstrated in full until the drama of the life, death,
and resurrection into Nothingness of Saïd.

Saïd has achieved the ultimate goal: he has accomplished the great escape. The ultimate Genetian goal is
the ecstasy (unfelt, of course!) of Nothingness. And
this goal is the logical conclusion of each of the basic
themes which are the stuff of Genet's drama. The theme
of the interrelatedness of reality and appearance is re-
solved as Saïd frees himself from all reality and moves
beyond even the last flickering appearance of appearance on to Nothingness, an uncondition beyond death.
The theme of the reverse mirror image is, in *The
Screens,* finally completed, for Nothingness is the perfect polar opposite of the whole created world so de-
tested by the Genet protagonist. As the Bible's first
chapter proclaims a creation *ex nihilo* and goes on to
speak of God's plenitudinous, Genet's last chapter pro-

claims the reverse process *ad nihilum,* the demonic Absence. Saïd has carried to perfection the role of the great Adversary. And the theme of distillation, abstraction, disembodiment, the filtering of the inessential, culminates in Absence, Nothingness. The whole of Genet's drama is the thinking out and working through to the climactic statement of *The Screens,* and each of Genet's protagonists is a part of the movement toward the perfect unhero Saïd. Genet sets, for his five plays, various texts, but perhaps all of them are simply variations on one basic text, that of the homily delivered on the unholiest day of his demonic calendar: "Blessed be un-Saïd, for he shall inherit Nothingness and there undwell."

The Glory and the Power

I

To ATTEMPT to comment in detail on the Genet of Sartre's *magnum opus,* or on the Genet chosen by Genet for presentation to the world, is a fascinating temptation. Yielded to, it would result in dispersal in a variety of directions, most of them alien to the intent of this chapter. That intent is an examination of Genet's development on his way to his aesthetic destination. The intent is simply defined, but the examination is unusually difficult, because of the tremendous shadow Genet casts on the literary scene through the magic lantern of publicity, licit and illicit. The task is made even more difficult by the almost inextricable snarl created by the tangling of the various strands of Genet's personality, character, public life, and what he chooses to tell us of his private life, with the thread of his published work. Even here, there is the relevant but separate thread of the autobiographical cast of his work outside the plays—the true or fictive accounts of his experiences given in *Our Lady of the Flowers* or *Thief's Journal,* for example. In order to discuss Genet's development and his success or failure in the plays, we must somehow detach this major section of his work from the Genet aura, attempting to eye all his work with the gaze we might accord an anonymous manuscript.

In the star-system of Hollywood, certain individuals become less actors than personalities, constant in their well-known quirks and foibles, draped and served by a succession of roles which never for a moment seem more or less than roles. In the case of Genet's work, there is the constant danger of watching, not the play, but the hovering image of the author, Genet, that Permanent Personality, with its notorious earmarks and its familiar history—the danger of listening, not to the dialogue, but to the echoes of publicity. It is difficult not to be distracted by our laboriously supplied knowledge of Genet, the reformatory of his childhood, his career as thief, his homosexuality, his "betrayals," his abject and desolate travels, his convictions, imprisonments, pardon, his gloriously unrepentant faith in his path, all of which chatter at us like importunate stations on some congested radio from which we try to trace the line of his communication. It is not a question of opting for one or the other method of analysis—that which considers the work *in vacuo* or that which attempts to place it in biographical and literary perspective. Here the interference is from circumstances, situations, and assertions pushed to such a bizarre insistence that unless some attempt is made to disentangle asseveration from accomplishment, scale will be completely thrown off.

Fortunately, Genet here occupies us as playwright, his novels impinging on consideration only as they lead us to, or clarify for us, Genet's intention as dramatist. This is indeed fortunate, for the novels are part of one long, not too varied, and pitilessly aggressive case history. In his plays, however, Genet's gifts have been directed and disciplined, at once curbed and enhanced, so that the best of his work, in its true testing-ground, is here visible. With the plays as our center of consideration, what are Genet's often commanding and sometimes valid holds on us? Why do we care? Is there a facet of truth so surely touched that we must respond, whether we will or not? Is he doing what he tells us he is doing? And is the result some fresh insight, through his art, into aesthetic truth? For obviously it is unfair to demand of Genet truth as we see it—to demand confirmation of our ideas, our predispositions, our assumptions. Does he convey *his* truth? And if so, what is it?

What does he tell us he is doing? No sooner are we involved in this first and crucial question, than we realize we must use any assertion by Genet as an ornament, rather than as a durable or responsible object in our progress; we may admire it, flourish it, but never for an instant may we depend on it as a staff. For, Genet tells us, he is a habitual liar; and his abilities as liar are involved in the richness of texture he often produces, in his color and nuances and shifts of emphasis, so that they enable him, called to account for self-contradiction and dizzy shifts in direction, to say with a child's triumph: "But I *told* you I was a liar." In other words: "You knew the rules of the game; lying was one of them; and now your indignation is really at your own stupidity in getting caught." But whatever the merits of the "I admit it . . ." school of honesty, the admission that truth to an aesthetic vision may be subverted at any time, does not remove our difficulty. Are we then, we ask ourselves, being heavy-handed, nailing the body of imagination on the Procrustes bed of veracity? Is this work a true fairy tale, in which it is perfectly legitimate that the stump be really an ogre and the hind an enchanted prince? Well, yes and no, says Genet. It is, and it isn't. It is a fairy tale; but you must not limit it to that. It is also a sacred play, and as such is meant to have its own majestic and pitiless logic—except, of course, when an impasse results, in which case it is a fairy tale once more, until the block in the mind is dissolved. Then it is sacred again, and its conclusions binding.

There are three specific stages in Genet's progress toward the Nothingness which he hopes will be the denouement of his search. What he is doing, he tells us at first, is defending himself by creating a system of values to which he can conform and in the practice of which he may, indeed, excel, inasmuch as we have precipitately closed to him that system to which the allegiance of the Other, the Just Man, has been given.

Because Genet feels that he cannot escape the category to which fate has consigned him, he will, like Green Eyes, dominate it; like Snowball, he will be carried by his chains. Sartre points out: "In limiting himself to willing proudly that which is, in transforming an actual situation ('I'm excluded from the group') into an ethical imperative ('Therefore, I must take the initiative of withdrawing'), the untouchable is playing the game of the privileged class. . . . A passage in *Funeral Rites* will help us to understand. Pierrot has inadvertently put a maggot into his mouth: 'He found himself caught between fainting with nausea and dominating his situation by willing it. He willed it. He made his tongue and palate artfully and patiently feel the loathsome contact. This act of willing was his first poetic attitude governed by pride.' "[1]

Genet writes always under the eye of the Other, that imaginary personification of the entrenched power of society, that Normal and Secure Man he posits as the figure which has consigned him to darkness. As we have seen, the first stage of his progress is that of self-protection.

The second stage, far more ambitious, but still strongly conditioned by self-defense, is that in which he links his system to the system of the Other, in which occurs the revelation that the Other needs the Outcast in order to be himself. Solange cries to Claire, of Madame: "Didn't you see how she sparkled? How disgustingly happy she was? *Her* joy feeds on *our* shame. Her carnation is the red of our shame. Her dress. . . . It's the red of our shame" (*M,* 80–81). And Village says to Virtue: ". . . you and I—were moving along the edges of the world, out of bounds. We were the shadow, or the dark interior, of luminous creatures." (*Bl,* 36) This stage, more fully relevant to *The Maids,* carries over clearly into the more complex relationships of *The Blacks.*

[1] Jean-Paul Sartre, *Saint Genet: Actor and Martyr,* tr. Bernard Frechtman (New York: a Mentor Book, 1964), pp. 66–67.

The third stage is that of the direct accusation, as well as of the bid for power. At the third stage, Genet is ready to reveal to us that the two faces—of the Other and the Outcast—are one, that what we watch as we meet the glance of the monster which Genet has created for our contemplation is not the gaze of Genet but our own terrible eyes in the mirror held up to us by his scarred hand. And we shall find that a moment later we are looking straight into the non-gaze of Nothing.

Why do we care, as we follow this progress? We are too constantly harangued for our lapses and crimes lightly to lend an ear to new strictures. It takes more than one more analyst, one more evangelist, one more adjurer, to make us listen. Relatively few people have read Genet's books; a fairly large number have seen his plays. But the shadow his name throws across the literary scene is greater than can be explained by the number to whom his written words have directly spoken. There is more, even, than can be explained by the *succès de scandale* of his criminal record, his publicized attitudes, his imprisonments, and his pardon on the eve of a life sentence, spectacular stuff though this be. There is more than can be explained by six hundred sixty-nine pages of Jean-Paul Sartre—without, in Alice's words, "conversation or pictures." That gargantuan exercise in brilliant ingenuity accounts for much—but far from all. Even Sartre's genius had to have something on which to work, something at the core, alive for the most skeptical reader. There is one thing, in addition to the shifting facets of his own talent, which Genet has had to his advantage, and it is a factor of enormous importance in the impact of his work. That fact is the collective conscience of his readers.

Genet has managed brilliantly to involve this conscience at each of the three stages—that of self-defense, that of the interrelationship between Outcast and Other, and last and most importantly, that of the final stage of naked accusation.

The loathing of, and shrinking from, hypocrisy, among intellectuals of the latter half of the twentieth century is the very atmosphere in which breath is drawn. The feeling is widespread that hypocrisy, conscious or unconscious, more than any other single defect has brought our century to the terrifying state in which most men of intelligence and good will believe we live. Whether it was the pitiful euphuisms of forty years ago mouthed to the graduates of military academies while the face of obscene and no-holds-barred war leered over them on the platform; or the sanctities of womanhood and race purity extolled by states which numbered among their dispossessed tens of thousands of illegitimate mulattoes; or close to two thousand years of lip service to Christianity still echoing as the mushroom sprang up on testing sites—everywhere one looked, the gap between what people claimed to believe and the practical beliefs on which they actually acted glared up from the abyss of disillusion into which we peered.

The belated revulsion was enormous. Religion, family relationships, the nature of freedom, private property, heterosexuality—the tacit assumptions about all these things were questioned. Above all, writers and artists everywhere began to examine the mask of reality and what lay behind it. What was human love—sexually, in friendship, in society? Does it even exist? Marcel Proust had already asked. How does the human imagination really function, mentally, and in its uses of language? James Joyce had asked. What is the significance of habit, and what is its power for distortion? asked Joyce and Proust and Beckett all together. Later these questions occupied the larger reading public. Some readers were seized by a tremendous unsureness, deep and varied, and this was especially so in the case of the noncreative, intelligent, diligent, and humble backbone of readers capable of disciplined thought. About the only thing of which the majority of these readers remained firmly convinced was that almost everything, on examination, proved to be a swindle—almost everything claiming to be otherwise, that is. With wider and prompter access to the miseries of the world, with millions of persons shaken by the loss of any sustaining belief, and with others, who clung to earlier assumptions, constantly urged to find substitutes for values treated as moribund, a large section of the intelligent reading public came up with one clear idea: that since humanity seemed to have been made a mockery of by so many professors of virtue, charity, high motives, and exalted principles, and since—worst of all—men as sensible and wary as they themselves had been taken in by others and (horrors of horrors) by their own smugness and obtuseness, then the safest, most honest reflex must be that of "guilty as charged." Whatever they were accused of—brutality, greed, belligerence, frigidity, sadism, self-righteousness—the chances were that it was true, and the quickest and surest way to avoid the sin of hypocrisy was to admit all. "Mon semblable! Mon frère!" they cried; but no one should call them "Hypocrite lecteur!" Genet's disinclination toward the conscienceless is well-founded. He realized clearly that in writing for a cynic, his power would be drastically reduced.

The scramble to escape this most repellent of all categories, that of hypocrite, and the gnawing sense that in the case of whatever crime, sin, or lapse has been committed, we are probably guilty, provided an enormously fecund ground for the accusatory artist. In our haste to disavow the self-satisfaction which had rendered us ludicrous and the blindness to our own recesses which had made us vulnerable, we became suspicious of any action or attitude which superficially seemed noble, generous, disinterested, full of the passion of charity; we examined ourselves for the stain of the hidden motive. But we went further. We developed a skepticism not only toward the appearance of our own virtue but also toward the appearance of virtue in others; too often it was only a name for some form of weakness, self-interest, or mental, spiritual, or material ambition. We were determined to purge not only ourselves but also our enemies and friends, of hypocrisy. If there were no God postulating such virtues, and their similitude in other human beings was merely decep-

tion or self-deception covering the appetites essential
for survival, then it was a short step to the world of
Genet—that world which starts as the fantasy of an outcast and ends as the pitiless regime of the all-seeing
leader.

Accompanied by their sense of guilt, Genet's readers
follow him stage by stage: first, the stage of the vivid
re-creation of the world of the rejected, that synthetic
world re-created to the pattern imposed on the Outcast,
in which the Outcast will learn to accept the role assigned
to him by fate acting through society and, in accepting
and willing it, will regain his domination of destiny; second, the stage in which the Other is implicated, owing his
luminous existence to that dark shadow against which he
shines; and the third and final stage, in which the Outcast, outcast no longer, says to the Other (now Other
no longer): "You are not my prime cause, nor the
luminance which shines because of my shadow; you *are*
me, under another name. Under all appearances there
is only one reality, and it is that which is to be found
under the mask, behind the screen, something smaller
and more powerful than the atom: in fact, Nothing."
Nothing—presided over by Genet, the only prophet,
priest, and president who can at once comprehend and
enforce its laws.

II

Has Genet been able to demonstrate through the body
of his work and in particular through its most successful examples, his plays, an aesthetic truth, no matter
how alien, valid under its own laws? It is obvious that
while Genet is alive, any summing up of the accomplishments of his art remains highly tentative. Whether he
moves forward to the irreparable crime he sometimes
posits for his future, or founders in a tide of critical
admiration, or continues his dazzling, provocative cir-
cles in a state of suspense, or penetrates through to the
far side of his stylized demonic ritual to emerge in an
orthodox position, only the future can tell. For the

present there are the plays—*Deathwatch, The Maids, The Balcony, The Blacks, The Screens*—and the auto-biographical novels which are the jottings of his processes of mind and work. There is something germane to the consideration of these which Genet does not tell us. He tells us certain things—things which continue to fascinate him, which remain relatively stable in the shifting emphasis of his work. He tells us that he will reveal to us the complicated relations between appearance and reality and that he will illuminate the world of the Outcast, that reverse mirror image of our own imagined virtues, that creature we must create in order to assure ourselves of being its opposite, "the shadow, or the dark interior, of luminous creatures." (*Bl,* 36) In the end he tells us that it is we who are the mirror images and that it is the dark interior, the shadow of Nothing, which is real. And it is here, in this last stage of the plays' development, that we are brought face to face with the accusation which is also a bid for power. We become aware of this domination slowly; Genet never speaks of it directly. It is indeed something we might not have expected to hear from him, and it is the key to all else. It is a key not often recognized—indeed it is hard to be sure to what extent Genet himself realizes it consciously. His supreme preoccupation is this: the *power* of Nothing. Power, the fascination of power, its adoration, the means whereby it can be procured, and the manner by which it can be enjoyed, maintained and protected—this is Genet's central concern.

It is power with which Genet is in love; it is power which obsesses him; it is power which he is intent on building and on using; and this once grasped, the virtues and defects of his work stand ranged primarily in their relation to power. Not for nothing are the pages of Genet's novels dominated by the soldier, the pimp, the super-hoodlum, the cop. Obviously this tendency has been exaggerated by, and is intertwined with, Genet's homosexuality and his embittering but beloved prison experience.

It is of power that Genet speaks, sometimes far more

freely than he intends. Hence it develops that in the
initial stages of his work, he tells us that he is doing one
thing, while in reality he is occupied with something
quite different. Our care is primarily for what he claims
to be doing. As we begin to conceive what, actually, he
is most interested in effecting, we care less and less
because our caring had its roots primarily in the sense
of our own guilt, rather than in our sense of his accomplishment; and the deadness and indifference which
often beset us in the end, in spite of all the ingenuity,
visual excitement, and sustained passion of will Genet
can command, are due to our discovery that we have indeed been dupes but not the sort of dupes we were
supposed to be.

Genet has told us that he is analyzing the method by
which the Outcast escapes, at least inwardly, his fate;
that he is examining the relations of appearance and
reality, with the final discovery that it is appearance,
the mask of Nothing, which is real. But what he does
not profess is that his own aesthetic purpose is domination—what Joseph H. McMahon refers to as the
rape of his audience.[2]

As this intention to dominate—by definition, by accusation, and finally by possession—becomes clear, our
reaction slowly alters. While Genet is brilliantly illus-
trating the conclusions of his first two stages, in spite
of whatever bouts of skepticism we may have to overcome, we are fascinated. But eventually we begin to
grasp his direction and ultimate destination, and at that
moment the work begins slowly to loosen its grip
upon our imagination. Faced with the question, "Has
fresh insight into any aspect of truth been given us?"
(inasmuch as it is with Truth and Falseness that Genet
has chosen to deal), we are forced to confront it with
another question: "How are we to be given fresh insight
into an aesthetic truth by something which reveals itself
as a power play?" But the initial question does not cease
to exist. Any method, any device, which stretches our

[2] Joseph H. McMahon, *The Imagination of Jean Genet* (New
Haven: Yale University Press, 1963), p. 167.

imagination or excites our wonder, changes us by some fraction, and Richard Gilman's criterion that the "serious is, in the end, whatever changes or replenishes us"[3] remains valid.

Genet's passion for and adoration of power is affected by both the criminal and the neurotic elements in his thinking. Anyone who has read, en masse, the literary outpourings, solicited for therapeutic purposes, of the inmates of mental institutions and prisons will recognize in Genet's work—distinguished from these by his strictly ordered and keen intelligence—similarities with that of the talented psychotic and criminal: the vanity, the shrewdness, the grinding logic operating pitilessly between false premise and reasoned conclusion, the secret elation, the enormous and tortured ego. There are also the gifts: disassociation from habit; the quick, wild, lucid glance which perceives bizarre resemblances; the sheer manic force of will and willfulness. These are great advantages and lend the work power.

Genet's writing is at its most vivid, its most effective, in those moments of outrageous recognition, in this reassembling of the materials of life. It is at its most dismal in the mechanical, predictable, meticulous performance of its Black Mass, its conditioned reflex to the forces it reverses.

In the beginning, Genet's preoccupation with power progresses in relation to the world of the Other, to society's implacable, functioning system, the values of which the practical man regards as reality. We have seen that in *Deathwatch* this concerns the acceptance, and through acceptance the domination, of fate; concerns the call to tragedy which, accepted and dominated, in the hands of the erstwhile victim turns to power which can be neither violated nor imitated. Snowball and Green Eyes are the supreme powers of their own environment, acknowledged as such even by the ostensible authorities of the prison. The jailor admits and negotiates with a power impossible to contravene, which is merely en-

[3] Richard Gilman, "End of Season: A Love Letter," *Commonweal*, Vol. LXXVI (June 29, 1962), p. 353.

hanced by chains and imprisonment, and will be supremely crowned by the formal death of execution.

The usurper is pitilessly destroyed. He will suffer punishment, but in his case the punishment will be fruitless and ignominious. The power structure (here mysterious, unevadable, personal as the call to sainthood) will be unshakable and know its own. Its potent sharers exchange glances of recognition and complicity. Lefranc, attempting to share, will die a failure.

The fascination of *Deathwatch* lies in its taut, single, ferocious line. It sets forth without a waver its principles of election, struggle, failure, and triumph. It is our introduction, from the world of grocery shops, fines, schools, and traffic, into the world of naked confrontation with destiny and with the pride which dominates that destiny. The play's inherent weakness, here scarcely more observable than the presence of a microbe in a lusty body, is that the still narrow but bottomless gap has already appeared between life and formula, between passion and system, between the human predicament and the spiritual *Führer*. Already Genet has taken us in hand, not as human beings but as case histories to help him understand his ultimate dictatorship of the spiritually elect.

At this stage Green Eyes and Snowball, Lefranc and Maurice, are still individual human beings, though already their individuality now and then thins to a mask worn by those archetypes in which alone Genet is interested. The archetype will ultimately be reduced to the gesture, and that gesture frozen in abstraction, as Warda's ugly gesture makes of her hatpin all whoredom. In great literature there are moments in which the crisis of a human being seems to extend itself into the illumination of a law. Is the final tableau of *Deathwatch* with its two victims, murderer and murdered, such a moment? Or is it rather the announcement of a pattern of education, as absolute as the admonition behind a political poster? There is still flexibility here. The premise is set; but the whole is in relation to the world of the Other; it is its product and its definition by shadow.

The line of communication with the world in which heterogeneous man breathes, struggles, loves, works, and breeds is still open.

In *The Maids,* a transition between the relatively simple stance of *Deathwatch* and that of *The Balcony,* the direction now taken by Genet's thought and art begins to become apparent. It is true that we have the devices which will become so familiar as they reappear in *The Balcony* and *The Blacks:* the play-within-the-play, the legerdemain of appearance turning into reality and reality into appearance; the abstraction of essence as the real glory and the true power; the interdependence of light on power and power on light. In *The Maids,* Genet deals, as in *Deathwatch,* with the emergence of the power of the individual under fate, the Called One, who can sacredly recognize and accept, and by accepting, dominate. In *The Maids* it is already beginning to be the emergence of the power of a category —a social, emotional, ornamental category. The struggle in *Deathwatch* takes place within the community of outcasts but still in relation to the world of the Other, and it is Genet's handbook of how the Outcast may obtain in his own world the reverse image of that glory and power attained by the Other in his world. But these worlds are still separate, though deeply related.

In *The Maids,* it is servantdom and madameness which are under consideration. Solange and Claire do not struggle to accept and dominate their individual destinies. They struggle to escape the category of the Outcast—of Black, of Hoodlum, of Prisoner (for Genet sees a profound consanguinity in all he sees as darkness). The servant, the prisoner, the Negro interest him primarily because of the ambiguous quality of their helplessness. Their helplessness, he will ultimately demonstrate, is fake because they hold within themselves the secret of power. Claire and Solange, by fake murder and suicide, do not attempt to scale the heights of servantdom but instead to become Madame, outshining and encompassing her privileges by the terrible distinction of their acts. Their fetidness, their repulsive condition, the arrogance which as maids they inspire, is not the ineluctable division providence has ordained between maids who "have it" and maids who "haven't it." It is far different. It is their servant essence, and this servant essence, this shadow, is dependent on the sun of Madame, as her sun is defined by their shadow. But if they cannot kill Madame, and with her, her madame-ness, they can, by destroying their servantdom, destroy her by the same stroke. And this is precisely their triumph.

Though raised to the class of heroes, Green Eyes is still strangely touched by human individuality. He is called to exemplify the large issue, but he must do it as an individual man. The maids, on the other hand, have already become those living categories, those important puppets, whose strings Genet will henceforth pull. In *Deathwatch* he is defending and exalting the outcast, the criminal elite. In *The Maids* he is already asking, "Who *is* the outcast?" as he will ask, in the epigraph to *The Blacks:* "But what exactly is a black? First of all, what's his color?"

It is completely impossible to think of Madame, Solange, or Claire as human beings; and indeed, this is the last thing Genet desires us to do. Already we are moving into the world of Mr. Worldly Wiseman, Christian, Mr. Faintheart. What we shall end with is Every-man—Everyman in Genet's image. The stages fluctuate and overlap. We are still primarily concerned with the second stage, but there are already strong intimations of the final one.

By the time we reach *The Balcony,* a major change has not only occurred, but actually been established. At first, we were the accusers; Genet, if not the defender, was the protector. He escaped the strictures of the Other by reversing values and becoming his own king-of-the-mountain in terrain functioning under reverse laws. In *The Balcony,* it is Genet who is the accuser, and his accusation, sprung like a switchblade at the end of that play, will become less an accusation than a cry of triumph.

With *The Balcony,* the theme of power has become so dominant that it has almost taken over. In the prison of *Deathwatch,* power was localized, localized at least in the world of criminals. In *The Maids* its consideration has moved into a wider context, that of all haves and have-nots—the gulf symbolized by the kitchen gloves versus the furs and perfumes of Madame. In *The Balcony,* it takes a giant leap; its arena becomes the Western world and those institutions which have shaped it —force, the law, the church. (Significantly, in the brothel of images, no one plays at being an Artist. It is impossible to make against art, which each artist creates according to his own ability, which freely yields itself and freely endures, the sort of case Genet has been forging against the Other and which he will finally use to trap us all. An interesting sidelight on this is the spectacular absence, in all of Genet's work, of response to art in any of its forms.)

It would of course be false to draw a straight line between one and another of Genet's plays and say, here ends stage one or here the second stage begins. One of the most effective characteristics of Genet's work is the extreme fluidity of its surface, playing in ripples, tides, and eddies over the solid stone of his purpose. One can go only so far as to say that with advances and retreats, and the constant shift of surprises, between the end of *Deathwatch* and the beginning of *The Balcony,* a major change has taken place. In the latter we find that an abstraction, a play which is power but which also wishes to remain *play* or appearance (since only in the play of reality does power reside) has taken over. Reality has failed and must be buttressed by appearance, but, as pointed out, appearance which ends by functioning in reality's place.

It is extraordinary how fully Genet throws down the challenge only just arrived at. No longer: We, the Outcasts (serfs, homosexuals, blacks, criminals) will excel you, the Other, by our outcasthood. Instead: Go back to your homes and consider; you will find yourselves in *The Balcony*. It is quite a leap. Genet's credentials as outcast, while not particularly distinguished, are authentic. As major prophet, they need perhaps more substance.

It is close to a truism that to be, or even deeply to comprehend, evil, one must retain a comprehension, however objective, of good. It is now, in *The Balcony,* that Genet begins the shift from his own Society of Dark Saints to the role of Jeremiah. First he warns us that the real power is in play. The ambition of Madame Irma's clients is not to *be* Judge or Bishop in real life (indeed, they are terrified when circumstances thrust them so far outside the brothel along this path as the ride to the city) but to be a permanent abstraction of these things, as the Police Chief becomes in his tomb a permanent abstraction. As the previous discussion of *The Balcony* has pointed out, reality fails the revolution, which must be salvaged by appearance; and in the end it is appearance which is power.

At this point in the consideration of Genet's advance, an acutely relevant side issue, that of betrayal, arises. Betrayal, along with power, is one of Genet's primary preoccupations. It is a direct offshoot of his juggling of appearance and reality, and it is one of his major bonds with the theatre. Any fakery is necessarily allied to betrayal. In his Introduction to *The Maids* Sartre comments: "It is the element of fake, of sham, of artificiality, that attracts Genet in the theatre. He has turned dramatist because the falsehood of the stage is the most manifest and fascinating of all." (*M,* 8) Betrayal is the sin of falseness, committed against someone or something; and of all sins, betrayal is the one that most consistently fascinates Genet. In this also, he is following his reverse image of Christian values; the Judas-figure is his greatest hero; his keenest admiration, he tells us, is reserved for informers and traitors.

Betrayal is obviously closely related to the second stage of Genet's progress. The Other is betrayed by Genet's discovery that the Other cannot exist save by virtue of his criminal shadow. Now we will be told the shameful truth which the pompous posture of the Other denied. It is betrayal, above all, which excites Genet. But betrayal, as he clearly realizes, is not simple. It has a precondition: trust. You cannot betray someone unless he is your lover, your friend, your confidant, your comrade-at-arms; you cannot betray a cause which has never been yours. Our homes, Genet tells us at the end of *The Balcony,* are false to our image of them as are the clients of *The Balcony* to reality. But what, in Genet's world, does he allow us to betray? Sartre discusses Genet's alleged betrayal of his "friends," those whom he "loves," but he adds: "Only an evil individual could love another evil individual for the love of Evil. But evil-doers do not love." (*M,* 17) Genet, by his own account, has no friend and loves no one, freely as he uses the word. Again and again he repeats it: "We love each other without love" (*OLF,* 110). His protagonist can betray no one—no matter how many rewards he steals—because he lacks the necessary antecedent.

To command deeply the interest and credence of an audience, to say nothing of its final acquiescence, one must compel it to believe that something is taking place, that an illusion is being exploded and hence a truth revealed, or that relationships are so acting upon one another that a new relationship, an alteration of relative positions, is being effected. But Genet's is becoming an increasingly static vision, expressed with recourse to an infinite variety of devices but incapable of true contingencies. It is, in a number of ways, like the patriotic or religious one-level play, in which a foreordained point is established by costumes, speeches, and admonitions. But the simplistic patriotic or religious performance may gain control of our interest by effecting another entrance. It may approach us through our love of—or dislike for—our country, by our reverence for—or distrust of—religion. But on this purely admonitory level, Genet will not work. No one is going to Declare for Genet, as though he were a revivalist, conducting services to lead us to himself; and for us to dislike and distrust the world he shows us scarcely involves an alteration of our basic concepts. Thus Genet's use of "blasphemy" or "betrayal" is ultimately rendered close to impotent by his inability to establish the prior sense of love.

But if the talk of "betrayal" lacks cogency, if nothing is happening to or within Genet, still there is a movement. Genet is gradually demonstrating how he will confront, control, and nullify us. More and more nakedly, he is saying: "Power is all important. You think power lies with you. I will show you, first, that it lies with the Outcast who understands his role, and even by this first step I will show you that ultimately all true power is the same: the dynamic ability to reveal Nothingness."

"Divine is a hole through which the world empties into nothingness; that is why she is called Divine,"[4] writes Sartre. Joseph McMahon has excellently analyzed Genet's attitude toward power in his discussion of Genet's shift from his "friend" Jean, the killed Resistance fighter, to Erik, the storm trooper in *Funeral Rites*. But perhaps McMahon's most astute observation in his entire book is the remark: "He [Genet] may have been bruised and knocked about in life, but the final victory was his, because he had learned that at the root of every shift within the dynamic was the transfer of a basic, capacitating energy: power."[5]

III

It is necessary at this point to discuss in more detail the increasing will-to-power in Genet's development, which was basic to even its first stage in *Deathwatch* but which becomes more overt, more strident, as the plays follow each other. In *The Balcony* and *The Blacks*, Genet examines more closely than heretofore the reality and appearance of power. In *The Balcony* he removes power from the world of outer reality and places it in myth; it is the *gestures* of law, theology, and war which, carried finally to permanence in their abstraction, will endure. In *The Blacks* the movement is circular, or

[4] *Op. cit.*, p. 411.
[5] *Op. cit.*, p. 96.

rather, its circularity is foretold, is inherent in the play's concept. In *The Blacks* there is still (in fact, in *The Blacks* more than in all the other plays combined) the poetry of positive praise. It is, true, the praise of power, but it is power clothed in images of physical and imaginative beauty, rather than, as in the previous and subsequent plays, in its own sparkling sterility. Diouf tells Archibald: "In my Negro solitude, I feel the need, just as you do, to glorify my exquisite savageness" (*Bl,* 33). Village exults: "The surfaces of my body were curved mirrors in which all things were reflected: fish, buffaloes, the laughter of tigers, reeds" (*Bl,* 45). And in a typical mélange of the erotic with the poetic and the pseudo-poetic, Felicity sings: "Tribes covered with gold and mud, rise up from my body, emerge! Tribes of the Rain and Wind, forward! . . . Are you there, Africa with the bulging chest and oblong thigh? Sulking Africa, wrought of iron, in the fire, Africa of the millions of royal slaves, deported Africa, drifting continent, are you there? . . . I call you back this evening to attend a secret revel. [*pondering*] It's a block of darkness, compact and evil, that holds its breath, but not its odor. Are you there?" (*Bl,* 76–77)

This is not merely Darkness exulting in its power to glorify itself as the reverse of that light which depends upon darkness for its luminance. This is a flare-up in Genet's poetic devotion to darkness before he consigns darkness also to the hole at the center, the hole which leads into nothing. It is this flare-up of poetic excitement, this refining of Africa to the gesture of a myth, which makes *The Blacks* easily the richest in texture, the most visually absorbing, the most aesthetically exciting of Genet's plays.

In the beginning of *The Screens,* the power of the Other, crumbling at the end of *The Blacks,* is already in full retreat. And here the device of the authentic object juxtaposed to the objects sketched on the screens is heavily employed. All the previous themes are echoed —reality dissolving into appearance; the filth and ugliness of Leila and Saïd conferring comeliness on the

Other; the belief in the assured permanence of power only on condition that it become an abstraction: the "skilful, vigorous heading towards Absence" (*Bal,* 1), toward that Absence which is the Royal prerogative. But this theme of the abstraction, illustrated by objects, begins to dominate and leads straight into the center of the hole.

The theme is set early, when Warda, arraying herself to practice her profession, comments: "A bracelet missing! As if I were a coffin and a hammerstroke were missing." (*S,* 18) It is that death-in-all-things, or Absence, which is under discussion. Death, with its *pompes funèbres,* is here rampant. In *Deathwatch* it was the climax; in *The Maids* it was climax and transfiguration. In *The Balcony* the funeral chamber of the Police Chief is his final triumph; in *The Blacks* it is the core around which all action revolves. In *The Screens* it *is* the core, the *raison d'être,* and final total solution, all in one. It is the archetype of the hole that Leila seeks in her blanket, of which her mother tells the Gendarme: "What interests her is the holes. The more there are, the better she likes it. In fact, what she likes best is to wrap herself for the night in a big hole." (*S,* 67)

Ugliness, it turns out in *The Screens,* leads to the ultimate Hole as rapidly as beauty led there; and grief is valuable because it is a form of ugliness: "And what's meant by going into mourning, gentlemen, if not to make oneself ugly? To cover oneself with crape, with ashes, with mud, with flies, with cow dung, to let one's beard grow, to let filth accumulate in the folds of the skin, to pluck out one's eyes, to scrape one's fingers, what's meant by going into mourning, gentlemen? [*Fervently.*] Blessed be Saïd!" (*S,* 133)

A contemporary of Genet's has written powerfully and persistently of the quest for the Void. This quest is one of the central themes of Samuel Beckett; another is that of Absence. It is instructive to look for a minute at the similarities and differences of writers so compelled by the same theme. The similarity is striking, but more striking still are the differences. Writing of the Beckett protagonist, in *The Testament of Samuel Beckett,* the authors note that he "seeks to escape himself and hence his pain; he will seek this escape in levels descending to the desired but never attained void of annihilation. He seeks it in love, in lust, in the return to the womb, in the mirage of death."[6] And later: "The void has marshalled its incentives: dissolving body, time's corruption, the travesties of love. . . ."[7] And still later: "This terrain, these circumstances, this clown figure, are all part, says Beckett bluntly, of a 'soul-landscape.' 'The soul exults in its rags.' The horrors of the Beckett landscape are moral horrors."[8]

The Beckett protagonist is drawn toward the void by the merciless realization of the horrors of his vision of life. His void is not an abstraction of evil, a supremely desired Absence, a Negation worshiped for its destructive power. It is on the contrary just the opposite; it is the passionately craved anesthetic to stop the pain exactly of the discovered, but hated, Absence—that Absence which causes the terrible laughter, laughter at that which is *not* good, at that which is *not* true, and the "*risus purus,* the laugh laughing at the laugh."[9] The Absence, glorified by Genet, here is seen as nemesis. Whereas the triumph of the Genet protagonist is that of utter destruction—by pulling all things with him through the hole, he has power to undermine reality and the very nature of existence—the despair described in Beckett's *Watt,* for example, springs from the fact that, although intimations of beauty, love, and truth exist, they appear deceitful, or certainly unobtainable, and that precisely to exist at all in the face of their absence has become unbearable. While Genet enthrones and worships Nothingness, it is the apparent power of Nothingness which drives the Beckett protagonist to his quest for the void.

[6] Josephine Jacobsen and William R. Mueller, *The Testament of Samuel Beckett* (New York: Hill and Wang, 1964), pp. 130–131.

[7] *Ibid.,* p. 134.

[8] *Ibid.,* p. 161.

[9] Samuel Beckett, *Watt* (New York: Grove Press, 1959), p. 48.

At that stage of Genet's progress in which the hole has not yet become the destination of beauty and ugliness alike, one may note that the power drive is again behind his insistence, in *Deathwatch* as in the novels, that his criminals, pimps, and hoodlums are without exception vivid examples of masculine beauty. One may counter with the pitiful, homely, stupid mugs on the walls of a thousand post offices. But Genet is ahead of us. He says bluntly that he knows that "the pale-faced corner hoodlums have pale souls" (*TJ,* 234). But for his own purposes they are uniformly of a dazzling beauty. They must be. For the men whom he desires to possess, to control, as the maids possess and control Madame, must, in the interests of Genet's power, be of an invariably startling beauty which, as their possessor, he can transfer to himself. It is thus that Claire envisages herself and Solange as rising to a supernatural loveliness. As Genet becomes more sophisticated, more experienced, he is able to dispense with this vulnerable myth of actual beauty, in which he never truly expected us to believe, and substitute in its place an arbitrary and *in*vulnerable beauty—the beauty of ugliness, which, once established, will draw him as fatally as ever Narcissus was drawn. By the last stage, that of *The Screens,* it has arrived. But in *The Blacks* it is already happening; rice, doves, sugar have become black: not because there is any inherent value in black or in white but because Genet not unnaturally associates power with whiteness, and, more unnaturally, does truly and personally associate black with evil.

Proust too was fascinated by the processes of power, most particularly by that particular facet of the power-wish which is the desire totally to possess and dominate the loved one. But he saw it clearly, thoroughly, and deeply for what it was, the caricature of love, which he came to believe could perhaps not exist at all between human beings. This perceived, he transferred his hope and his final commitment to art, which exacts and confers all.

The elements of Genet's own make-up drive him

deeper and deeper into the whirlpool of power. He wishes to control systems, lovers, society, nomenclature, and—above all—the resisters of Genet, for, as McMahon points out, Genet rejects the historical process because it "would . . . imply a willingness to tolerate the existence of competitive views; and that simply cannot be, for in the church of Genet's imagination one tolerates neither the error nor the man who perpetrates it."[10] The cause of Genet's revulsion from the aura of servantdom goes far deeper than the matter of haves and have-nots. The idea of even true and voluntary humility rouses his sharp contempt, unless he can reanalyze it as inverted pride. A Francis of Assisi, an Angelo Roncalli, a perceptive and dedicated worker in the areas of human distress, disgusts him. The jackboot, the Sam Browne belt, draw him; the compass-needle of his fascinated admiration turns toward the metal of the bully, the guard, the pimp, the storm trooper. Explaining that this is in part due to his type of homosexuality cannot alter the importance of the result.

Genet's obsession with power is at the base of his profound preoccupation with ritual and the sacred. Unable to believe in a God, he believes passionately in religion—his religion. We are irresistibly reminded of the Preacher in Flannery O'Connor's *Wise Blood,* who preached The Church Without God. Among its advantages, ritual has that of the gesture—that earliest, clearest, and most comprehensive form of communication. As Sartre constantly points out, Genet's conception of life is sacred. In other words, the mysterious, valuable, inherent quality is miraculously expressed through the material object, Genet's regard for the latter often verging on fetishism. It is not difficult for Genet to believe that fire can be sacred, or water holy; indeed it is impossible for him to believe otherwise. But what the power of its sacredness means, Genet will decide, and its significance will be the result of his own traumatic experience.

The accumulated potency of ritual is tremendous. It

10 *Op. cit.,* p. 209.

imbues gestures, objects, sounds, clothes with enormous power. Aura will linger a long time after its source is removed, but ultimately, like a brilliant and exotic cut flower, it will soften and collapse. Even the Black Mass, to which Sartre has accurately compared the ceremony of *The Maids* (*M,* 23), functions only in relation to its prototype in reverse. We react strongly to the forces to which our history and convictions, past or present, have conditioned us. As Genet employs every device of ritual (and his use of ritual rises steadily), we do react, mentally and emotionally. At first its use does help to make his plays exciting, rich in texture, provocative, and haunting. Genet's art keeps the flower in water; it looks almost as real as it did yesterday. But on the third morning—alas, what has happened to the outline of the petals? For Genet, counting on our being preconditioned, is inevitably unconditioning us. The significance of the gesture, the costume, the word, which evoked the desired reaction, is gently, imperceptibly wilting.

In order to maintain the power of both his use of ritual and his gospel of the interrelationships of reality and appearance, Genet must harp on both evocation and exposure. He must evoke the emotion related to the ritual object, but he must at the same time remind the audience of that emotion's falseness—hence the instructions that the maids shall if possible be played by boys masquerading as girls; that the actors must always seem to be acting; that the masks must not completely cover the identity of the masked; and that there be a juxtaposition on the stage of the fake and the authentic detail. He is acutely aware of the significance of clothing; not Bergson or Beckett sees more clearly the relation between material and mind. Genet is insistent that the *gesture* of clothing (that ritualistic homage which understands that both the material and the symbolic gesture must embody the action which is taking place) is a kind of sacred sign language.

The imagined picture of a college president clad in shorts, presenting a parchment to a student clad in pajamas outrages something far deeper than our sense of social suitability, although the parchment's authenticity and the recipient's accomplishment would be unaffected. It is also our sense of connotation, our sense of the symbolic gesture, which is being outraged. Nor does it require a vision of a soldier in a tuxedo bayoneting a boy in tennis clothes to force our realization that the ritual gesture of clothing reaches our deepest commitments to form, to law, to ethics, however bizarre a turn these commitments may take, or however dangerously oûr conscience or awareness may be lulled by our conditioned reflex, even when the gesture represented by the clothing may be no longer true or permissible. Genet knows that the form of clothing expresses by its gesture our attitude—that clothing is the product of our attitude, and in accepting it, we accept its symbolic significance.

The blackness of Genet's Blacks is a sort of theatrical clothing. There is an ominous tendency on Genet's part to freeze the poetic flavor which he finds in the Negro into racial characteristics. Negroes are all a sort of pantomime to Genet. They interest him only insofar as they evince the characteristics of blackness—that is to say, of his conception of blackness. It is their primitivism which he savors. The Blacks are no more human beings than the Whites.

Negroes have no age. Mlle. Adeline could explain to us that when they try to count they get all mixed up in their calculations, for they are quite aware that they were born at the time of a famine, of the death of three jaguars, of the flowering of the almond trees, and these circumstances, mingled with the figures, make it easy for them to go astray. (*OLF,* 166)

Musing on the figure which reaches its apex in Snowball of *Deathwatch,* Genet says: "I have tried to recapture, in the cell where I am now writing, the odor of carrion spread by the proud-scented Negro . . ." (*OLF,* 166). And in the same book, the nauseous dawn after the murder sees Genet's Ideal Couple: "The costumed Negro and the murderer staggered a bit and leaned

THE GLORY AND THE POWER

against each other" (*OLF,* 222). Genet's elite, his figures of the power of darkness, are abroad.

This use of race, gesture, clothes, and words in the
interests of power is the basis of Genet's claim—and of
Sartre's oft-repeated claim for Genet—that he is a poet.
In justice to Sartre, it should be made clear that he
believes Genet to have created himself as poet, not that
most of what Genet writes in the poetic vein is poetry.
The latter, however, is a conception widely held, and no
one holds it more firmly than Genet himself. In any discussion of the functioning of Genet's theatrical devices,
the issue of poetry looms large. But what concerns us
at the moment is that in Genet's mind poetry is prac-
tically interchangeable with power—a persuasive and
by no means original conviction. He correctly believes it
to be that which can alter and rearrange. In his list of
the "creators of poetry"—dancers, Negroes, boxers,
prostitutes, soldiers—four out of five are images of
power: the dancer, who must dominate his body, the
laws of gravity and rhythm, and impose on them his
own pattern; the Negro, associated for Genet with the
force and ferocity of the primitive; the boxer; the soldier.
And indeed there are many ways in which the prostitute
may belong to the image of power. In the end, Genet's
characters, his language, his gestures, all illustrate that
image.

IV

Having followed the emergence of Genet's dominant
theme in the stages of his plays' development, one is
moved to ask why the plays are so superior to the novels
—those longer, more intimate, more passionately asserted records of experience real or invented. There are
two well-defined reasons. One of these is that Genet's
imagination is supremely visual; he is a born pantomim-
ist. His mind swarms with visual images. He sketches
things with movement; he sketches things with chalk,
with costumes, with colors. Primarily he does not say
"Listen!" or "Think!" or even "Feel!" He says "Look!"
His steadfastly pursued objective of extracting the

essence from a living entity and then asking from that essence an abstraction leads him, it is true, to a formula, but to a formula conceived as a property or gesture. In *The Screens,* the pigskin glove of Sir Harold, the empty trousers of Saïd, tell us all that he wishes us to know. True, they tell us very little—just a formula; but the formula is hollow and will hold as much or as little as we can put into it. It is as isolated and visible and attention-catching as a man on a tightrope.

A second reason for the superiority of the plays is that the theatre imposes its own restrictions on Genet. Three of these are the restriction on stasis, the restriction on obscenity, and the restriction on homiletics. On the stage events move. On the stage there are flexible but ultimate limits to erotic detail; on the stage there is a limit to the amount of admonition an audience is capable of absorbing—though it must be said that in this latter consideration Genet's confidence in his audience's capacity is superb.

In the novels, no matter how much characters and incidents may proliferate, the effect of Genet, motionless and engaged in a circular monologue, is overwhelming. In the plays, the characters may have no more life or reality of their own, but they *look* different—see, here is a General, here a Black, here a Hoodlum, here a Policeman, an Arab, a Prostitute. And if they do not move, inside themselves or in our minds, they move on the stage—indeed, they perform startling acts of confrontation and juxtaposition. Always something at least seems to be happening, and if a great amount of this is what the theatrical profession calls "props" and "business" (gloves on wires, flames drawn on screens, tiers, levels, blackouts), still it is all part of an animated illusion, which partakes of the very nature of theatre.

The restriction on obscenity is no less important. Occupied with his Sainthood, in the novels Genet repeats obscene detail as a religious novice might repeat the religious exercises which will add up to a state of mind or heart. These exercises may operate as he wishes on Genet's consciousness—but they do something else.

They gradually numb the sense of shock—indeed, of any sensation whatsoever—into the atrophy of helpless boredom. The theatre's restrictions force Genet to that limited use of the obscene which maintains its effect.

The last point, the theatre's restriction on homiletics, is supremely important. Saint Genet may address our wicked ears with his burning revelations, but he simply cannot stand in the middle of the stage and admonish us for three hours. Our salvation (that violation of our identity and convictions by Genet's identity and convictions which, as McMahon points out, is the object of Genet's effort and which McMahon characterizes as our rape by Genet) has simply got to be accomplished indirectly, by means of actions performed and dialogue exchanged between the actors. He cannot merely tell us both what he means and what we are to make of it—he must so demonstrate it before our eyes that its significance voluntarily appears to our perception.

A crucial point in any discussion of Genet's functioning in the theatre is the matter of language. The question of his relations with language is so surrounded by myth—like most things about Genet—that the general impression has grown that he is a master of language. In the theatre, language is important, but obviously not nearly so important as it is in poetry or fiction, where it is unsupported by flesh and blood, sets, motion, and the physical presence of an involved audience. It may be objected that plays are judged also in their reading, but it remains true that the final judgment on them must be that of how they function on a stage.

Genet's language operates on three levels. The first and least satisfactory level is fatally reminiscent of the exposés common to the poorer pulp magazines: "I am planning for the near future a perilous outlaw's life in the most dissolute quarters of the most dissolute of ports" (*TJ*, 234). But interestingly enough, very few pure examples of this sort of blood-and-sequin prose exist in the plays. A considerable cut above this ham-elegance is Genet's middle manner: an imaginative prose, marred by purple passages, but lit by an imaginative flair. Its quality can best be summarized by one of Genet's favorite words: *glamor*. Though, repeatedly, the weight of evocation is heavier than the context can bear—"A more ancient and more Greek Antigone was making me scale a dark, steep Calvary" (*TJ,* 42)—on this level his language is more resilient, more justly used.

There is a third level, the best, the most original and compelling Genet has to offer, the infrequently attained level of an almost miraculous invocation. This usually occurs when he is describing or explaining something which relates immediately to an intimate or traumatic personal experience or obsession. It is as though an almost visceral reflex of the ego has ripped through into the element of language. A few quotations can serve as examples:

"The silence was a peculiar silence, a silence that was present, which sounds from the outside could not penetrate. They squashed against the thick walls of the church like rotten fruit thrown by children. Though they were audible, they in no way disturbed the silence." (*OLF,* 172) Here speaks that positive absence of outer sound, the presence of Absence. There is nothing, really, about Genet's work, about his Church of Evil, which is not implicit in this paragraph. Nothing can communicate through this silence which is the presence of Absence. This language fits, like its own mold, the shape of Genet's alienation.

"Think of the moonlight tinkling of the toad; at night it is so pure that the vagabond on the highway stops and does not go on until he has heard it again" (*OLF,* 279–280). The purity of the sound, the tinkling of the toad—that epithet, that term of abuse, that clammy, abhorred possessor of the jewel-like eyes, that hero of fairy-tale transformations—is one of the examples in Genet's prose of the beautiful fusion of language and concept.

In phrases, in short sentences, the frequency of this language is highest. Solange speaks of going back to her "belching sink" (*M,* 46), and, in her role of Madame, cries: "I myself am both the thief and his slavish shadow.

I move alone toward the brightest shores." (*M,* 88)
Africa queries the West: "Answer, Diouf. Seen through
their eyes, what are their kings like? What do you see
from the height of your blue eyes, from the height of
those belvederes?" (*Bl,* 89) Genet speaks of the place
where "illustrious ash-weddings are celebrated" (*TJ,*
10), and, in his final and best fiat, of the Royal prerogatives of Absence (*Bal,* 69). Silence, the silence of ashes,
of absence; he is dominated by this.

The connotations from which language never escapes
are precious to Genet's use. He wishes dazzlingly to
violate those connotations; and until they are established, how are they to be violated? It is for this reason
that he leans so heavily upon biblical and liturgical
language, and even when he is not misparaphrasing a
familiar phrase, he will often adopt a biblical tone: "I
shall go to Tangiers, I said to myself, and perhaps I
may be summoned among the traitors and become one
of them" (*TJ,* 73).

The quintessential condition for a writer's mastery
of language is that, exemplified by his style, his personal
relations with language inspire confidence in the reader
—the sense that, although his language may infuriate
us, wound us, horrify us, it will not *fail* us. Again and
again, in a sustained passage of the novels, the language of Genet does fail us. He wishes to shock, but
by the monotony of repetition, and the lack of scale,
he succeeds in numbing us. He wishes to instruct in his
articles of faith, but by naked haranguing and the determination to bully, he stiffens our resistance. He
wishes to reconstruct our world, from its boast to its
dark fact, but his will-to-power chooses the words of
absolutism rather than of persuasion. He wishes to
move us; over and over again, in isolation from all contact with another, he reiterates the word "love." It is
permissible to ponder Genet's trustfulness in banking
so heavily upon this word "love," with which he has
tampered with great effect. Beckett almost never writes
overtly of "love," but its great presence-in-absence is
implicit, in the child fallen under the wheels of the

train, the escaping love affair in the boat among the rushes. It cries out in absence from Watt's wild garden.

In *The Screens* Sir Harold announces: "And to tamper with language is sacrilegious" (*S,* 74). This is one of those sly reminders Genet enjoys. He is telling us both what he is doing and under what category of sin it falls. But one of his chief difficulties lies in just this tampering. His relations with words are often less those of a poet than of an animal trainer: they may jump through hoops, lift tremendous weights, play cornets and clap their flippers, and carry monkeys on their backs through flaming paper—but it is an overt and alien force prevailing over them, and suddenly they may balk, spit, or, even worse, lie down.

When we have once grasped the formula by which language is used, emotionally and connotatively, to reverse its original trend, the effect often misfires to an almost embarrassing degree. The pattern is too consistent. The Mother of *The Screens* shouts to the audience: "I'll recite a hundred and twenty-seven insults a hundred and twenty-seven times, and each insult will be so beautiful, ladies, that it'll make you gleam" (*S,* 44). Mr. Blankensee muses: "I love my cork oaks. There's nothing more beautiful than a forest of cork oaks when the men circle round the trunk to strip it of its bark. And when the flesh of the tree appears, raw and bleeding! People may laugh at us, at our love of this country, but you [*He is moved.*], you know our love is real." (*S,* 73) The condemned man who has murdered his mother, reflecting how he could improve on the crime, could he re-enact it, decides: "I'd have . . . delicately opened her belly, I'd have lifted up the curtains of the skirt to watch the guts flow and I'd have toyed with them as fingers toy with jewels." (*S,* 83–84)

If the lesions of pseudo-poetry noted by Sartre in Genet's use of language—lesions in its very substance —cause it to fail him, and hence us, repeatedly and disastrously; if words, dominated out of their nature and often raped to provide Genet with the monsters we must adopt, take their own revenge by hostility or collapse, this coercion with its brilliant side-effects, its dazzling *tours de force,* achieves willy-nilly in the long run the result, if not the effect, Genet wishes. Like the words, we are bludgeoned into a fictive harmony, for the trainer's purpose. We are indicted. This display of pyrotechnics, this knowledgeability as to our vulnerable points, this persuasion by *force majeure,* arrests us, dazes us into a sort of half-eager, half-shamefaced compliance. The lights go up, and *"Mea culpa!"* we cry.

Is this guilty reflex of ours the test of Genet's stature? Sartre's intelligence is far too keen and his intention far too honest to allow him to ignore the blocks, irrelevancies, deceits, shifts, and the flowery glue present in much of Genet's writing. Understanding fully these qualities, he constructs a laborious and ingenious framework for them, in which they seem inevitable, or at all events, demonstrably explicable. But it is just here that a substitution may occur, a sleight of hand which will turn the analyst of Genet's work into the analyst of Genet's nature. Since the issue is not to explain, blame, or exculpate Genet but to watch and to listen to him, it must be his success or failure which remains.

At his best, in the incantatory passages, how valid is that vivid effect upon the reader or audience? Often, though not always, it is not Genet's vision, not his concepts, not even his flair for controlling the motion of words, which, in the main, account for the magic which lingers in these passages; it is the appropriated magic of terms weighted with the cargo of ages, and now used with skill in a violent reversal. Sartre is never weary of pointing out that it is the power of rites that draws us in Genet's work. The omnipresent terms of worship and liturgy, torn out of emotional context and placed in situations bizarre enough temporarily to enhance their immediate effect, ultimately silently withdraw themselves. Worse, there is so often an intimidating conventionality about Genet's use of language. The sterile quality of this conventionality appears persistently and battles against any natural poetic instinct he possesses, tending to dominate it. The accidental and stupid cruel-

ties in which life abounds are not represented by this
perverse but rigid formula. Those cruelties evidence deficiencies of the moral imagination. Genet's inversion of
moral values shows adherence to a strictly conceived
moral code. This rigid adherence gives to his work
both a substance and a monotony which the unpredictable lacks. It is, after all, the negation of and reflex to conventional "virtues" and, as such, has a built-
in quality of the mechanical. Far from showing the
wayward ferocity of art, his concepts manifest an extraordinary docility in the custody of the entrapping
formula. His words are trained to point to a generaliza-
tion. In the Barrio Chino we have paraded before us
the conventional generalizations: "Beggars," "Whores,"
"Thieves," "Fairies." The human identity has escaped.
A man may be a beggar or a pimp, a woman a trans-
vestite or a whore. But of the essence which makes
whore differ from whore, pimp from pimp, of this his
language gives us no trace. Even though we concede
that the archetype is the object of Genet's efforts, we
shrink from such labeled identities—the sort of identification which enables the human being to be summed
up in the word "thief" or "fairy," as Hester Prynne was
summed up by the inhabitants of Salem in the letter
"A."

Without these classifications, these dazzlingly manipulated generalizations, much of Genet's language would
collapse. Actually, he examines no identity, since for
him none outside his own exists, and himself he is
unable to imagine other than as Outcast, Thief, Homosexual. So here are Criminals, Servants, Brothel-Keep-
ers, Blacks, Arabs. Over their stylized exposure glitter
coruscations of words which were never intended to
communicate discoveries but to ornament the underside
of the conventional social fabric. For all his near-fetish-
ism, nothing could be further from the pragmatic world
of the materialist than the world of Genet, in which
everything is expressed in moral or religious terms. In
almost every word formed by his pen, he borrows from
those positive values of which his language celebrates

the negative, those values which hang heavy over his head. When he writes of the supreme beauty of betrayal, one knows that he is once again serving himself of a gigantic religious image; he is evoking the Judas prototype. He writes, in the tone of a saddened, good bourgeois: "I know nothing of her who abandoned me in the cradle" (*TJ*, 21).

Genet has not intended to communicate discoveries. Genet, Sartre consistently repeats, does not wish to communicate at all on any significant level; it is indeed a major part of his purpose to fail to do so. He will instead communicate on a level lacking in significance, but available as is no other to Genet's own mind—that mind which he tells us has been relegated to the outer darkness where he explodes his sulphurous fireworks and throws up his Indian rope trick into the air which seems to sustain it. He will show us a blazing, livid truth about ourselves, which, if it turns out not to be essentially the truth in any ascertainable way, will, he retorts, be as much or more truth than we see in the brightly lit cells of our own complacency, in which we exist as helpless and far stupider prisoners.

In the plays, this noncommunication has one impact; in the novels, another. Has it, can it have, sufficient force and direction to qualify Genet for inclusion among the writers who have made significant and aesthetically formidable comment on the human situation? In the case of the novels, the answer would seem to be an unqualified "No." The resolute boredom which ultimately overtakes us would seem to be in itself an answer. The law of diminishing returns hounds the footsteps of the writer dedicated to detached outrage— outrage not springing in hot blood from within the text but superimposed upon it as a device. The towering sense of tragedy which survives the deluge of catastrophes in Greek drama, in Shakespeare, is sustained by the interaction between the events of the story and the painful experience of the spectator or reader, who most likely has not suffered the counterpart of these catastrophes but who now suffers them by emotional par-

ticipation, by intuition, by the generosity of the imagination. Distress and horror, compassion and wrath, are
translated alive into the language of mind and nerves.
When once this imagination fails, the spate of disasters
or shocks will evoke, instead of a profound and terrible
credence, the helpless mirth, or embarrassed apathy,
with which Sick Jokes are received, according to the
temperament of the hearer. You cannot maintain the
sense of the monstrous without the sense of proportion.

The valid contribution made by Genet in his novels
could be compressed to the length of an autobiographical essay without losing a shred of its effectiveness. Its
brilliant glimpses of a nightmare world, its baroque
excursions into the imagery of spiritual and social disease, its exhibition of the nature of one enemy of life,
contribute a brief, vivid, and traumatic passage in the
literature of the underworld of the spirit. To expect it
to expand, to develop ramifications in the areas of human experience, and the world literature which springs
from that experience, is asking of it not only the impossible but the irrelevant. Genet is no more interested
in literature than in human beings; the very existence
of literature he acknowledges only in a few misin-
terpreted misquotations or references, such as those
from Pope and Dickens.[11] Great literature reaches very
far down, and this depth is conceived by Genet to be
achieved by the violence in the details of his own ego's
war. His novels never penetrate to any genuine depth;
they do not work their way down, through whatever
bizarre and unexpected distortions, to the great basic
hungers and drives which feed the growth of literature,
any more than they forsake their shallow subworld to
reach upward to the motions and accidents of human
fortunes. They function instead in a special soil, at once
rank and ersatz, growing by fiat of their creator in an
oxygenless vacuum. They are surrounded, truly, by
Nothing. Here are no countries, no cities, no human
beings, no fortune, no fear, no hope. Here is only the

[11] See Sartre, *op. cit.*, p. 22, and Genet, *The Thief's Journal*,
p. 197.

writer; and as writer he has achieved his ambition and ceased to exist—because he writes in a determined effort not to communicate. He will appear to excoriate, to bombard us, but it is not so. For him we do not exist —any more than Divine or Stilitano exists. We were always phantoms, to be apprehended only as screens on which the images that are the fragments of Jean Genet can for a moment be thrown, so that the grim and minute entertainment by Genet, through Genet, and for Genet can take its course. The novels are the seeding ground for the plays.

And the plays? Here is a different matter. If in the novels Genet has been incapable of relating, or unwilling to relate, his work to any organic life which would give it ultimate relevance or power, in the case of the plays he has made brilliant contact with a deep-rooted, long-lasting human need: the theatre. His novels are not novels—not because they ignore or subvert the conventions of the novel but because he does not wish them to be novels and because, pursuant to his wish, they remain within the ranks of sermons, or primitive incantations. He does, however, wish his plays to be theatre—and so they are, though *The Screens* comes almost full circle and to some extent bogs down in its own theatricality. It becomes at too many points an accumulation of devices, an accumulation of *things,* of props, so that the actors and the characters they portray tend to disappear into the tiers, drawings, screens, offstage sounds, floating objects, and the like, which all too often form the motor action of the play.

Genet—as both he and Sartre repeatedly assert— takes his path to Nothingness through the sophisticated frauds of theatrical illusion. Genet, says Sartre, delights in the theatre because the theatre is the science of fakery (*M,* 8). It is much more besides, of course; but it is obvious that illusion, overt or invisible, masks appearance, and stage effects are crucial to its life. Exhibitionism, the *trompe d'oeil,* the wig, the mask, the costume are not its progenitors, but they are its legitimate progeny. Genet, faithful to his theme of the falseness of reality, of the power of appearance, is spectacularly at home on the stage. He wishes to exhibit broken fragments of himself until (like the Queen who is simultaneously sewing, sleeping, and drying the dishes, until in the balked mind she is canceled out and ceases to exist) he achieves extinction. He wishes to dominate—a single, controlling figure in the light, before a hushed, docile, and faceless multitude. He wishes to play at appearance until there is nothing left, not even himself, when a tell-tale curtain will descend. He wishes to use language violently, so that, issuing from the lips of phantoms, monstrous shadows, and archetypes, it will acquire a color and force it lacks in its own right; and in all these things he succeeds. Irridescence, transparence, Absence. The irridescence of his volatile, inventive visual imagination; the transparence of the theatrical illusion's reality; the ultimate Absence, when the curtain softly descends on what never existed.

It is quite possible that *Deathwatch* concealed the seeds of all he has subsequently had to say to those faceless listeners. It is fascinating to analyze how the plays have matured in technique, in sureness of touch, in the ability to exploit all facets of theatre. For this reason *The Balcony* and *The Blacks* are more exciting, more visually rewarding, offer more interest in terms of the stage than does *Deathwatch*. In *Deathwatch*, power, its presence, its absence, the struggle to achieve it, its intransigent and pitiless essence, were considered. There power in its purest sense, set free from the appurtenances of locks, keys, sentences, walls, punitive apparatus, is seen as a gift, from above or below or within; a gift unsought, unprocurable, immutable, impossible to earn or imitate. In *The Maids* power will yield itself to those who are willing to kill, or die, for it. Again it consists in a spiritual triumph or knowledge: the "eternal couple of the criminal and the saint"[12] merge and become the saint-criminal. In *The Balcony*, power, by what is really the slightest of mutations, is the grip of Appearance, which slowly and forever con-

12 Sartre, *op. cit.*, p. 86.

sumes reality, and those who comprehend the nuances of Appearance are the true holders of power. In *The Blacks,* power openly moves from its imagined holders, the pale sunlit masks of law, religion, history, and martial convention, to the dark masks of primitive power, to those cast as murderers, rapists, and savages, in order that their monitors, judges, and punishers can exist. In *The Screens,* darkness—that darkness superficially recognized as ugliness, violence, treachery, obscenity, and degradation—is already absorbing the languishing remnants of those outmoded power-holders, and we are face to face with what has been more clearly implied at each step: nothing truly exists except power, and the only indestructible power is that of ugliness, beauty's Absence, that ugliness which is in reality the hole at the center of all. It is a simple, small hole, once reached. It is banal in the extreme; its banality—that absence of astonishment—is dazzlingly suggested by Genet. Each of the newly dead arrives at the hole's center with the same small, mingy exclamation: "Well what do you know!" And we know. We know Nothing, the silent, triumphant answer.

This theatre is stimulating and often exciting. It can and does command respect on its own level of intention. But given its complete contempt for the audience, the characters, and the author himself, and—far more important—its path toward domination, toward the power-play which ultimately wrenches from the dominated the "Yes! Guilty as charged!" of the third-degree, how seriously can the plays be taken? Seriously enough, certainly, to make of Genet a fascinating dramatist impossible to ignore. Yet it remains a question whether the plays Genet has so far written will successfully endure the grinding motion of time. Our sense of guilt varies as surely as does our sense of political morality. It is impossible for the audience or reader of this decade, caught in the turning of tremendous tides, to assess the force these plays will exert fifty years from now. But there is one touchstone in the examination of the work of serious writers which is not apt to fail the examiner: the *desire* to communicate. Of itself it is little; it is in its absence that it becomes formidable. The entire theatre of the absurd is more directly concerned with the breakdown in communication than with any other single concept. In *The Silence,* Ingmar Bergman explored in fantasy the results of the silence of God. In the Roman Catholic missal, the words run, "If Thou goest in silence, who shall save us?" In Beckett, Estragon and Vladimir desperately wish to hear and to be heard by the absent Godot. Winnie, in *Happy Days,* confesses to a near-silent Willie that she could not bear to face the day when she should have to talk all to herself. The burden of Ionesco's plays is terror at the rupture between speaker and listener; the terror inspired by the puny, feeble Killer lies in his changeless chuckle and his slight shrug, no more responsive to reason or pleas than to a breath of air. The sinister ambiance of Pinter's *Dumbwaiter* lies in the impossibility of communicating in regard to the smallest puzzle. Kafka created the archetype of the accused who is unable to communicate with his accusers. The list could go on endlessly.

But in the case of Genet, what is occurring is quite different. He is interested in communication only to the degree which permits him to explain to us that there is nothing *to* communicate, and, in any case, no one *with whom* to communicate. He functions, as he enjoys doing, within a paradox: he will use words to lead us toward that Royal prerogative which he will grant us. He says to his audience: I shall speak to you only in order to explain that you do not exist. Your identity is that of Nothing. You are Nothing, and it is in the knowledge of this that my power lies. I communicate with you *as audience,* only in order to demonstrate the essential nothingness of communication between human beings, whom I shall cause to disappear into that hole into which I, too, shall vanish.

Genet is not interested in suicide because for him suicide is redundant. Inasmuch as life is merely the mask of death and all things are the mask of Nothing, there is no life from which it is necessary to escape; one has only to realize what Sartre calls the "Nay," which Genet is dedicated to constructing. One needs only, first, the power the knowledge of Nothing gives one over those dupes who misread it as Something, and second, the use of that power consciously to draw the hole about one's audience and oneself. We are back to the Mother's comment on her daughter-in-law Leila, that quintessence of negating ugliness: "What interests her is the holes. The more there are, the better she likes it. In fact, what she likes best is to wrap herself for the night in a big hole." (*S*, 67)

Iridescence, transparence, the invisibility which is Absence. A thing shows the colors of life; it breathes. It is a rabbit, a bat, a whore picking her teeth. Becoming transparent, as life and its colors fade out, it reveals itself as the *gesture* of rabbit, bat, whore. Under Genet's power, rabbit and bat become transparent, reveal their secret: "A sprint setting in the shape of a rabbit, a flight in the shape of a bat" (*S*, 113). A sprint, a flight, into the hole of Absence.

As Genet has progressed, he has abandoned mask after mask en route. Surer of himself, more frankly dedicated to the concept of power, he has attempted to dominate even poetry, so that once reduced to a result of the will's exertion, it too can vanish with its tamer into the hole. There can have been few falser definitions of poetry than that which Genet frankly produces for us: "Poetry is a vision of the world obtained by an effort, sometimes exhausting, of the taut, buttressed will. Poetry is willful." (*OLF*, 226) Genet's poetry is to be an effort of his will, its triumph, taut and buttressed. Now that he possesses it, poetry is under his control. Having made it by an act of will, he can unmake it, carrying it along with his other possessions into Nothingness.

Sartre writes, in his Introduction to *Our Lady of the Flowers:* "We sense . . . the maniacal will—which has become exacerbated in prison—to regard the Nay as the symbol of the Yea and the Nought as the symbol of the All" (*OLF*, 47). Elsewhere he amplifies this: "For the medieval philosophers, 'life is only a pilgrimage to God: the physical world is the road that leads us to Him. The beings along the way are signs, signs that may at first sight seem puzzling to us, but if we examine them carefully, faith, with the aid of reason, will decipher, under characters that are always different, a single word, a call that is always the same: God.' Replace God by Genet, and you have the universe of *Our Lady of the Flowers,* whose only reason for being is to express Genet—who has written only in order to be read by Genet—and to recall him constantly to love of Genet." (*OLF,* 39–40) In the novels, this obsessive quality is more overt. In the plays, theatrical skill and the discipline imposed by the stage mitigate its obviousness. But it is a flower of the same root. Genet's lovehate for Genet will confer upon him ultimately the Royal prerogative of Absence; and with Genet goes all. Saint Genet has earned his halo. "Like beauty—and poetry, with which I merge it—saintliness is individual. Its expression is original. However, it seems to me that its sole basis is renunciation." (*TJ,* 209) He has not in mind the saint's joy, that consummation for which renunciation is endured. To him the renunciation *is* the saintliness, and we must and shall renounce with him. "But since non-being *is not,*" writes Sartre, "how can it *no longer be?* It is this perverse intuition that Genet prefers to all else: it makes the *nothing* shimmer at the surface of *all.*" (*M,* 29) This diabolic-puritanism is consistent. Genet states quite truthfully, "I make of sacrifice, rather than of solitude, the highest virtue. It is the creative virtue par excellence. There must be damnation in it." (*TJ,* 215)

As the completeness of Genet's inability to believe in the predicaments of others is frightening, so is our involuntary eagerness to justify him frightening. Our all too largely justified self-mistrust, our suspicion that we are hypocrites, or brutes, or both, creates a perfect opportunity for Genet's special brand of negativism to take over. As we progress through Genet's work, we begin to realize that a good proportion of the shocks we originally sustained came from the belated acknowledg-

ment of areas of guilt and self-distrust within ourselves
—and this is likely to be true of most encounters with
living literature. But it is by the power to illuminate
these existing, but often unexplored, interior areas that
literature must trigger its shocks. When the accusations
inherent in Genet's writing lose all proportional relationship to our sense of our own weaknesses, failures,
and culpability, the force of our reaction flags. Genet's
kingdom of the hole and its darkness is too remote from
even our subconscious, and his purpose too special,
genuinely to reveal us to ourselves or even, ultimately,
to stir our sense of guilt at all profoundly. Less and
less are we able to acknowledge recognition of ourselves in the image presented to us. In the last analysis,
it is left to him to impose this image upon us from
without, not by its validity but by his dictum. True
shocks must come from valid and inescapable revelations.

Yet it is obvious that Genet feels he has possessed
us, that that rape of audience by playwright, which Mr.
McMahon has postulated as Genet's intention, has in
Genet's eyes been accomplished. Mr. McMahon is
demonstrably correct in pointing out that beneath the
similarity of thesis, there is an almost complete metamorphosis from the guilty, self-loathing, and resentful
Genet, idealizing in reverse that world to which he feels
himself condemned, to the Genet of *The Balcony* and
The Screens, who says in effect: This is also your
world. There *is* no other, and this is built upon a system
of values of which I alone am lord and judge, and
which leads where I say it shall lead. Genet's imagination progresses from physical love-hate of self, through
mental love-hate of self, and is finally clamped and
sealed in spiritual love-hate of self. McMahon notes
that, in Genet's later plays, the "tone is no longer incantatory; it has become tough and aggressive. Beneath
the aggression there is a mixture of anger and the snick-
ering laugh of the practical jokester."[13]

Like Ionesco, Genet challenges our habits of thought.

[13] *Op. cit.,* p. 116.

Like Ionesco, he reverses and re-reverses the roles of reality and appearance. Like Ionesco, he explores the submergence of the individual in the prototype. Like Ionesco, he rejects the realistic event in favor of the revealing fantasy. Like Ionesco, Genet believes in the terrifying power of nomenclature and examines its divorce from truth. How far two contemporary playwrights, so related in a dozen details, can move in opposite directions is noteworthy.

Perhaps the outstanding point of divergence is one impossible to overstress. It is that Genet has passed from identifying himself with the dispossessed to identifying himself with Everyman—or, more accurately, that for him Everyman has *become* Genet. All who are not with him are fakes—as he has felt Gide's "immorality" to be "suspect." Aloof from others, he preaches the virtue of uncommunicative silence. Ionesco, on the other hand, has retained his vehement solidarity with others and with the cause of communication. He has joined those who strive to restore to human beings—addled by double talk, stifled by conformity, and paralyzed by rigidity—their capacity to speak and be heard, to move independently and of their own volition. If the reservoirs prove to be dry, if the silence is unreasonable, it is not with Ionesco's acquiescence.

Because the issue of Genet's work is so complicated by the difficulty—amounting to impossibility—of extricating it from Genet's nonliterary career, and the exploitation of that career, one can only hope to read him with a disciplined and uncommitted eye. At what point do consideration of the thief, the dedicated homosexual, the effects of physical and mental suffering, and the long chronicle leading from the reformatory at Mettray and proceeding through the Barrio Chino and the prisons of three countries, to the bourgeois affluence and the respect accorded an internationally recognized writer, cease to be legitimate parts of an attempt at dispassionate discussion of a body of work and instead merge into the sort of territory entered by the classic approach of a dust-jacket line: "The famous underground best seller! . . . An extraordinary erotic masterpiece for the first time in an American paperback edition! . . . Jean Genet . . . has spent time in the prisons of nearly every country of Europe. After ten convictions in France alone. . . ." That "in France alone" is a fine stroke; one can hear in it the perennial voice of the Barker at the flap of the sideshow.

Sartre's enormous work, undertaken with characteristic intelligence, command, and skill, gives a more exhaustive analysis of the mind, spirit, and talent of Genet than has been accorded any other living writer. Yet in it, the works are always subordinate to the case history. To assess, or at the least discuss, the quality of Genet's plays requires above all else the ability to listen, and to watch, and to forget for the moment all else but the listening and the watching. Even the novels, those detailed blueprints for "sainthood," can be considered only as, in their concepts and their determined progress, they prepare us for the moment when the curtain rises on the prelude to Nothing. It is the plays, not the case history, or the exploits, or the dossier, which will decide Genet's stature as playwright.

The Unreasonable Silence

THE THEATRE has always been the least private of art forms. It is not necessary to have a companion in order to receive the communication of a painting, to listen to a concerto, or to read *A la Recherche du Temps Perdu*—indeed, there are those who will argue that solitude is the happiest prerequisite. But any chronic theatregoer knows how essential is the rapport among audience, players, and playwright, which in combination produces that curious, complex entity, a living piece of theatre. A sketchy, obtuse, or indifferent audience can and does drain off the force of a tragedy; a comedy it can destroy, for basic to comedy is often the playwright's understanding with the audience at the expense of a character or characters. Waves of applause which still sweep relatively sophisticated New York audiences when some sentiment peculiarly acceptable to their current temper is pungently expressed can show how easy it is for members of a group publicly to demonstrate an attitude which individually no one of them would ever rise to express.

The plays of Jean Genet remain, in a special sense, private plays. They are, as Jacques Guicharnaud has pointed out,[1] exclusive and excluding, relevant to the general human knowledge only in painful fragments of the recognition of predicament or in a sense of guilt too all-embracing to be cathartic. But the profoundly inclusive character of human life does exist; it does continue to renew and refresh itself. It does carry with it

[1] *Modern French Theatre from Giraudoux to Beckett*, p. 171.

218

aspirations—however defeated and embittered—for companionship, for beauty, for the dangerous privileges of love. This sense of common humanity, at once strange and deeply related to the observer, and which is so lacking in Genet's work, in the most acute sense threatens that work's validity.

Ionesco reiterates, through every theatrical device, that we are losing the ability truly to communicate anything whatsoever, because we have lost the ability to believe. No convictions: no language. Albee has demonstrated that hatred and violence are often attempts to break through the intolerable steel of loneliness. Beckett, Albee, and Bergman, in totally different idioms and by totally different methods, point to the imminent threat of total silence. Their work is never private in the same sense as is Genet's; however bizarre the protagonist, or distorted his image of life, this very bizarreness, this very distortion, is utilized in an appeal to maintain or reestablish the relationship of human beings to each other, to some central significance.

Work such as Genet's, which has at its core, not the cycle of birth and death with which humanity has always been confronted but instead a special and desired core of private death seen at the center of all living things, breeds a solipsism essentially hostile to the theatre. Wilfrid Sheed recently wrote:

A "public" play does not in fact need to be a thesis play at all. . . . What it does require, though, is a public imagination—and by this is meant not simply a polite interest and a willingness to sign things, but a sense of politics, of how things work when more than a few people are involved in them; and beyond that, a sense of life going on outside this particular bedroom or bathroom and forcing its way through the cracks. . . .
[The plays of "hermetic privacy" have their sights] trained on the individual psyche, as though the individual psyche existed in a vacuum and were not also a locus for social forces: and because of this limited view, they are dubious guides even to the individual psyche.[2]

[2] Wilfrid Sheed, "The Undercover Play," *Commonweal,* Vol. LXXXIV (July 1, 1966), p. 418.

Ionesco has pointed out that he searches within himself in solitude for his plays, just because he believes that he is so related to all men that it is within himself that he can mature his knowledge of them. The plays of Genet pursue their way within the vacuum. They close themselves into the void, that void which has the quality of silence once heard by the child Genet in a violated church.

Beckett's couples—Nell and Nagg, Didi and Gogo, Mr. and Mrs. Rooney—go down together into the huge, dim void of the Beckett universe; their problem is a joint problem. The luckless, loveless couples of Ionesco —Amédée and Madeleine, Bérenger and Daisy—hurt, betray, and lose each other, but they envisage a quite different sort of communication. The Genet character is alone. Even Green Eyes, emulated and fought over, is quite alone; basically, his admirers wish only to become him, instead of being themselves. Claire and Solange each needs the other only in order to fulfill her own individual role. Saïd and Leila require each other in order to assure his or her individual degradation.

Certainly it is not required of a writer that his relationship to humanity take the form of his being a literary progenitor. His work may, or may not, fecundate a future series of playwrights or poets, so that work which would not have existed except for his genius, or would have existed differently, results. But this is no part of his obligation as writer, which is simply that of giving in its finest form what he has it in him to give. Genet has a dazzling visual imagination, and like Ionesco, he believes in exploring and exploiting every possible theatrical device to make what we are watching peculiarly *of* the theatre—magic, not fully explicable, unrealistic. Ionesco writes: "I personally would like to bring a tortoise onto the stage, turn it into a racehorse, then into a hat, a song, a dragoon and a fountain of water" (*NCN*, 46). But if Ionesco is equally concerned with stretching the limits of the stage, it is, as he repeats, magically and immediately to present a contemporary aspect of his classical themes. Unlike those of Genet, all of his de-

vices are enlisted in the service of a vision related to the
history of humanity.

If Genet uses his devices to implement his private
vision of destruction, and Ionesco his to break through
habit and indifference, to the quick of human attention,
it is interesting to note that Beckett, on the contrary,
as though passionately convinced that devices unsupported by spontaneous vitality are traps, has steadily
stripped his stage, as he has stripped his novels, of all
appurtenances, showing but the tiny endangered flame
of life flickering alone upon a sterile stage. Ionesco is
interested in showing us that objects, out of control, are
sinister; Genet that what we see is a brilliant screen
which will dissolve while we watch: iridescence, transparence, Absence; Beckett, that we are bereft and
stranded inside the landscape of our skull.

The silence implied in Ionesco's plays differs sharply
in quality from the silence achieved in Genet's. In Genet,
the long history of literature and art is speechless. Only
dying echoes of its privileges conferred become part of
the dying echoes of the Queen, the Missionary, the
Judge of *The Blacks*. It is not the windows of Chartres
or the themes of Palestrina which concern Genet but
the privileges their *possession* has conferred.

There is, truly, great fascination in destruction, the
precursor of silence. From the house partly bulldozed,
with ragged, exposed rooms still tilting scraps of furniture, which arrests the passerby with the fascination of
witnessing the silencing of a pattern of human life, to
that explosion in the form of a giant rose which gripped
the imagination of Count Ciano, staring down from his
bomber, the violence of destruction is potent dramatic
material. Most of that fascination comes from the sense
of power at work, and there is no question that the
destructive power of Genet's work makes a dark appeal.
But in the case of Genet, the power turns out to be not
so much sinister or constructive, or even purposeful, as
to be the last of the masks of nothing. There is an eerie
deadness to the silence which ensues.

It is quite possible that it is silence which will ensue

from Ionesco's plays, that Roberta's "cat, cat, cat, cat" and Choubert's "Heu . . . glu . . . you . . . kno . . . clem . . . neeg . . . erls . . ." will be succeeded by the silence of the Orator, the silence which closes in on the Tenant. But this is not what Ionesco hopes; and, as he has said, if he believed communication to be foredoomed by silence, he would scarcely continue to practice an art dependent on language. It is obvious, on the contrary, that he has faith in the *possibility* as well as the desirability of human communication, and indeed that above all he wishes this communication between his characters, now almost lost, not only to be restored but also to be reinforced. He wishes it to be reinforced and sustained by his protagonist's communication with that stronger illumination, that "governing light" which served, in the recollected moment, to represent with a strength all too ephemeral the design which it seems to the protagonist must somewhere exist outside of himself because it corresponds to his most profound inner need.

But if silence and indifference are to be overcome, if the end result of all is not to be that of Bérenger on his knees before the shrugging and chuckling Killer, then conviction of some sort or other must, as Ionesco clearly sees, oust them. And it is here that Ionesco treads on tricky ground. Orson Welles has written that neutrality is the enemy of art, and fundamentally Ionesco is in complete agreement. But so anxious is he not to let conviction harden into formula, choice into trap, that in much of his comment, he is trying simultaneously to defeat indifference and to deny the necessity of choices based on formulated belief. However, in his plays no such conflict exists. They demonstrate irrefutably that to playwright Ionesco some men *are,* to our faulty powers of judgment, better men than others; that one course of conduct *can,* by the same token, truthfully be said to be preferable to another. He never wavers in his view that the artist must be uncommitted, *as* artist, but this is because of his belief in art as a source of light rather than an admonition, a dynamic principle rather than a resulting theory. J. Bronowski writes: "Poetry does not move us to be just or unjust in itself. It moves us to thoughts in whose light justice and injustice are seen in fearful sharpness of outline."[3] There, Ionesco feels, the artist's role ends.

Injustice is a basic form of giving the lie to truth, and the attempt to disentangle the truthfully reported phenomena of human speech and behavior from the rigid travesties which are our accustomed fare is, in Ionesco's view, his function as writer. It is admittedly a dangerous occupation. There is in it danger to language, danger to the theatre, danger to the concept of human individuality. But it is laboring the obvious to assert that one of the indelible marks of pseudo-art is that it is safe.

Ionesco has not been able to locate the re-entry to that street whose radiance was vital, not ersatz; but he has indicated repeatedly that of his three great themes —love, death, and wonder—it is that of wonder which he views most optimistically as a possible thread through the labyrinth of mirages, icy and sordid cities, and the meaningless jargon of people no longer communicating even with themselves. Death he loathes and dreads; so far it promises him nothing. Love is nonexistent or foredoomed. But wonder, the marvelous sense of the strangeness of all things, the unforeseen and unforeseeable manifestations of flexible life, is the one thing which seems capable of maintaining its essence. In Ionesco, wonder is the corrective to indifference.

It is passive acceptance, by those who have lost the capacity to marvel, which is the tell-tale symptom of the terminal disease. It is not strange to the Smiths that Bobby Watson should be both dead and alive, or that Mrs. Watson should be both tall and short, both pretty and ugly; nor does it seem odd to Jean that rhinoceroses have become the established paragon; nor is it strange to the Architect that the Killer, unmolested, strikes afresh every day: that is the Way Things Are.

[3] J. Bronowski, *The Poet's Defence* (Cleveland: World Publishing Company, 1966), p. 16.

But the young Amédée is amazed at the beauty and freshness before him—his exclamations on radiance, greenness, blossoming, the voices of children, bells, are those of wonder; and Bérenger, before his disillusion, naively and rapturously exclaims over the prodigies produced by the Architect of marvels. The wonder is, certainly, not exclusively for the radiant and the pseudo-radiant. The child in the darkening street, terrified and sickened by the confused and incomprehensible shapes of violence and hostility, continues as an adult to marvel at the forms floating in the Ornamental Pool, at the policeman's unmotivated hatred, at the malice which pains and maims Choubert, the Pupil, Bérenger. But as long as that wonder is alive, the question Ionesco has asked is also alive: If this were truly our home, how would we know that we are aliens here?

It is fascinating to see what divergent conclusions are reached, through the use of an identical device, by Genet and Ionesco. By her simultaneous action of sewing and not sewing, sleeping and washing dishes, the Queen exercises the Royal prerogative and, disappearing into Absence, ceases to exist. Genet has snatched her into Nothing. But in the case of the chameleon Bobby Watsons, Ionesco is commenting not on the absence of Bobby Watson but on the indifference of the Smiths. Far from finding the absence of identity in Bobby Watson to be a Royal prerogative, Ionesco finds it merely the ludicrous but horrifying demonstration of the blind indifference, the rigidified acquiescence, of the Smiths.

Though their flavor, their methods, even their basic premises are in many aspects far apart, the work of Ionesco has striking similarity to certain facets of the work of the greatest and earliest figure among those playwrights attacking the conceptions of the *théâtre du boulevard*—Samuel Beckett. As early as *Murphy,* in 1938, Beckett had taken the path which was to lead him inevitably through the wastes of *Endgame, Embers,* and *Happy Days.* Many of the similarities which, as we noted, are shared by Ionesco and Genet, apply also to Beckett: the mélange of the grandiose and the sordid, the protagonist as outcast from an order he never established, the belief in the virtues of pantomime and in the resources of burlesque and farce, the sense of isolation. We have already touched on the differences between Genet's Nothing and Beckett's Void. There is a similarity, breeding a divergence, between Beckett's and Ionesco's theme of the Recollection of Good Things Past. It is a theme repeatedly emphasized by both. For the Beckett protagonist, the recollections of happiness are fugitive, brief, extremely fragile: a boat becalmed in the rushes, a blue afternoon on Lake Como, a vision of a shepherd with his sheep. They are specifically, or by implication, directly related to love. For Ionesco, the recollections are more exuberant: luminous streets, green and blossoming valleys, the felicities of hope. But the sense of a loss which is, in the literal sense of the word, unbearable is common to both. The interesting divergence is in the aura of what is desired. Bérenger passionately desires a warm, joyous, human sense of life; his guilt, his distress, his perpetual cold, are symptoms of a discontent with a life which bears no resemblance to life in the true Radiant City. The thirst of the Beckett protagonist is both deeper and less definable. He is desperate not because a happy life has been interrupted or lost but because a significance appears to be lost or dead, because the "hypothetical imperative" ("charming things, hypothetical imperatives") *is* hypothetical, and its dubious manifestations are indistinct and capricious as well. His, Beckett has said, is a "moral landscape." That of Ionesco is a social landscape, in which people, beset by matter which is uncontrolled by any conviction, lose their way, become rigid, are lost to life. The enormous thirst which permeates all of Beckett's work is a more drastic affliction, having at its source a deeper vision of refreshment: ". . . in your thirst, your hunger, no, no need of hunger, thirst is enough . . . talking without ceasing, thirstier than ever . . . thirsting away . . . what have I done to God, what have they done to God, what has God done to us . . . dying of thirst . . . it's I am talking, thirst-ing. . . ." So speaks the Unnamable. As Ionesco has himself observed, much of Beckett's writing is akin to the Book of Job. There is a formidable austerity in his progress toward the irreducible.

The progress of the plays of both Ionesco and Genet, like that of the Beckett protagonist, is characteristically circular. This is an important similarity. The circle has two distinct aspects. It has been often the symbol for eternity, the symbol of the indestructible. Its associa-tion with rhyme, with the motion of a timeless dance, of the end which is also a beginning, with the cycle of the seasons, has deeply involved it with the sense of renewal. Its other face is that of a trap, that of motion never fulfilled in arrival, that of the stone of Sisyphus which ends where it began, that of the jungle animal circling in its cage. It is this aspect of the circle which the Beckett protagonist endures and exploits. The whole of Beckett's work is a nightmare of wheels, fruitlessly turning in a sort of frenzied stasis.

Genet and Ionesco have caught the affliction. As a recounted rape and murder are re-enacted in *Death-watch,* as the minuet recommences as the circle of *The Blacks* ends only to begin again, so the new Pupil rings the Professor's doorbell, one Bobby Watson replaces another Bobby Watson, and the Smiths and the Martins exchange places in the rounds of their puppet-dance.

That three contemporary playwrights, as different in genesis and outlook as Beckett, Ionesco, and Genet, should share a number of common assumptions gives a specific shape to the outline of serious international theatre. A world in which old assumptions are frag-mented; a world of cruelty, violence, and indifference, in which the real is perpetually hidden behind a gro-tesque and deceptive mask; a world in which shelter, warmth, and human contact are so difficult to come by as to be virtually unavailable: this is their common vision. Genet is the first to break off from this commu-nity of conception. Though chaos seems to obtain, he reports magic laws for controlling it. The knowledge of

Nothing is the secret which confers power; and with power, a system of domination can be established which will assist us to the final consummation of negation.

Both Beckett and Ionesco are in total disagreement with this. Beckett, by every searing description, by what Hugh Kenner has called his "ecstasy of disgust," postulates, by their brilliantly implied absence, the dignity, charity, and significance without which all dwindles and darkens. Ionesco rejects, with anger and scorn, the rigidity, the disingenuousness, the cancerous indifference, all of which break down communication between human beings and render them the prey of objects, of moribund language, ultimately of silence.

We come now to the final consideration. What is specifically common to Genet, to Ionesco, to Beckett, is that predicament has overwhelmed identity. In the great tragedies of the past, the human identity involved was so much a part of that tragedy (being in fact its core) that the tragedy would have been unrecognizable had its especial protagonist been replaced merely by an undelineated human figure. In the cases of Beckett, Ionesco, and Genet, we are confronted by a predicament (incommunicability, coldness, indifference, the blindness bred from habit) rather than by a fully conceived human being, whose nature and characteristics we understand, and who—only *after* our interest has been engaged by him as a specific human being—is placed in a predicament which is of interest to us primarily because we care what happens to *him* personally and because his nature is itself deeply a part of his tragedy. In a predicament of coldness, indifference, and blindness Beckett, Ionesco, and Genet set the shape of a man. The accent is far less on the human individual than on the desperate circumstances in which man may find himself. The predicament looms so large, so universal, that the individual caught in it is dwarfed; indeed, it is hard to imagine his existence apart from the problem he is designed to illustrate. Character, as it has traditionally been conceived, scarcely exists here; the man is little more than the manifestation of his predicament. He is not a man of certain tastes, temper, defeats, joys, and the mysterious molding of human life, but The Man Who Is Trapped, the man who is surrounded by mushrooms, or screens behind which is the void. It may well be that the vision of a life without significance or the possibility of communication does preclude any further definition of character; perhaps, in this final state, we have reached this bleak and terrifying common denominator. But, regardless of its truth or falseness, it most certainly does constitute a giant problem for the future theatre to solve.

In Beckett, we have the conception of the clown-tramp, struggling to make, to speak, as he is stripped and immobilized in an unanswering and destructive universe. In Genet, we have archetypes, masks, all held up before the face of Genet. In Ionesco, we have the personified predicaments of human beings isolated from each other by habit and by that indifference which is the lack of the capacity for wonder. This common stress on predicament over individuality is so basic, so undeniable, so important that it encompasses the whole question of human identity in the theatre of the present, let alone the future. The question clearly is this: Are we to—indeed, should we *desire* to—re-create from this personified predicament a human being who is more real, more alive, because he has been stripped of all incidentals and put through the humbling test of a predicament conceived as universal; a human being who can now, properly placed within his predicament, say, "I have at last forced his name from the angel; now I exist and shall continue to exist and to put on identity, in ways you have never dreamed"? Or does the predicament, having sucked the lifeblood from its victim, hold only a puppet, whose significance is totally limited to what is done to it? Are we inevitably face to face with the Happening or its heirs—not as a diversion, not as a limbering-up process, not as fun-and-games but as our manipulating and only guide into future theatre?

It is no use calling on Shakespeare, on Molière, on Ibsen to come and save us. Each artist, always, advances by means of respectful patricide—a practical if bloody arrangement, by which the traditions and enlightenment of the work are venerated after the outmoded form has been discarded. The question is not, "Can we return to what Lear taught us?" but, "What is Lear's storm saying now?" Genet's work does not involve interest in his predecessors or in his heirs. Beckett has finally reached the apparently irreducible point from which there is no further retreat; his clown-tramp is already there, keeping his appointment which shows no signs of materializing to reward and relieve his endurance. Ionesco does specifically insist that we recur constantly to the classic themes under new guises. He does specifically look to a theatre which will refresh, renew, and illumine them. But whether those themes can continue to draw life from the deracinated, fragmented, marionettelike world of his plays is another matter. It is interesting that two of his portraits of Bérenger come closer to recognizable human identities (for they depict those dimensions of life by which we distinguish a man from an argument) than do any of his other characters, and that they are relatively recent creations. Unquestionably what we are left with is the question of a belief. No civilization has existed without one, and it is certain that none ever will.

There now exists an ideological-ethical belief, in its heyday a quarter of a century ago, which is perhaps the most commonly held hope: the brotherhood of man without a common father. This was to be expressed sociologically, and often, as in the case of Camus and Silone, with the accent of love. Interestingly enough, neither Beckett nor either of the two writers discussed in this book has the slightest interest in this solution to the problem of belief. Genet is not interested because he sees all such gestures of amity and responsibility as power moves by the Ins and, more fundamentally, because they are hostile to the *raison d'être* of his own work. Ionesco is not interested because he is intuitively and intellectually convinced of their ineffectuality. Will political panaceas, ideological systems, sociological concern ever protect men from lovelessness, human pain, longing, and the presence of death? This he repeatedly asks and gives his own answer. He is, in fact, almost unreasonably hostile to the expression of any codified effort for the amelioration of *anything*.

Beckett, in his thirst and enduring wait, is even more drastically contemptuous of organized ameliorations; his most scathing ironies have been directed at the efforts of science, education, and all the machinery of civilization to quench the ravaging thirst which is his protagonist's unwavering lot. (Incidentally, Beckett, unlike Ionesco, clearly separates the exigencies of daily life from the problems of metaphysics. He has demonstrated in his own life that every possible effort must be made along practical lines to ameliorate the human condition—but without the illusion that this effort can cure the sense of isolation, longing, and death detailed by Ionesco.) It is demonstrable that in relation to these problems, Ionesco and Beckett find ethical-social action a palliative so weak as to be ludicrous. In an image of Beckett's, it is like a man dying of cancer, who is forced to visit his dentist.

If, then, the scientist, educator, and social worker do not hold the solution, where does the playwright turn in search of hope? Genet hopes for Nothing. Ionesco hopes for a wonder which will perhaps revive love and postpone the paralysis of death. He does believe the great themes are inexhaustible and that each age is overshadowed by a different aspect of the same questions. Whether, however, he has led the way toward an exit from his preoccupations—death, violence on the one hand and indifference on the other, the contention of shadows—back into a clarified consideration of the human being, a specific, many-dimensional human being linked to a past and a future, is more open to dispute.

One sign which has been little commented on, but which it is impossible to ignore, is the element of poetry so strongly present in the avant-garde playwrights. It is a poetry so allusive, so colloquial, so little fitted onto the Procrustes bed of form, that it can easily pass unobserved. But the essence of poetry is its special ways of employing language and its uniquely individual and elliptical approaches. *Who's Afraid of Virginia Woolf?* may or may not be bad poetry but its final scene is purely poetic incantation, and *The Zoo Story* is closer to being a macabre and forceful poem than to being a play. Pinter's portentous and mysterious characters have all the clear yet evasive power of an unglossed line of poetry; Genet deals almost entirely in the trappings and aura of poetry; and Beckett is a poet long before and after he is a playwright or a novelist—probably one of the handful of major poets now writing. The corpse in *Amédée;* the floating man, child, and woman of the Ornamental Pool, with their medal, hoop, and waving hair; the rhinoceroses milling splendidly below Bérenger's window; the icy mountain heights glimpsed by Choubert, do not belong by their nature to prose.

This strong element of poetry, where it might be least expected, is highly significant. It is the instinctive attempt simultaneously to achieve that penetration to the depth and that universality which are the earmarks of true poetry. Technical poetic form in the theatre, which not long ago had a strong but brief vogue, has bogged down; what appears in its stead is that characteristic which John Ciardi happily described as "As If." It is the basis of most of Genet's happier effects; it is implicit in all of Ionesco's most successful work. In the case of Beckett, it cannot be considered merely as an element, for Beckett is primarily a poet. This element of poetry in Genet and in Ionesco is one valid reason for the vitality of their plays.

It is the similarities and differences noted in their work which constitute an especial reason for considering a comparison of these three playwrights important and interesting to anyone concerned with contemporary theatre. As we have seen, the difference in their viewpoints and objectives is so wide as to constitute a philosophical and aesthetic hostility. It is precisely for this reason that the similarity of so many of their theatrical assumptions is impressive. When you have three playwrights differing so radically in tenets, temperament, and vision as Beckett, Ionesco, and Genet, it is obvious that such agreement is apposite to any discussion of the ideas shaping our theatre. It is an agreement certainly not common to the more optimistic of our humanists. But it is definitely common to these three playwrights, probably the most influential now writing.

One assumption is that existence without significance, or existence whose apparent significance dissolves under examination, is intolerable to the human heart and mind. A concomitant assumption is that in such a situation, identity ceases to be valid, and characteristics and formulas established by habit and precept are revealed as terrifying or ludicrous masks for the same robotlike predator. Since this situation is an intolerable one, it follows that the protagonists seek a way of escape. Genet, alone of the three, has found one: he will escape into the hole that gives on Nothing.

Ionesco clings stubbornly to the notion that an appetite implies the existence of a related satisfaction, that a specific and gnawing hunger is functional and implies the existence of nourishment. We reject what we see, he repeats, with the profound and instinctive reaction of a legitimate searcher, cheated. We know that this is not where we belong. We know that it is not our home because the relations of all around us, in Ionesco's eyes, are compounded of violence, a heartless rigidity, and worst of all, a consuming indifference, ravaging our human possibilities. He sees no hope in any form of organization; love can come truly to exist only if we can find our way back to the luminous intimation which at some point visited our past. A prerequisite to that return is wonder—the sense of the strangeness, the flexibility, the unforeseeable genius of life. If we are to possess wonder, if we are to be conscious of non-fabricated marvels surrounding us, we must have the basic conviction of the constant presence of the marvelous; we must have this belief to counter the chuckle of the Killer. If we fail in all conviction, we are siblings of the man, woman, and child in the Ornamental Pool. Language will fail us because we have truly nothing to convey; vision will fail us because we cannot see the person to whom we speak.

Interestingly enough, it is in Beckett, whose work Ionesco has likened to the Book of Job, that we find the implication that however chaotic and obscure the conditions, however cryptic the "hypothetical imperative," however desolate our stripped and debilitated state, the fault, if in our stars, may be also in ourselves. There is no opportunity here to develop the theme of guilt which runs through Beckett's work, but it is omnipresent, and it gives a sort of small and enigmatic hope to his atmosphere of despair. If there is something which we have done and for which we are responsible, perhaps there is something we can rectify. There is in Beckett's work a deeper thirst, a larger demand, and a more acute sense of a lost, defaced, and misunderstood compact that has gone woefully wrong. As Vladimir says: "We have kept our appointment. . . . We are not saints, but we have kept our appointment."

Genet has gutted the sacred of its core and kept its trappings. Like the Architect, he has substituted for the miracle, the fake marvel; he tells us so. Ionesco has allowed his hunger for any transcendental values to appear only in his sense that an Eden existed and that in order for life to be bearable, it must be regained. But it is a natural Eden, without commands, or penalties, or promises; in the cool of the evening, only the happy protagonists walk there. Beckett alone manifests the insatiable desire for a coherence, a compact, the presence of Dante's primordial love. It is this which, even from the purely literary viewpoint, gives his work its resonance, its marvelous and dramatic sense of *listening*.

In any summation it is essential to remember that there is danger inherent in limiting consideration of a play to its author's conscious intent. Every good writer is surprised by elements in his own work. The deep wells of the subconscious, the parts of the completed work never wholly subject to analysis and evaluation, contribute to the secret of its life; and this is especially true in the case of writers such as Ionesco and Genet, who are acutely aware of the element of strangeness in all things. Genet, like Antonin Artaud, turns toward an Eastern form of theatre, a theatre of ceremony and ritual, which invests its material with the mystery of the sacred. Both Genet and Ionesco share the conviction that poetry and wonder are elements needed for the revitalization of the contemporary theatre.

It is the similarities, rather than the differences, between Genet and Ionesco which indicate the importance of isolating the area of their agreement. The presence of Absence is common to the work of both; the absence which makes reality a nightmare for Ionesco, the Absence which for Genet is the Royal prerogative. The Genet protagonist escapes through the hole of holes. The Ionesco protagonist (like the dual personalities of Bérenger: on his knees before the Killer and precariously clinging to his humanity as the herd mills and trumpets below him) still, in one of his aspects, struggles. It seems obvious beyond argument that some new impulse of conviction, some undiscovered bridge back to the great themes named by Ionesco, back to a death which might be tragic because it might also be heroic or significant; to the theme of love which might confront and endure death, illuminate the individual, and show itself as the inexhaustible source of joy; to the theme of wonder not merely at the strangeness and unpredictability of life, but at its sudden revelations of human daring, compassion, and grace—some fresh approach to these themes must be forthcoming if life, as reflected on the stage, is not indeed to become an immense, an intolerably boring Happening. Is there the slightest hint, in the work of Genet and Ionesco, of what might prove a prelude to such a revitalizing concept, of what might break the "unreasonable silence"?

There would seem to be two elements which do, perhaps, constitute such a hint. One is the element of poetry —that sudden illumination from the unpredictable quarter, that strange light striking the familiar so that it is at once the new and the recognized.

The second element is that of stage magic—that return

to the deepest roots of theatre, that attack on realism which includes in its catholicity the fakir, the circus-clown, the miracle play, the tightrope-walker feasting from the table on the highwire over the narrow street of an Italian town. Theatrical wonder begins here, and there is no foreseeable limit to its growth.

The nobility, courage, charity, and generosity which ferment ceaselessly in human life—along with its less appetizing traits—can no more be permanently ignored than can the restlessness of the human spirit be contained, trapped in the circularity of a sterile cage. One is driven to ask whether there are no new ways of reflecting those qualities which seem dormant or non-existent in today's serious theatre, no new ways germane to the genius of the medium. Poetry and wonder, at least, are not contained in that cage. Fortunately, they are uncontainable.

Selected Bibliography

Principal Translated Works of Eugène Ionesco

Four Plays, tr. Donald M. Allen. New York: Grove Press, 1958. (Includes *The Bald Soprano; The Lesson; Jack, or The Submission; The Chairs.*)

Three Plays, tr. Donald Watson. New York: Grove Press, 1958. (Includes *Amédée, or How to Get Rid of It; The New Tenant; Victims of Duty.*)

The Killer and Other Plays, tr. Donald Watson. New York: Grove Press, 1960. (Includes *The Killer; Improvisation, or The Shepherd's Chameleon; Maid to Marry.*)

Rhinoceros and Other Plays, tr. Derek Prouse. New York: Grove Press, 1960. (Includes *Rhinoceros; The Leader; The Future Is in Eggs, or It Takes All Sorts to Make a World.*)

Plays, Volume V, tr. Donald Watson. London: John Calder, 1963. (Includes *Exit the King; Foursome; The Motor Show.*)

Notes and Counter Notes, tr. Donald Watson. New York: Grove Press, 1964.

Plays, Volume VI, tr. Donald Watson. London: John Calder, 1965. (Includes *A Stroll in the Air; Frenzy for Two.*)

Principal Translated Works of Jean Genet

The Maids and Deathwatch, tr. Bernard Frechtman. New York: Grove Press, 1954.

The Balcony, tr. Bernard Frechtman. New York: Grove Press, 1960.

The Blacks: A Clown Show, tr. Bernard Frechtman. New York: Grove Press, 1960.

The Screens, tr. Bernard Frechtman. New York: Grove Press, 1962.

Our Lady of the Flowers, tr. Bernard Frechtman. New York: Bantam Books, 1964.

The Thief's Journal, tr. Bernard Frechtman. New York: Grove Press, 1964.

Works in English on Eugène Ionesco and Jean Genet

Barish, Jonas A., "The Veritable Saint Genet." *Wisconsin Studies in Contemporary Literature,* Vol. VI (Autumn, 1965), pp. 267–285.

Brustein, Robert, *The Theatre of Revolt.* Boston: Little, Brown & Company, 1964.

Cismaru, Alfred, "The Antitheism of Jean Genet." *Antioch Review,* Vol. XXIV (Fall, 1964), pp. 387–401.

Coe, Richard N., *Ionesco.* Edinburgh: Oliver and Boyd, 1961.

Cohn, Ruby, "Bérenger, Protagonist of an Anti-Playwright." *Modern Drama,* Vol. VIII (September, 1965), pp. 127–133.

Cruickshank, John, "Jean Genet: The Aesthetics of Crime." *Critical Quarterly,* Vol. VI (Autumn, 1964), pp. 202–210.

Doubrovsky, J. S., "Ionesco and the Comic of Absurdity." *Yale French Studies,* No. 23 (1959), pp. 3–10.

Driver, Tom F., *Jean Genet.* New York: Columbia University Press, 1966.

Eastman, Richard M., "Experiment and Vision in Ionesco's Plays." *Modern Drama,* Vol. IV (May, 1961), pp. 3–19.

Esslin, Martin, "Ionesco and the Creative Dilemma." *Tulane Drama Review,* Vol. VII (Spring, 1963), pp. 169–179.

———, *The Theatre of the Absurd.* Garden City, New York: A Doubleday Anchor Original, 1961.

Greshoff, C. J., "A Note on Eugène Ionesco." *French Studies,* Vol. XV (January, 1961), pp. 30–40.

Grossvogel, David I., *Four Playwrights and a Postscript: Brecht, Ionesco, Beckett, Genet.* Ithaca: Cornell University Press, 1962. (Republished in 1965 as Cornell Paperback under title of *The Blasphemers: The Theater of Brecht, Ionesco, Beckett, Genet.*)

Guicharnaud, Jacques (in collaboration with June Beckelman), *Modern French Theatre from Giraudoux to Beckett.* New Haven: Yale University Press, 1961.

Killinger, John, "Jean Genet and Scapegoat Drama." *Com-*

parative Literature Studies, Vol. III, No. 2 (1966), pp. 207–221.

Lamont, Rosette C., "Air and Matter: Ionesco's 'Le Piéton de l'air' and 'Victimes du devoir.' " *French Review,* Vol. XXXVIII (January, 1965), pp. 349–361.

———, "The Proliferation of Matter in Ionesco's Plays." *L'Esprit Créateur,* Vol. II (Winter, 1962), pp. 189–197.

McMahon, Joseph H., *The Imagination of Jean Genet.* New Haven: Yale University Press, 1963.

Phillips, William, "The New Immoralists." *Commentary,* Vol. XXXIX (April, 1965), pp. 66–69.

Pronko, Leonard Cabell, *Avant-Garde: The Experimental Theater in France.* Berkeley and Los Angeles: University of California Press, 1962.

———, *Eugène Ionesco.* New York: Columbia University Press, 1965.

Pucciani, Oreste F., "Tragedy, Genet and *The Maids.*" *Tulane Drama Review,* Vol. VII (Spring, 1963), pp. 42–59.

Reck, Rima Drell, "Appearance and Reality in Genet's *Le Balcon.*" *Yale French Studies,* No. 29 (1963), pp. 20–25.

Sartre, Jean-Paul, *Saint Genet: Actor and Martyr,* tr. Bernard Frechtman. New York: New American Library, A Mentor Book, 1964.

Schechner, Richard, "The Enactment of the 'Not' in *Les Chaises* of Eugène Ionesco." *Yale French Studies,* No. 29 (1963), pp. 65–72.

———, "The Inner and the Outer Reality." *Tulane Drama Review,* Vol. VII (Spring, 1963), pp. 187–217.

Smith, J. Oates, "Ionesco's Dances of Death." *Thought,* Vol. XL (Autumn, 1965), pp. 415–431.

Strem, George G., "Ritual and Poetry in Eugène Ionesco's Theatre." *Texas Quarterly,* Vol. V (Winter, 1962), pp. 149–158.

Svendsen, J. M., "Corydon Revisited: A Reminder on Genet." *Tulane Drama Review,* Vol. VII (Spring, 1963), pp. 98–110.

Swander, Homer D., "Shakespeare and the Harlem Clowns: Illusion and Comic Form in Genet's *The Blacks.*" *Yale Review,* Vol. LV (December, 1965), pp. 209–226.

Watson, Donald, "The Plays of Ionesco." *Tulane Drama Review,* Vol. III (October, 1958), pp. 48–53.

Zimbardo, R. A., "Genet's Black Mass." *Modern Drama,* Vol. VIII (December, 1965), pp. 247–258.

Index